A Philosophy of Prayer

Series Board

James Bernauer

Drucilla Cornell

Thomas R. Flynn

Kevin Hart

Richard Kearney

Jean-Luc Marion

Adriaan Peperzak

Thomas Sheehan

Hent de Vries

Merold Westphal

Michael Zimmerman

John D. Caputo, *series editor*

Perspectives in
Continental
Philosophy

GEORGE PATTISON

A Philosophy of Prayer
Nothingness, Language, and Hope

FORDHAM UNIVERSITY PRESS
New York ■ 2024

Copyright © 2024 Fordham University Press

All rights reserved. No part of this publication may be reproduced, stored in a retrieval system, or transmitted in any form or by any means—electronic, mechanical, photocopy, recording, or any other—except for brief quotations in printed reviews, without the prior permission of the publisher.

Fordham University Press has no responsibility for the persistence or accuracy of URLs for external or third-party Internet websites referred to in this publication and does not guarantee that any content on such websites is, or will remain, accurate or appropriate.

Fordham University Press also publishes its books in a variety of electronic formats. Some content that appears in print may not be available in electronic books.

Visit us online at www.fordhampress.com.

Library of Congress Cataloging-in-Publication Data available online at https://catalog.loc.gov.

Printed in the United States of America

26 25 24   5 4 3 2 1

First edition

Contents

	Preface	*xi*
1	Annihilation	*1*
2	Unknowing	*17*
3	Mystery	*34*
4	Words	*51*
5	Preaching	*68*
6	Promise	*83*
7	Height	*96*
8	Homecoming	*110*
9	Humility	*123*
	Postscript	*141*
	Notes	*143*
	Select Bibliography	*163*
	Index	*171*

> Domine, Jesu Christe,
> qui me creasti,
> redemisti, et preordinasti
> ad hoc quod sum,
> tu scis quid de me facere vis;
> fac de me secundum
> voluntatem tuam
> cum misericordia.
> Amen.
> —*A prayer of King Henry VI*

Religion ist Ehrfurcht,—die Ehrfurcht zuerst vor dem Geheimnis, das der Mensch ist.

—**_Thomas Mann_**

Preface

The essays collected here were presented over a period of nearly twenty years (2000–2017) in a variety of academic and church contexts. Although several of them were planned as parts of a work on the philosophy of prayer, these are ultimately independent essays, and although I have tried to indicate some of the ways in which they are linked, their unity is not that of a systematic development but relates more to *die Sachen selbe*, the things themselves, that they address.

The original plan was overtaken by what became *A Phenomenology of the Devout Life* (Oxford University Press, 2018), and the present work can be read as a kind of companion piece or perhaps a foil to that. Although there are significant commonalities, there are also striking differences. *A Phenomenology of the Devout Life* drew the larger part of its material from the French School of the seventeenth century (notably de Sales and Fénelon), albeit reading them in a horizon developed through the resources of post-Kantian philosophy. Here, the focus is more concentratedly on post-Kantian traditions of religious thought, especially those that can be described as "existential"—Kierkegaard, Dostoevsky, Buber, Berdyaev, Heidegger, Marcel, Tillich, Weil, and Levinas are all major points of reference. For thinkers such as these, the possibility and meaning of prayer is from the outset challenged by the multiple questions and dissonances characteristic of nineteenth- and twentieth-century modernity. This is not to say that the world of de Sales and Fénelon was an oasis of calm. On the contrary—as the bitter controversies that stymied Fénelon's court career show. Like the twentieth century, their time was a time of wars, persecutions, ideological challenges, and cosmological disorientation. All the same, they did not face, as the post-Kantian thinkers did, a series of basic challenges to the very possibility of religion and, therewith, of prayer. Theirs was not yet—or did not yet understand itself as—a secular world, whereas the main interlocutors of the present collection were all fully aware of how the horizon of faith was not immediately accessible to their contemporaries, and, consequently, they understood the intellectual obligation to reconstitute that horizon in new ways. This has direct implications for their approach to prayer because, at the very least, it requires parking any supernaturalist understanding of prayer, whether as a form of personal consciousness or as religious practice.

It is certainly not the case that those assembled here did or even could agree on some common doctrine or theory of prayer. Nevertheless, I suggest their witness is significantly convergent and provides at least some indication as to how prayer might become possible in a secular world. That this testimony also reveals significant resonance with older traditions (Augustine, *The Cloud of Unknowing*) is scarcely surprising, given the ongoing presence of ancient and medieval sources across broad swaths of Christian culture. My position is certainly not that only the "moderns" can help us. It is simply that as we attempt to do our best at engaging in the practice of prayer, we are necessarily involved with our human past—although, at the same time, we can only relate to that past as the people that we are now, in this case "moderns" (or "postmoderns," or "second moderns," etc.).

Of course, for many who may read this, not only Kierkegaard and Dostoevsky, writers of the nineteenth century, but even my twentieth-century dialogue partners may seem like ancient history—and it is certainly true that they both require of us and educate us in a different kind of attention from what is needed for participating in the world of social media. But that's not a bad thing, and I don't think anyone is incapable of learning such attention. In a certain perspective, this is not so different from the situation in which philosophy first set out on its pursuit of wisdom in a marketplace dominated by the multiple voices of sophists, priests, oligarchs, populists, poets, and comedians. Let's see.

Chapter 1 is based on an unpublished lecture given in Liverpool's Anglican Cathedral as part of the program "Philosophy in the City, Liverpool 2010." Chapter 2 was originally published under the title "Desire, Decreation, and Unknowing in the God-Relationship: Mystical Theology and Its Transformation in Kierkegaard, Simone Weil, and Dostoevsky," in *Subjectivity and Transcendence*, ed. Arne Grøn, Iben Damgaard, and Søren Overgaard (Mohr Siebeck, 2007), and I am grateful to Mohr

Siebeck for permission to reproduce this article. The part of Chapter 3 dealing with Berdyaev and Marcel is based on a paper given at the conference "Discourses of the Unsayable: Apophaticism and Literary Praxis," held at the Royal Flemish Academy of Science, Brussels, June 17–18, 2009; the part dealing with Tillich is developed from the colloquium "Philosophy, Mystery, and Love" commemorating the fiftieth anniversary of the death of Paul Tillich, held at the University of Glasgow in 2015. Chapter 4 is a much revised version of the paper "Language and the Revelation of Silence: Reflections on Mystical Theology," a version of which is in *Invisibility: Reflections upon Visibility and Transcendence in Theology, Philosophy, and the Arts*, ed. Anna Vind (Vandenhoeck and Ruprecht, 2020). Chapter 5 is based on a lecture given in a series of summer lectures held in Christ Church Cathedral, Oxford, in 2011; Chapter 6 is the English-language version of a paper given in Russian at the conference "Image and Symbol in Jewish, Christian, and Muslim Traditions," at the Jewish Museum and Tolerance Center, Moscow, April 2016. The basis of Chapter 7 is previously unpublished, though a related section appeared in my *A Rhetorics of the Word* (Oxford University Press, 2019), 204–6. Chapter 8 has evolved from a paper presented at the 'D' Society, in the Cambridge University Faculty of Divinity in 2000. Chapter 9 is an unpublished seminar paper, given at the University of Essex, 2016, as part of the project "The Ethics of Powerlessness." I am grateful to all who organized the events at which I was able to develop my thinking into its present form, and I am especially grateful to Jack Caputo for suggesting collecting these essays into a single volume.

I am, as ever, grateful to Hilary for being with me throughout a lifetime of unforeseeable trials and joys.

1

Annihilation

Kant's Embarrassment

In his *Religion within the Boundaries of Mere Reason*, Kant has some harsh words to say about prayer. "Praying," he writes, "conceived as an inner ritual service of God and hence as a means of grace, is a superstitious delusion (fetish-making); for it is only the declaring of a wish to a being who has no need of any declaration regarding the inner disposition of the wisher, through which nothing is therefore accomplished nor is any of the duties incumbent on us as commands of God discharged; hence God is not really served."[1] It is true that he immediately contrasts this with what he calls the "spirit of prayer," namely, "a sincere wish to please God in all our doings and non-doings, i.e. the disposition, accompanying all our actions, to pursue these as though they occurred in the service of God," to which he adds that this "can and ought to be in us 'without ceasing'" (alluding to Paul's injunction in 1 Thess 5:17 to pray without ceasing). However, he insists that if this spirit of prayer is genuinely active within us, then the "letter" of prayer should fall away and that, if it persists, it becomes actually harmful, since it "weakens the effect of the moral idea (which, subjectively regarded, is called devotion)."[2]

This last comment indicates that what really offends Kant is not simply the illusion that we are talking to another (God) when we are really talking only to ourselves but the effect of this illusion on the moral will. Where morality requires us to maximize the operation of the good will by freely affirming and enacting the moral law and, in doing so, to believe that "I ought" entails "I can," prayer—according to the "letter"—seems to presuppose that we are not capable of giving effect to whatever elements of good will are at work within us and that, even if we ought, we cannot. Whereas morality requires us to suppose the center of personal life to be an active will transcending all external influences, prayer seems to suppose a fundamental passivity beyond, behind, or beneath whatever signs of self-motivating activity we may nevertheless display. Or: Morality regards human beings as essentially autonomous, whereas prayer—and, more broadly, the religious view of life in which prayer is embedded—judges us to be subject to a power, not ourselves. In strictly Kantian terms, therefore, Matthew Arnold's definition of God as "a power, not ourselves, that makes for righteousness" is self-contradictory, since it is only what we do, of ourselves, that makes for righteousness (or not). Even prayers of thanksgiving seem to be redundant, since the only good in which we ought truly to delight is the power of moral striving, whereas thanking an Other for this good is once more to undermine the conviction that we ourselves are indeed capable of such striving. For Kant, religion is justified to the extent that it can be integrated into a program of moral autonomy, but it would seem that prayer undermines the very basis of such a program. From the Kantian perspective, then, prayer entails the belief that we are not and cannot become fully morally responsible for ourselves and are condemned to remain in a state of moral tutelage or heteronomy.

Yet prayer is, clearly, one of the basic features of Christian life. Of course, there are many forms and practices of prayer, from liturgical prayer, possibly in Latin, Church Slavonic, or another nonvernacular language; through the spontaneous outbursts of charismatic prayer; to the silence of private or monastic contemplation. Whether or not Kant's embarrassment is justified, his comments confirm that prayer is a privileged site for examining the further anthropological and ontological implications of Christian faith. As a first step in such an examination, I shall consider how two of Kant's successors, J. G. Fichte and F. D. E. Schleiermacher, developed or contested his thought. A key issue is what we might call the passivity of prayer. For the self that exists as the maximum realization of pure practical reason is a self that approximates to the *actus purus* of medieval theology. That is to say, it is a self that is the source of its own actions and, in a sense, of its own world. If Kant never quite said this, some of his heirs, notably Fichte, did. But such a self would seem incapable of the petitions and expressions of gratitude and reliance that characterize so much of Christian prayer and that, as I have suggested, bespeak a certain passivity in the basic orientation of the one who prays.

Fichte or Schleiermacher?

In an article "On the Basis of Our Faith in a Divine Governance of the World," published in 1798, Fichte addresses the question of how we might justify the belief that the world is such as to allow for the fulfillment of moral purposes. His answer is simple: It is human beings' direct and immediate experience of freedom: "I find myself to be free from all influences from the sense world," he writes, "absolutely active in myself and through myself, thus as a sublime power over everything sensuous." Such freedom is not only freedom *from* external constraint but freedom *for* acting as a free agent might wish to act. As he puts it: Freedom "as a goal [*Zweck*]: only this is not derived from something external, but it posits it through itself."[3]

Freedom of this kind is thus something very different from mere freedom of choice. You are offered a choice between a glass of white and a glass of red wine. You did not yourself "posit" the objects between which you now have to choose. They are put before you, and, to that extent, your freedom is limited in relation to them. You might really want a beer, but that is not on offer. What Fichtean freedom wants, however, is quite simply freedom itself, the conviction that I am capable of realizing whatever I might want to achieve and that I am able to do what I ought to do and be what I ought to be. As moral agents, we cannot allow ourselves to believe that the world of the senses—"our common stage," as Fichte calls it—can in any way prevent such fulfillment. If I commit myself in love to a lifelong relationship with another human being and believe that I do so freely, then I must also believe that I and human beings in general are capable of making such choices and promises. Conversely, it is inconsistent with the nature of such a commitment to believe that there is something integral to human nature—such as a tendency to sexual promiscuity, emotional instability, or simple selfishness—that would make such choices and promises impossible. In adopting a moral point of view, we must therefore believe that the world of sense-experience is ordered in such a way as to permit and even enable the fulfillment of moral purposes: The world-order is a "moral world-order," and the history of this world is the history of the "revelation" of duty, or moral freedom.

Fichte sees this as entirely compatible with Christianity. In fact, he says, it is the essential idea of the petition "Thy Kingdom come" in the Lord's Prayer.[4] But who is Fichte's "thou" in this case? His "God" does not seem to be a power external to human freedom but is more or less identical with the power of that freedom itself. "This is the true faith; this moral order is what we accept as divine," he writes.[5] Still more radically, he affirms that "That living and effective moral order is itself God, we need no other God and cannot apprehend any other."[6] On this basis, Fichte rejects the idea of a divine legislator external to the world, since the idea of such an external God would be an abstraction from our own direct and immediate experience of personality and freedom. Faith, however, holds to what is immediately given, to what has no "proof" other than its own self-experience. This doesn't make God uncertain: On the contrary, it grounds our faith in God in what is most certain of all. However, as Fichte's critics were swift to point out, it is questionable whether the God of such a faith is in any recognizable sense the God of Christianity. Could this God, in any nonequivocal sense, be a God to whom one might *pray*?

Kant himself understood that freedom is a problematic concept. We do not experience our own freedom, and it is not an object of possible knowledge.[7] Moreover, it is constrained, though not determined, by the fact that we are also corporeal beings who are subject to laws of nature over which our freedom has no direct control. Furthermore, we are not alone in the moral universe but can only exist as free moral agents by virtue of being members of a moral community, which in turn requires us to respect the freedom of others and not to reduce them to instruments in the service of our own egotistical ends. Also important is that Kant assigned freedom to the realm of noumena, or things-in-themselves, that cannot be known but only postulated as ideals. Even in its Kantian formulation there is something mysterious about freedom, something that eludes all representation and conceptualization. This is not yet the passivity of the one who prays, but as we shall see in this and subsequent chapters, it may have a certain proximity to it.

F. D. E. Schleiermacher, a defining figure of modern theology, took the Kantian inheritance in a very different direction from Fichte and did so in a way that brought to the fore the mysterious and ultimately unknowable impulse at the root of prayer. If we read Schleiermacher's theology as a kind of phenomenology of religious feeling, one of the conclusions to which it leads us is that, in the end, passivity is more ultimate than activity in the genesis of the self.[8]

Schleiermacher was a central figure in early German Romanticism, and in many respects his presentation of religion as an alternative to ethics and metaphysics sounds almost indistinguishable from what a more purely idealist Romantic might say: Religion, he says, in his *Speeches on Religion* from 1799, "is the sensibility and taste for the infinite."[9] However, whereas Fichte bases consciousness of the infinite in the immediate awareness of the self-activity of the will, Schleiermacher insists that such consciousness cannot be derived from the analysis of the will alone, any more than it can be deduced from any purely theoretical position. It must be received, and it is in our receptivity rather than our activity that we are more truly linked to the infinite. This receptivity is religion, and to want to enter into communion with the infinite without religion is to be like Prometheus, stealing the holy fire in "insolent enmity against the gods."[10] If we genuinely long for the infinite and revere it, if we have a feeling for it, then it will bestow itself upon us—but it must be given to us. We are what and as we are as a part of the universe, and we must accept our individual lives as a part of the whole, a limited and finite form in which, nevertheless, the life of the whole is manifest. As Schleiermacher repeatedly insists in the *Speeches*, the means by which we realize this is neither will nor knowledge but feeling, or, as he puts it still more precisely, that moment in psychic life before intuition and feeling have become separate.

Even if Schleiermacherian passivity or receptivity marks a shift from the thoroughgoing activism of Fichte, the position set out in the *Speeches* was criticized by many theologians for dissolving the transcendence of God into the infinity of the universe. His later, more doctrinally precise work, *The Doctrine of Faith*, is therefore more careful and, probably, more orthodox. Here Schleiermacher sets himself the task of expounding what he takes to be the feeling or self-consciousness of Christian piety in a rigorous and systematic way. The first and most basic element of Christian faith, he says, is "the consciousness of being absolutely dependent, or, which is the same thing, of being in relation with God."[11] He arrives at this point by an analysis of the conditions of human life, which, he argues, show that every relation we have to our world and to the various entities within it will always be a mixture of activity and receptivity in varying degrees. Our relations to our parents or to our country are predominantly receptive, yet in both cases we are also active in some degree, maybe extremely active, for example, by engaging in political life on behalf of our country. But "there can . . . be for us no such thing as a feeling of absolute freedom. He who asserts that he has such a feeling is either deceiving himself or separating things which essentially belong together."[12] Why not? Because freedom always requires an object, an other, upon which or toward which its action is directed, but it itself creates neither objects nor others. "Therefore in any temporal existence a feeling of absolute freedom can have no place"[13]—a position that clearly contradicts point-blank the position of Fichte's early philosophy. But won't the same thing apply to receptivity? Won't every single experience of receptivity also have a certain admixture of freedom? Indeed, Schleiermacher concedes, this is how it is with regard to finite objects. Even in our relation to the stars our freedom is in play, no matter how minuscule its part. But absolute dependence does not mean dependence on any particular entity within the world, not on our parents, or our biology, or our physical constitution. Absolute dependence refers only to the totality of our being-in-the-world, a totality comprising both our activity and our passivity. Thus, Schleiermacher argues, the one on whom we are absolutely dependent is and can only be God, as (what he calls) "the *Whence* of our receptive and active existence," and this "Whence" "is not the world, in the sense of the totality of temporal existence" any more than it is "any single part of the world."[14]

These last points are crucial. Schleiermacher is not arguing, as many Christian critics of Enlightenment and modern values argue, that the individual should submit his or her reason to any other human being or institution. He is not conceding the right of religious organizations to direct the consciences of individuals. Only in relation to God are we absolutely dependent, but in relation to God we can only be and must only be absolutely passive: Freedom is in play in every other relationship in our lives, and we need both to know that and to accept the responsibility that goes along with that. Our feeling for God is therefore not to be confused with how we are to be in relation to any purely human expressions of religion, but the God-relationship is determinative for the whole of our lives, inclusive of our religion. If this is the case, however (and even if there are other routes to the same insight), the moment of surrender, submission, or passivity that is integral to prayer is potentially revelatory of a deep structure of human life as such, what Heidegger might have called an *existentiale*.

Striving in Prayer—Kierkegaard

Kant, Fichte, and Schleiermacher constitute a significant part of the intellectual context in which Kierkegaard developed his original account of human existence, an account that in turn had a near-incalculable impact on the development of twentieth-century philosophy and theology. As we shall now see, the questions we have been considering take us right to the heart of Kierkegaard's thinking about what it is to be human.

The way that prayer reveals the relation of active and passive forces in the self in the self's God-relationship is well expressed by Jean-Louis Chrétien, who writes, "To ask is actively to acknowledge that we are not the origin of every good and every gift, and it is actively to acknowledge that the one whom we address is what he is. All prayer confesses God as giver and, by dispossessing us of our self-centeredness, is a speech that at every instant the addressee alone, in our eyes, makes possible."[15] Chrétien then proceeds to illustrate the point by referring to one of Kierkegaard's *Upbuilding Discourses*, "One Who Prays Aright Struggles in Prayer and Is Victorious—in That God Is Victorious." We shall shortly return to this discourse, but first it might be helpful to remind ourselves of the basic shape of Kierkegaard's conception of the self and of the God-relationship. His most concise definition is to be found in the opening pages of *The Sickness unto Death*. He writes:

> The human being is spirit. But what is spirit? Spirit is the self. But what is the self? The self is a relationship that relates itself to itself or is that in the relationship that the relationship relates itself to itself; the self is not the relationship but that the relationship relates itself to itself.... In the relationship between two, the relationship is the third as [their] negative unity, and the two relate themselves to the relationship and in the relationship to the relationship; thus, in terms of the attribute of "soul," the relationship between soul and body is a relationship. If, however, the relationship relates itself to itself, this relationship is the positive third, and this is the self.[16]

To be ourselves, we must choose ourselves, and to that extent we must be active in self-affirmation. However, Kierkegaard immediately goes on to insist that the dynamic relational movement is only completed when "in relating itself to itself and in willing to be itself, the self is transparently grounded in the power that established it."[17] To be a self is freely to choose yourself, but it is freely to choose yourself from the hand of God, as infinitely, absolutely dependent on God. Being present to yourself, being who you are, here, now, is simply being in the presence of God, here, now, seen from another angle: Knowing yourself as living in the presence of God is simply knowing yourself as who you are in your aspect of absolute dependence.[18]

This pattern is exemplified at many points in Kierkegaard's religious writings, which should not be read as merely illustrating the philosophical positions developed in his pseudonymous writings. On the contrary, they are better seen as the crucible in which that philosophy was formed. A discourse that especially highlights how the relationship of activity and passivity in the self is configured in the specific context of prayer is the discourse to which Chrétien refers. This is the last of the first series of *Eighteen Upbuilding Discourses* and is entitled "One Who Prays Aright Struggles in Prayer and Is Victorious—in That God Is Victorious."[19]

Kierkegaard opens the discourse by drawing attention to a scenario that has some analogy with Hegel's dialectic of master and slave. People, he suggests, are always hungry for recognition, and recognition is never more fully given than to those who have proved themselves victors or champions in some competition or conflict. It follows that there is always a ready response when someone calls us to some serious struggle and especially when we are inspired to believe that victory is certain. Even likely defeat can inspire us, if such a defeat were to earn us a crown of glory. What matters is not the victory itself but the recognition that we have "stepped up." If, however, the speaker added that the battleground was a person's own inner being and that the battle could be fought at home as well as anywhere else and then further add that the battle was prayer, the listeners would be puzzled and amused. This is because praying is generally assumed to be "the very opposite of struggling; praying is a cowardly and faint-hearted business, left to women and children, but struggle is to a man's liking."[20] If it is further added that "victory" in prayer is the "realization that one has lost," the listeners will be completely disillusioned. But is it at all appropriate to call prayer a "struggle," "since prayer, after all, is not a weapon of war but on the contrary the quiet pursuit of peace; prayer is the weapon not of one who attacks another or of one who defends himself but of one who yields"?[21] In any case, if the "struggle" is said to be between human beings and God, this introduces further difficulties, since "God is in heaven and man is on earth, and consequently the distance is too great" for them to fight—yet insofar as both are brought together in prayer there is also no possibility for a "struggle," since "if a person yields himself completely in prayer, he does not struggle, but if he does not yield himself at all, then he is not praying, even if he were to stay down on his knees praying day and night."[22] So, Kierkegaard asks, "Who is the praying one who struggles with God in prayer and therefore simultaneously preserves a relationship of deep and inward devotion to God because he prays but is also so separate from God that he is able to struggle?"[23] Such a one will, at the very least, have sufficient belief in God's goodness to want to strive with rather than against Him and will wish to see God's will fulfilled in their lives. As regards the specific content of their prayer, it can be extremely varied, the happiness of the beloved or their own happiness at the side of the beloved, the fulfillment of a wish or deliverance from a past guilt. If it is really assumed at the outset that the God to whom prayer is made is both good and loving (and why would we pray to a God whom we did not believe to be well disposed toward us?), what, then, does the one who prays seek? It is, Kierkegaard suggests, "a matter of making oneself clear to God, of truly explaining to him what is beneficial to the one who is praying, of truly impressing it upon his mind, of truly gaining his consent to the wish."[24]

But if prayer is in this way essentially a matter of explaining oneself to God, what exactly makes it *prayer*? What makes it different from simply trying to think clearly about one's situation on one's own and for oneself? Perhaps it is that the words spoken in prayer have the quality that Franz Rosenzweig called "vocativity," that one speaks them "to" or "as if" *to* "someone." Not "I wonder what I should think or do about x" but "What am I to think or do about x?" And note: In this latter case, it is not just that the words are addressed (as if) to another but that the "I" is itself involved and committed in a quite different way. It is not pondering the alternatives in semidetachment but is implicitly declaring itself ready for whatever claim the answer might hold. And perhaps, whether or not God is named, it is this quality of "vocativity," crying out for a self-understanding that the self cannot give itself that makes what is going on here prayer and not simply an act of reflection. And whether it is to God or to "the cosmos" or just "life," the cry of the praying self expresses its desire to be in accord with that power greater than itself: that is, to know itself as acceptable to God and accepted by God.

What, then, happens in the prayer or, more precisely, in the praying of the prayer? Kierkegaard recalls trying to explain himself to a wise friend. Having ignored his friend's initial advice, he now gets more and more worked up in explaining why he did what he did and justifying the action that he took. He seems to himself to be becoming more and more forceful until, finally, he brings all his arguments to a head "very briefly and with unaccountable force."[25] But what does the friend say? "He shook his finger at me and said: Your present view is just what I said from the beginning, when you could not and would not understand me."[26] In other words, what the one who struggles for in prayer seeks has already been given. How? Because we are always already the objects of God's unconditional love and care—long before we even begin to pray. In Schleiermacherian terms, being infinitely and absolutely dependent on God means that, since we cannot be without being sustained in existence by God, the mere fact of our being is already the primordial sign of God's love toward us. Or, as Kierkegaard puts it, "Should not a person who prays, indeed, one who prays aright, be one who says: Lord, my God, I really have nothing at all for which to pray to you; even if you would promise to grant my every wish, I really cannot think of anything—except that I may remain with you, as near as possible in this time of separation in which you and I are living, and entirely with you in all eternity?"[27]

In prayer, we have only to seek God; the struggle of prayer is to find God; victory is finding that the struggle was superfluous, since God is already found or, more precisely, we have already been found by God.

In a further illustration of his point, Kierkegaard pictures God as an adult who stands behind a child who is drawing and, without the child noticing, directs the pencil to draw what the child is really wanting to draw but is unable to effect. The adult rounds off the curves, straightens out the wobbly lines, adds in eyebrows and nostrils until the face looks like a face.[28]

Those who pray in order to understand their lives and what they should be doing are like the child, and the prayer is like the drawing. That is, the prayer is an attempt to picture their situation to themselves, to see themselves as they are. But, says Kierkegaard, there is a dissimilarity in comparison with the child and its drawing. For the adult perfects the child's drawing by adding to it, but those who pray find that more and more is taken away from them in the struggle. What maybe began as a question about their lives in the world and what they should think or do about this or that becomes solely about whether what they want is really in harmony with God's will. As the prayer goes on, the content becomes less and less important, and just this question as to whether they are as God wants them to be remains. And, in the end, even this must be given up.[29]

> At last it seems to him that he has become an utter nothing. Now the moment has come. Who should the one who thus struggles wish to be like if not God? But if he himself is anything [in his own eyes] or wants to be anything, then this something is enough to prevent the likeness [from appearing]. Only when he himself becomes utterly nothing, only then can God shine through him, so that he becomes like God. Whatever he may otherwise amount to, he cannot express God's likeness but God can only impress his likeness in him when he has become nothing. When the sea exerts all its might, then it is precisely impossible for it to reflect the image of the heavens, and even the smallest movement means that the reflection is not quite pure; but when it becomes still and deep, then heaven's image sinks down into its nothingness.[30]

The victory is not what the one praying expected, yet it is after all a victory. "Or was it not a victory," Kierkegaard asks rhetorically, "that instead of receiving an explanation from God he was transfigured in God, and his transfiguration is this: to reflect the image of God?"[31] In classic Christian theological terms, to know that we are made in God's image and cannot exist as human otherwise than as bearers of that image is already to have the assurance that we have and always have had God with and even within us—if we paused to notice it. In the distraction of the world as it is, however, it is an assurance we typically find only by struggling our way back to it. Simple passivity—going with the flow of the world—is amply criticized elsewhere by Kierkegaard, but the fact that we must exert ourselves to go against the stream of societal expectations about how it is good for us to be cannot undo the fact that "the answer" (or "victory") is only found when, having struggled, we give up the struggle and become as nothing.

But where has this got us with regard to what prayer shows us about the ontology of human being?

The first point to make is that the limit at which the soul struggling in prayer arrives when it surrenders its self-understanding to a "divine" interpretation of the situation is defined in terms of its being made in God's image, its being "like" God. That it must surrender itself to this new understanding is clearly indicative of a moment of passivity, yet what it acquires in this moment of surrender is the realization that it lives in what Fichte might have called the supersensuous world, that is, in the relationship of mutual freedom that is called "love of God" and, inseparably from that, love of the good.

In another discourse, on what he called his "favorite" biblical passage, "Every good and perfect gift is from above," Kierkegaard emphasizes that what is good for human beings can only be understood and accepted as a gift from God, since God is the sole source and essence of goodness. But, he asks, "What is the Good? It is what comes from above. What is perfection? It is what comes from above. Where does it come from? From above. What is the Good? It is God. Who is it who gives it? It is God."[32] Our capacity for doing the good, then, is a capacity we must receive from God. And yet, as other Kierkegaardian texts make clear (perhaps especially the long discourse known in English as "Purity of Heart"),[33] this capacity is inseparable from our will or desire to do the good: Purity of heart, as he repeatedly puts it, is to will one thing, and the only thing that can be willed with complete single-mindedness and single-heartedness is the good. The good cannot be an object of theoretical knowledge but exists only insofar as it is willed or chosen.

Kierkegaard seems now to be coming into extremely close proximity to Kant. Yet, against Kant, he insists that the good will can come about only as something given and received—as a gift. However, as "gift," the good will, that is, moral freedom, is received as having been given, genuinely given, and given away in such a way that the receiver is genuinely free in making it his or her own. The gratitude that, from a strictly Kantian viewpoint, would seem to indicate a residual element of heteronomy is therefore conceived of by Kierkegaard as a free act, that is, as the free decision that gratitude is a more worthy expression of the possibility we have of living as free beings than simply enacting freedom as if it were a self-generating function of the ego. In this respect it is closer to Nietzsche's *schenkende Tugend* than to the forced thanks of an economic exchange. In the mutual freedom that allows for and expresses itself in the free act of gratitude, the divine-human relationship thus becomes a relationship of love, such that the only thing that we, as it were, "get out of it" by attending to it is, to revert to the story of the struggler in prayer, to be near to God.

The Kantian picture has been significantly modified, not least by the acceptance of an ineluctable element of passivity in the constitution of the self. But how can we envisage the point of union of the *actus purus* of freedom and the passivity of having to receive every good and perfect gift—and freedom itself—from the hand of God, passively? How can we describe a state in which "I can" emerges out of "I cannot" or in which "I can" and "I cannot" are effectively saying the same thing? Kierkegaard depicts the zone in which activity and passivity converge and, ultimately, combine as a place where annihilation, transparency, pure luminosity, gift, and gratitude merge into a single, simple, but nevertheless differentiated way of being. As is well known, Kierkegaard was not one to be scandalized by the fact that the "explanation" of how the self can be "transfigured" in God cannot be rationally explicated at a single level of discourse and has what he elsewhere calls a "paradoxical" character. But can we give more human depth and breadth to Kierkegaard's account?

From Kierkegaard to Dostoevsky

To do so, I turn now to Dostoevsky's *The Brothers Karamazov*. Here we find the account of a life-changing religious experience had by his "hero," Alyosha Karamazov. Alyosha is preparing to become a postulant and is devoted to the saintly Elder Zosima, who has told him that he must leave the monastery and go to fulfill his destiny in the world. On account of the violent crises in his family, Alyosha is already in a state of great emotional turmoil when Zosima dies. What is worse, the expected signs of sanctification do not occur, and there is a great scandal scene in which some of the community loudly denounce Zosima as an impostor. Although the experience about to be described is not narrated as a prayer, the whole narrative context allows us to see Alyosha as enacting the story of a Kierkegaardian struggler in prayer, as he struggles with his conscience and his God-relationship for an "explanation" of what the catastrophic sequence of events mean for him and for his future vocation.

Keeping vigil by Zosima's body, Alyosha dreams that he sees his mentor mingling with the guests at the wedding at Cana in Galilee and bathed in the divine light of Christ. Waking up, Alyosha rushes out into the still, early autumn night.

> The silence of earth seemed to melt into the silence of the heavens. The mystery of earth was one with the mystery of the stars . . .
> Alyosha stood, gazed, and suddenly, threw himself down on the earth. He did not know why he embraced it. He could not have told

why he longed so irresistibly to kiss it, to kiss it all. But he kissed it, weeping, sobbing, and watering it with his tears, and he vowed passionately to love it, to love it for ever and ever. "Water the earth with the tears of your joy, and love those tears," echoed in his soul.

What was he weeping over?

Oh! In his rapture he was weeping even over those stars, which were shining on him from the abyss of space, and "he was not ashamed of that ecstasy." There seemed to be threads from all those innumerable worlds of God, linking his soul to them, and it was trembling all over, "in contact with other worlds." He longed to forgive everyone and for everything, and to beg forgiveness. Oh, not for himself! but for all men, for all and everything. "And others are praying for me too," echoed again in his soul. But with every instant he felt clearly and, as it were, tangibly that something firm and unshakable as that vault of heaven had entered into his soul. It was as though some idea had seized the sovereignty of his mind—and it was for all his life and for ever and ever. He had fallen on the earth a weak boy, but he rose up a resolute champion, and he knew and felt it suddenly at the very moment of his ecstasy. And never, never, all his life long could Alyosha forget that minute.

"Someone visited my soul in that hour," he used to say afterwards, with implicit faith in his words . . . [34]

This is a long, complex, and vivid passage that, as the quotation marks in the text indicate, plays extensively on earlier parts of the novel, especially the homilies of Zosima.[35] It would be plausible to read this as an account of a "religious experience" in a Jamesian sense, and although the whole context is strongly Christian, having been initiated by the vision of Cana in Galilee, the experience itself is not described as having a specifically Christian content, and some recent commentators have seen in it an example of post-Christian "minimal religion."[36] But whether it is strongly or weakly Christian, it illustrates the convergence of activity and passivity that I am taking to be a central feature of the life of prayer. The passage is marked by repeated indications of uncertainty and ambiguity, of something that cannot be said or written. This ambiguity has three salient dimensions: cognitive, emotional, and moral. Let us examine these more closely.

As regards cognitive ambiguity, the tone is set by the silence that encompasses the whole scene. What takes place is beyond words. The "experience" commences with a sudden fall to the ground. Garnett's translation suggests that Alyosha "threw himself down on the earth," but the Russian text speaks of him being "cut down," like grass or hay being mown or scythed. It is not a voluntary act of self-abasement. "He did not know why" he was embracing the earth or try to understand. Words and phrases ring in his soul, but it is almost as if he is not saying them. "Something" descends into his soul, and "someone" visits it—but what or who? We are not told. "Some idea" takes control of him—but what sort of idea? Again, we are not told. Perhaps there is here an echo of the apophatic dimension of Russian Orthodox spiritual writing, but as far as this passage is concerned, this is not expressed in directly negative or paradoxical statements, only in terms of the elusiveness and ambiguity of Alyosha's experience.

The link to the apophatic tradition is further strengthened if we turn back to Zosima's homilies, where he speaks of the sense of being linked to other worlds, a key feature of Alyosha's experience. "Much on earth is hidden from us," says the elder, "but to make up for that we have been given a previous mystic sense of our living bond with the other world, with the higher heavenly world, and the roots of our thoughts and feelings are not here but in other worlds. That is why the philosophers say that we cannot apprehend the reality of things on earth."[37] The world is an abyss of mystery for which the abyssal night sky is a powerful symbol, an abyss that human knowledge can never plumb.

The ambiguity of Alyosha's experience is also emotional. He is, from the outset, "weeping, sobbing, and watering [the earth] with his tears," and his soul "is trembling all over." Much could be said about the role of both tears and trembling in Dostoevsky's novels and in the Christian tradition more generally, but what they underscore in this passage is that the firm boundaries that a well-developed ego-self maintains in its dealings with the external world have become suddenly porous.[38] When we weep, our inner state becomes manifest in our external appearance, as when we speak of someone being "disfigured" by tears. Conversely, tears register the body and/or the mind being overwhelmed by external events such as a physical injury or a bereavement. Tears literally blur our vision in such a way that we can no longer see the world for tears and, being unable to see it, cannot put it at the distance required to act upon it. This inhibitory effect may be connected with why men in particular have been discouraged from weeping openly, since, in modern Western culture, men have been defined through their power of action, as opposed to the supposedly feminine tendency to "yield" the self (a contrast reflected in Kierkegaard's remarks about the tendency to regard prayer as a feminine business). Yet Alyosha's tears, while not unconnected with the state of grief in which he has spent the past few hours, are "tears of joy," and if tears are often reckoned as belonging to the childish things that men must put away, Alyosha's tears are central to an experience in which "he fell to the earth a weak boy, but he rose up a resolute champion." In this respect, his tears are a sign of his coming of age and, as such, of his transition from passivity to activity. Less emphasized in this passage is the motif of trembling, where a similar logic reigns, since trembling disrupts the well-defined bodily contours of the efficiently functioning ego-self and therefore indicates that the self is at the mercy of whatever is coming upon it and occasioning its trembling. Rodion Raskolnikov, the central character of *Crime and Punishment*, who spends much of the novel in a state of trembling, declares his aim as being to triumph over all trembling creatures, that is, to assert the sovereignty of the ego over its passive, sensuous environment.[39] In Alyosha's tears and trembling, then, we see that the ambiguous convergence of activity and passivity in the self is not simply cognitive (although that, naturally, is generally what most interests philosophers of religion) but also emotional—which could scarcely be otherwise if we once realize all that it means for us to be, really to be, embodied beings.

Finally, Alyosha's experience puts him in a space of moral ambiguity. He wants "to forgive everyone and for everything"—but he also wants to be forgiven, and for everything. These words too refer back to what has been a major theme of Zosima's teachings, deriving from the deathbed testimony of his brother Markel and restated in slightly varying formulations thereafter, namely, that we are each guilty before all, for all, and for everything and must regard ourselves as more guilty than all.[40] This, we may say, is Dostoevsky's analogue to Nietzsche's "beyond good and evil." The stance of entire acceptance of complete guilt indicates a moment of extreme moral passivity, a state in which I can no longer answer for myself or take it upon myself in any way to be the representative or agent of the good unless or until my guilt is absolved by another. Yet for Markel and Zosima, "guilt" is also acceptance of what Bakhtin would call "answerability," that is, acceptance of moral responsibility for the totality of our relation to the world. What we see Alyosha being initiated into here is a stance analogous to that of the unconditional affirmation of the other expressed in Jesus's saying that God sends his sun to shine equally on the just and unjust (Mt 5.45–47). The forgiveness he seeks and wishes to communicate is precisely a forgiveness that lives in and from the freedom of an utterly gratuitous and unmerited gift-relationship. As Markel says, if we could live from the standpoint of such a forgiveness, "tomorrow there would be paradise the world over." Although for the present we mostly do not want to know this, we could, each and all of us, freely choose to know this and to enter paradise—precisely by surrendering the moral yardstick by which we conventionally judge and are judged.[41] Kant could scarcely agree that this would be an optimal move on the part of the human being.

For much of this chapter, the emphasis has been on the God-relationship. However, implicitly in Kierkegaard and explicitly in Dostoevsky, we can see that the zone of convergence of activity and passivity in the self that is revealed in prayer has important implications for interpersonal relationships. The self that has surrendered the desire to define itself exclusively in terms of its individual freedom and that becomes the image of God only in its entire self-surrender to God will also recognize that every other human being is more than the ego by which we define ourselves in relation to one another, that each of us, whatever our personal, intellectual, emotional, and moral conflicts, also has a life hidden with God, whether we recognize it or not. That is, it knows that its God-relationship is not a reason to regard itself as elevated into the company of elect spiritual aristocrats but more a matter of coming into a deeper solidarity with all other human beings. In a Christian theological perspective, we might wish to further define this solidarity in terms of a solidarity in sin of all for whom the gates of paradise are now closed, and a closer reading of both Kierkegaard and Dostoevsky would, I think, show that this too is indicated in their work. "We are all guilty" is the obverse of our being free to take on responsibility for the transformation of the world.

We began with Kant and the famous Kantian charge that prayer leads to moral indolence. Whether the path we have followed suggests a simple rejection of Kant will depend in large part on how we understand Kant and how far we see his thought as open to dimensions of moral and religious mystery. But the phenomenon of prayer allows us—invites us—to see more in the basic configuration of being a knowing, moral, and emotional self than the Kantian model immediately suggests. As we draw closer to God in prayer and discover that God was always there and was always close to us, if only we had known it, we experience the mystery of God not simply in terms of God's transcendence over all worldly intuitions and concepts or of God's ontological otherness but also as intimately connected with the mystery of our own being—with the emphasis on *our*. To live with knowledge of that mystery is not to weaken our sense of moral obligation toward others or the urgency of maximally willing the good to the extent that we are able, but it is to infuse the life of freedom with the oxygen of gratitude and acceptance. In the following chapters, we turn to a number of modern writers who have been especially conscious of the mysterious dimension of our being and have given this a defining role in their account of human existence. This will further underline how the issue of religion, specifically Christian faith, in the modern world is not only a matter concerning the putative existence of an extramundane being, "God," but a question concerning who and how we ourselves are, in our very being.

2

Unknowing

> Can any praise be worthy of the Lord's majesty? How magnificent his strength! How inscrutable his wisdom! Human beings are your creatures, Lord, and their instinct is to praise you.... The thought of you stirs them so deeply that they cannot be content unless they praise you, because you made us for yourself, and our hearts are restless until they rest in you.
> —St. Augustine, *Confessions*

Into the Cloud of Unknowing

We have seen that the movement of prayer is a movement that brings those who pray to acknowledge their essential passivity and even nothingness in relation to the God to whom they pray. It is just this that, probably, lies at the root of Kant's distaste for prayer, since such a self-accounting is the antithesis of the attitude of the rational moral agent, who, in his view, effects the optimal realization of our human capacity for willing the good. Seen from the Kantian perspective, prayer means abdicating our innate moral responsibility. The praying self is an abject self, and abjection is the ruination of what is most authentically human. All of this is understandable, yet it oversimplifies. The passivity and nothingness presupposed in prayer do not straightforwardly imply the subjugation of the self to some external force, since their actualization in prayer is in accordance with the praying soul's own desire, as the words from Augustine's *Confessions* just cited show, words that are among Western Christendom's most quoted postbiblical words. Does the soul, then, desire its own annihilation? It seems that it does. Yet at the same time, Augustine sees this desire as related to the desire for *knowledge*, the Platonic *eros* that lies at the root of philosophy. But what can a soul that has become "nothing" know? An obvious answer would be: nothing. If it is in any sense a "knowing," it is a not-knowing, or an unknowing. Here, then, is a threefold relationship between the praying soul's desire for God, the realization of this desire in an "experience" of nothingness, and the condition of not-knowing inherent in such an "experience."

I shall attempt in this chapter to illustrate and explore something of the dynamic of this threefold relationship, with particular reference to three post-Kantian thinkers: Kierkegaard, Dostoevsky, and Simone Weil. First, however, I shall briefly indicate how their approaches are anticipated in both ancient and medieval sources.

In Augustine it is often hard to distinguish the longing of the restless heart from the Socratic *eros*, and in many passages he has difficulty in keeping these apart, as in book X, where the passionate longing to be united with God in love is processed through the question "what do I love when I love my God?"[1] As many have pointed out, one thread in Augustine's complex personal and intellectual development is the transmutation of Platonic philosophy into Christian spirituality. Yet Augustine's very (and very Platonic) eagerness to *know* God is constantly bringing him up against the limits of what human beings can know. Often this brings him to the point of denouncing those who presume to a knowledge of God that is different from the knowledge that Godself gives in the incarnation. Left to itself, the Platonic *eros* leads only to a one-sided and abstract knowledge, and if this is identified with a true knowledge of God, it results in a hubristic overestimation of what we are capable of achieving by ourselves.[2]

The idea that the God-relationship requires displacing the claims of knowledge in favor of the exigencies of love is, if anything, even more strongly marked in many other patristic writings. This can entail a negative view of knowledge, as in the apophatic dimension of theology that is especially (but not solely) characteristic of the Eastern tradition. Whereas positive, or cataphatic, theology seeks to name God in positive terms (as Lord, King, Father, Shepherd, Rock, etc.), negative, or apophatic, theology proceeds by "unsaying" all that the positive theology says. God is Lord—but not like any other lord we know, a King, but not like any earthly king, etc. The classic text in this line of thinking is *The Mystical Theology* of (Pseudo-)Dionysius, where we read of God that

> It [N.B.!] is not soul or mind, nor does it possess imagination, conviction, speech, or understanding. . . . It cannot be spoken of and it cannot be grasped by understanding. . . . It has no power, it is not power, nor is it light. It does not live, nor is it life. It is not a substance, nor is it eternity or time. It cannot be grasped by the understanding since it is neither knowledge nor truth. . . . There is no speaking of it, nor name nor knowledge of it. . . . It is beyond assertion and denial.[3]

In the Middle Ages, Dionysius was as influential in the West as in the East. Yet it has to be said that there is a constant tension between theologians' acknowledgment of the inescapability of some kind of apophaticism and their desire to vindicate the church's very specific and often very graphic descriptions of God. Theories such as that of analogy attempt to bridge the gap, but whether they entirely succeed may be questioned. But if scholastic theology itself got into a logically and ecclesiastically awkward situation at this point, a text such as *The Cloud of Unknowing*, produced with a more immediately practical aim than any Summa, Commentary, or Questions, gives freer rein to the apophatic voice.

The text is anonymous and dates from the second half of the fourteenth century. It has the avowedly practical aim of helping those seeking to make progress in the spiritual life, and the author beseeches his readers not to "read, write, or mention it to anyone, nor allow it to be read, written, or mentioned by anyone, unless that person is in your judgement really and wholly determined to follow Christ perfectly."[4] Theological writing of the Middle Ages was, of course, not so naïve as to be ignorant of literary conceits, but I think that the whole style and content of the book support the author's claim that this is not intended as a book for debate but for souls seeking God, a genre that was being rapidly developed in England in just this period and that was beginning to be directed to readers beyond the walls of monastic life (Margery Kempe comes to mind). The author himself was not theologically unlearned, and there are clear references in the text to such sources as Richard of St. Victor, Augustine, and Dionysius (generally referred to in the West as "Denys").

Nevertheless, *The Cloud of Unknowing* has a clear practical orientation that is manifest in the sharp distinction it draws between love and knowledge. "All rational beings, angels and men, possess two faculties, the power of knowing and the power of loving," the author writes, to which he adds: "To the first, to the intellect, God who made them is forever unknowable, but to the second, to love, he is completely knowable, and that by every separate individual."[5] Furthermore, he continues, "one loving soul by itself, through its love, may know for itself him who is incomparably more than sufficient to fill all souls that exist."[6] Love, then, would seem to have its own knowledge. Indeed, "the soul, when it is restored by grace, is made wholly sufficient to comprehend [God] fully by love."[7]

Love, however, is not to be confused with producing or stirring up feelings. Instead, it is a matter of finding out or responding to the movements of divine grace that are already at work in the aspirant's life. This, it is suggested, is something quite different from the "inventiveness of the imagination" or "manufacturing an experience." It is not an "activity of the mind," and "intellectually" it must be "left alone."[8]

At this point, the author begins to radicalize his argument. After all, we can very well imagine that whether his love is directed toward a human or a divine object, a lover will still have a certain consciousness of loving and of the object to which that love is directed. Poets have always been fertile in describing the perfections and attractions of their beloved objects of desire, and the same goes for religious poets. But now, our author tells us, we must even abandon thoughts of God's "kindness and worth." We must, it seems, not even think about God at all, even in the act of desiring God: "Therefore I will leave on one side everything I can think, and choose for my love that thing which I cannot think! Why? Because he may well be loved, but not thought."[9] The author even seems to offer something like a direct rebuff to Augustine's procedure in the *Confessions*.

> Should he [the thought] ask, "What is this God?" answer that it is the God who made you and redeemed you, and who has, through his grace, called you to his love. "And," tell him, "you do not even know the first thing about him." And then go on to say, "Get down," and proceed to trample on him out of love for God, yes, even when such thoughts seem to be holy, and calculated to help you find God.[10]

The grammatical content of what can be said about God is reduced to a minimum. The author virtually insists not merely on restricting oneself to a single word but on that word itself being no more than one syllable—a word like "God" or "love," as he says.

Yet though he warns against thoughts in general, he also urges the one who prays it to "really mean God himself who created you, and bought you, and graciously called you to this state of life. And think no other thought of him. It all depends on your desire. A naked intention directed to God, and himself alone, is wholly sufficient."[11]

Clearly, then, what is being proposed is not mindlessness. What is called for is a very definite mental action that is intentional in the double sense that it both requires the subjective action of the one who intends it and is also directed toward a definite intended object. It is not just a call to "let go your mind, relax, and float downstream": We must direct our thought godward. The author is not unaware that we are likely to want more information about what this means and to fill the intention out with a specification of its conceptual content, but this must be resisted. "Don't study these words," he warns in chapter 39.[12] "See to it that there is nothing at work in your mind or will but only God. Try to suppress all knowledge and feeling of anything less than God, and trample it down deep under the cloud of forgetting."[13] Yet interestingly, this is never treated as if it were the application of some systematic ascesis. It is not so much a matter of climbing the ladder of contemplation or of passing through a series of prescribed stages of noetic development but of constantly being engaged in purifying the intention, of returning to and holding fast to the originating intention that sets the religious life in motion—a view consistent with the author's assertion that those impulses that move us to want to pray are themselves the work of grace: In returning to them and holding them fast we are responding to the movement of God himself within the soul.

The Cloud of Unknowing is not, of course, a philosophical text—we might almost be tempted to smile at the naivety displayed by the writer when warning his reader against imagining that he is using terms like "cloud" or "darkness" in a literal sense, as if the "cloud" or the "darkness" were something that could itself be experienced. But before we get too condescending, perhaps we might consider whether we too are not constantly at risk of importing into the text some of our own ideas as to what a mystical text is or should be saying. It could, for example, be tempting to think he is proposing some sort of programmatic interiorization of consciousness, as many "mystical" writers doubtless do. But note the following: "And so it is that where another man might tell you to withdraw all your powers and thought within yourself and worship God there—and he would be saying what was absolutely right and true—I do not care to do so, because of my fear of a wrong and physical interpretation of what is said. But what I will say is this: See that in no sense you withdraw into yourself. And, briefly, I do not want you to be outside or above, behind or beside yourself either!"[14] The author never conceals that the practitioner is to go on living in the world, with others, and constantly warns against understanding the vocabulary of inwardness as being somehow in competition with the realities of bodily existence. We should similarly refrain from assuming that he is trying to instruct us in how to have a certain kind of experience. It would go against the whole logic of the book to hold that there was, in fact, any single or definable experience or mental state that could be regarded as the fulfillment of the intention to desire God and nothing but God. In the same vein, he cautions against attempting to excite oneself in an emotional way, to work up feelings of devotion and to strain at producing what the overeager learner mistakenly regards as an appropriately aroused spiritual state. The emphasis is precisely not on attaining mystical states but on the orientation of the intention.

This can be understood as strongly accentuating the subjective dimension of the religious life. Although the author never denies the legitimacy of the "objective" scriptural, doctrinal, or ecclesiastical dimensions of religion, he clearly qualifies all of these by his intense focus on the question of intention. At the same time, it is not subjective in a sense that might be natural to us in the wake of modern ideas of subjectivity as requiring perspicuous self-consciousness or moral and other forms of autonomy. Nor is the intended reader one who is concerned with being developed into a personality through internalizing the rich resources of a given culture. The intention of *this* subject, the subject who wills to enter into the cloud of unknowing, is by no means to live for-himself but for-another. His subjectivity is nothing other than the intensification of the intention to be for-another, that is, for the quite definite other who is God. Nor is this solely a matter of an autonomous self choosing to abandon its own presuppositions, since the basic impulse that takes shape in and as the intention to love God is not itself an original decision on the part of a ready-made, pre-existent self: It is a response to a movement or prompting of grace. This subject is not only for-another but from-another. Such a subject does not so much intend the love of God as allow the intention of loving God to become the defining formative drive of the (non)subject that it is. One might well ask at this point whether this is "subjective" in any recognizable sense, and, then, of course, one might recall the author's warning as to being misled by the implicit spatial metaphors indwelling our conventional religious language and remember that even such pure philosophical words as sub-ject and ob-ject are themselves saturated by the metaphorics of spatiality.

A Person's Highest Perfection

The spirituality of *The Cloud of Unknowing* and other late medieval schools of mysticism lived on via Teresa of Avila, John of the Cross, and the French School of the seventeenth century, and there is much to say about all of these, but I now wish to turn now to developments in the post-Kantian tradition.[15]

In the period following Kant, something analogous to the medieval "unknowing" again begins to be encountered. This is not unconnected with Kant's own reflections on the limits of knowledge and is manifested in the upsurge of interest in medieval mystical texts that seemed to their immediate post-Kantian interpreters to offer something like a way beyond the limits of reason laid down by Kant.[16] Kierkegaard explicitly disavowed mysticism, but at many points his own writing reflects the influence of older spiritual traditions, including those of a mystical character.

The threefold relationship of desire, nothingness, and unknowing is especially clearly illustrated in Kierkegaard's discourse "A Person's Highest

Perfection Is to Seek God," where Kierkegaard describes how, in its course through life, the self reaches a point at which it feels the need to be more than a link in the chain of endless becoming, "a string being played by the hand of obscure moods," that is, a mere reflex of natural, worldly processes, biological, social, or psychological.[17] At this point, the self bestirs itself to reflect upon itself and becomes concerned with directing its own life, rather than merely being pulled and pushed by instinct and social habit. But this isn't so easy, says Kierkegaard. For what is it that the self thus seeks to master: It is nothing but—itself! Although it might seem inappropriate in the midst of an "upbuilding" discourse, Kierkegaard now plays something that looks suspiciously like a logical trick: How can a self possibly "master" itself, he asks, since it is a matter of two equal forces? The self equals the self, and the one self can therefore never "overcome" the other. In the effort to get a grip on itself, then, the self is brought to an impasse. The two equal parts of the divided self fight each other to a standstill in a fearful internal war of attrition. The subject is annihilated, but "in this annihilation is his truth," since he has discovered that he does not have the power to be the ground of his own being: If he is to *be* at all, this being can only come to him from somewhere beyond the circle of his own power, from another.[18] Putting this another way, the experience of nothingness, the annihilation of the self, is also the moment in which a new possibility of being will be opened up, the possibility of a God-relationship, in which he is restored to himself on a new and unshakeable basis. The shipwreck of human will and understanding clears a space for a foundational dependence on God that encompasses and permeates every aspect of the subject's life in the world. "He who is himself altogether capable of nothing, cannot undertake even the smallest thing without God's help, that is to say, without being aware that there is a God."[19] The zero-point of not-being-able becomes the moment at which one knows oneself as rooted and grounded in the power that Kierkegaard elsewhere defines as "that all things are possible." Knowledge of his nothingness is thus the obverse— could we say "the incognito"—of the soul's discovery that the love, the need, the longing for God is what, with Heidegger's translators, we might call its "ownmost possibility."

In the last chapter, we considered the discourse "One Who Prays Aright Struggles in Prayer and Is Victorious—in That God Is Victorious," which is the last of a set of *Eighteen Upbuilding Discourses* to which "A Person's Highest Perfection" also belongs. There, I discussed this discourse with regard to the way in which it highlights the passivity of the praying self. Here, however, we note another aspect: the distinction between the desire for knowledge and what the one who prays rightly is striving for. Kierkegaard now describes the struggle of prayer as beginning with the desire of the one who prays as a desire to understand the meaning of what he is experiencing in life. In this regard, what he wants from God is not some external benefit (health or success for himself or another, for example) but an "explanation" or "clarification" (*Forklaring*) from God. But the final outcome is not an explanation or a clarification in a theoretical sense but what Kierkegaard, using a deliberate wordplay, calls a transfiguration (*Forklarelse*), in and as he consents to being nothing. This becomes clear if we extend the passage cited in the previous chapter in both directions:

> The outer world, and every demand he ever made on life, was taken from him, so now he struggles to find an explanation, but he cannot fight his way through. At last it seems to him that he has become an utter nothing. Now the moment has come. Who should the one who thus struggles wish to be like if not God? But if he himself is anything [in his own eyes] or wants to be anything, then this something is enough to prevent the likeness [from appearing]. Only when he himself becomes utterly nothing, only then can God shine through him, so that he becomes like God. Whatever he may otherwise amount to, he cannot express God's likeness but God can only impress his likeness in him when he has become nothing. When the sea exerts all its might, then it is precisely impossible for it to reflect the image of the heavens, and even the smallest movement means that the reflection is not quite pure; but when it becomes still and deep, then heaven's image sinks down into its nothingness. Who, then, triumphed? It was God, since he did not give the one who was praying the explanation he desired or he did not give it in the way that the striver desired it. But the striver too triumphed. For was it not a triumph that instead of an explanation from God he was transfigured in God, the transfiguration involved in mirroring God's image?[20]

In the later set of discourses entitled *Upbuilding Discourses in Various Spirits*, Kierkegaard makes clear that what this involves is nothing short of the recreation of the self in the image of God, in the paradoxical mode that the human self becomes "spirit" precisely by renouncing its characteristics of mastery or dominion and becoming "nothing in the act of adoration ... [for] adoration is precisely that wherein humanity is like God ... it is only when God has infinitely become the eternally omnipresent object of adoration, and humanity remains forever the one who adores, that they are 'alike.'"[21] Also in *Upbuilding Discourses in Various Spirits*, Kierkegaard recurs to the image of a transparent sea perfectly reflecting the radiance of God, but where the passage cited from the *Eighteen*

Upbuilding Discourses could seem to suggest an almost entirely passive condition, as if one had exchanged the passivity of being an instrument in the hand of obscure moods to being the passive matter of God's action, Kierkegaard now emphasizes that this condition is also characterizable as that of the heart that truly wills the good, in purity and single-mindedness.[22]

It is hard not to resist figuring the passages that have just been cited about becoming transparent to God as involving some kind of experience. If the meaning of our lives is dependent upon a right ordering of our God-relationship, if the secret of this is in recognizing and taking to heart our own incapacity to produce our own being and, with all our heart, seeking after God, won't the moment in which we become aware of this be of immense significance for us? Won't it be a discovery that shakes us to the marrow, that makes our hearts grow strangely warm, a moment to remember all our lives? Indeed, as we know, Kierkegaard was not silent about "the moment" (*Øjeblikket*) of intersection of time and eternity, a moment that is both temporal (and therefore an event within the flow of human experience and consciousness) and eternal (and therefore beyond all possible comprehension). This moment, whether spoken of as an atom of eternity in time, or as the moment of awakening of self-concern in which the self becomes "older than the moment," or as the moment in which the heart grows still and pure and becomes transparent to God, would seem to be a necessary requirement if time itself is not to be mere flux, a bad infinity, or one-damned-thing-after-another. And, from another angle, doesn't Kierkegaard's repeated insistence on *actuality*, on the actuality of religious existence, as opposed to the merely theoretical attitude of speculative philosophy also cry out for some kind of experiential element in becoming religious? Yet typically Kierkegaard is anxious to avoid talk of "experience," fearful, as was the author of *The Cloud of Unknowing*, of confusing emotional excitement and creative imagination with the simple dart of longing love. Any possible "experience" would need to be hedged about with ironic, ambiguous markers, making clear that if there is to be talk of experience, then it can only be of an experience that was not an experience but a resolution made actual in time.

Certainly there is no question for Kierkegaard of positing some kind of "state" at which the aspirant might hope to arrive. It is the desiring itself that is to be desired: To know one's need of God is a person's highest perfection, to will the Good. It is intention, not "state," that matters, a position, I suggest, entirely in keeping with what we have read in *The Cloud of Unknowing*. This means, equally, that whatever form of "mysticism" Kierkegaard might allow could not be used as a basis for smuggling some kind of "knowledge" about God into human consciousness, as some of his contemporaries hoped it might. In this regard, there is essential agreement between Kierkegaard's "upbuilding" works and the sharply worded limitations placed on knowledge in such pseudonymous works as the *Concluding Unscientific Postscript*. God is not known otherwise than in the terms of the intention itself.[23]

This specification of what is truly worth desiring in religion is linked to two further elements that we might, with Heidegger, call "equi-primordial": first, that the person who grows in love for God is also bound to grow in love toward others. In love toward God we are to learn to love others, and this is what it means "to be strengthened in the inner being." Secondly (and this applies both to desire and to the obligation of love), what is sought and might be found in the religious life is to be sought and found and held in the patience that creates continuity in, with, and under the flow of time: No possible moment of ecstasy can, of itself, resolve our life's questions unless or until it is made real in time itself, becoming temporal in such a way as not to lose itself in time but to become itself in time; humbling itself under time, living in time with an expectation of the eternal, acquiring and preserving the self in the patience that is the subjective correlate of time's diachronic distention. If, however, what we are talking about is not a state, extended through time, then, to use Kierkegaard's own term, it can only exist as a "repetition," a repeated renewal or recreation of the intention to be-toward/from God. Of course, even terms such as "intention" or "subjectivity" might seem to be saying too much at this point, especially if we hear in them connotations of "resoluteness" or "decision." Kierkegaard's insistence on the annihilation of the self as the obverse of its recreation in the image of God powerfully undermines any voluntaristic tones we might be tempted to hear in (or read into) what he is saying here. Yet it remains the case that the annihilation, the repetition, the recreation are to be *lived, owned, inhabited*. This cannot be a process that merely happens to us, as if we had no active part in it. If the content is determined in terms of being-for-another and being-from-another, that content is still experienced in the mode of a certain intentional comportment, and this is no less the case if I reformulate that—as, similarly, in the case of *The Cloud of Unknowing*—in terms of finding myself intended in it and by it, a very decentered sort of intention.

Simone Weil and the Spirit of Attention

The aphorisms of Simone Weil's *Gravity and Grace* present us with a very different kind of text from what we experience in the slow, cumulative flow of Kierkegaard's *Upbuilding Discourses*. The assertive tone of the aphorisms invites contradiction at every turn yet at the same time frustrates argument. Each aphorism is, in a sense, its own conceptual world, so that what is said in the one can easily appear to contradict what is said in another. Thus, in the section on "The Self,'" Weil writes: "We possess nothing in the world—a mere chance can strip us of everything—except the power to say 'I.' That is what we have to give to God—in other words, to destroy. There is absolutely no other free act which it is given us to accomplish—only the destruction of the I."[24] At the beginning of the next section, "Decreation," however, she contrasts decreation with destruction: "Decreation: to make something created pass into the uncreated. Destruction: to make something created pass into nothingness. A blameworthy substitute for decreation" (28). At the purely verbal level, then, there would seem to be a complete contradiction between the attitude taken to "destruction" in these aphorisms.[25] Yet if we are prepared not to insist on absolute terminological consistency and to allow for the role of context, they give expression to a coherent religious vision that is significantly congruent with what we have been reading in Kierkegaard. How so?

Like Kierkegaard, Weil does not see the destruction of the "I" or "decreation" as merely negative processes or events. Whether we assess them in positive or negative terms depends ultimately on our own God-relationship. Seen from the side of the conventional ego, they are, of course, negative, but seen theologically, they have a very different value:

> We are born and live in an inverted fashion, for we are born and live in sin which is an inversion of the hierarchy. The first operation is one of reversal—conversion.
>
> Except the seed die. . . . It has to die in order to liberate the energy it bears within it so that with this energy new forms may be developed.
>
> So we have to die in order to liberate a *tied up* energy, in order to possess an energy which is free and capable of understanding the true relationship of things.
>
> (30)

It is in this spirit that we are to understand such paradoxical formulations as "Moral gravity makes us fall towards the heights" (4).

Simone Weil's own life and fate could be taken as evidence of the danger of overemphasizing the negative aspect of this situation (and one could say the same of Kierkegaard), but this does not of itself invalidate the conceptual structure of her thought. In this regard, it is vital to hold on to her insistence that the destruction of the "I" is and must be a free act, to be sharply distinguished from the destruction of the "I" perpetrated by, for example, Nazi persecutors. The I is to be given up, but it is to be given up freely rather than being compelled by hunger, exhaustion, or torture. Destruction is not to be sought for its own sake but only in the context of the self's free love-relation to God. It is not suicide but detachment.

Weil has an unusual concept of creation with roots in the Kabbalah. According to this concept, we should not envisage God creating the universe in some kind of empty metaphysical or physical space external to God's own being. Rather, God creates by withdrawing into himself, and the world springs into being to fill the void thus left. This world is governed by the law of what Weil calls gravity or heaviness: Whereas God has the freedom to withdraw from himself, to rise above himself, as it were, the world exists in a constant process of sinking down into inertia. Without the elevating movement of grace, it would become altogether subject to necessity and, as such, inert and lifeless. Fortunately, it never is entirely without some relation to grace, since it is already, in some sense, "in" God. The dynamic tension between the "light" love of God—grace—and the heaviness of the world permeates Weil's thought. In giving up the "I," we are, precisely, freeing ourselves from necessity and becoming light and free. Our renunciation of this "heavy" being is thus, seen positively, "Imitation of God's renunciation in creation" (29). Here too might be mentioned the comment that it is "of no importance whatever" that I come to share in the divine joy, since such sharing cannot be a matter of necessity and, therefore, of importance (33)!

However, there is a further element in the process that has to be noted. Weil does not merely contrast God and the world in terms of the duality light/ heavy. The very lightness of God makes it possible for God to be gracious—not merely to rise, endlessly, as if by some law of lightness. That would make God too subject to the law of necessity. God's lightness is demonstrated precisely by his possibility of making a movement of descent: to be in the world of necessity without being subject to it. "Grace is the law of the descending movement" (4). Or as she puts it in a comment on art that could equally well be applied to God: "A double movement of descent: to do again, out of love, what gravity does" (137).

There is thus a double paradox. First, the renunciation or destruction of self is also the supreme act of freedom. Second, it is in allowing ourselves to be decreated that we realize the movement of grace that is also the movement of creation. "To re-establish order is to undo the creature in us" (30): Yet in this "undoing," "we are co-creators," and "we participate in the creation of the world by decreating ourselves" (29). That is to say, we allow the world to be as God wills it to be, not as we will it. Only so can it truly exist. What we "create" under the domination of the ego is only an illusory world, even if the necessity to which the ego and its productions are chained inspires in us the belief that this pseudocreation is "reality." Weil illustrates this with the reference to the Spanish Civil War, stating that the crimes of the fascists (and others) are "real," but since they do not reflect the creation willed by God, they are in a theological perspective "unreal." Thus, she comments that "the crimes in Spain were actually perpetrated and yet they resembled mere acts of boastfulness" (16).

Weil's readers might well ask how it is possible to annihilate myself or make myself pass into nothingness. How can God love himself in me or create through me? Weil's response to such questions interestingly distinguishes her approach from what we have seen in *The Cloud of Unknowing* and in Kierkegaard, since it establishes a possible role for intellectual inquiry within the overall trajectory of the religious life. One way of practicing decreation, she suggests, is simply by learning to be attentive, suspending the productive outpourings of the imagination by paying a disciplined attention to the world as it exists outside the orbit of the ego—"To see a landscape as it is when I am not there . . ." (37). Precisely because we are, as Weil puts it, born upside-down, we have to pay our attention to what seems to us to be the lowest, the dullest, the most necessity-bound forms of existence. Importantly, this refocuses the idea of religious intentionality away from the voluntaristic paradigm that might seem to characterize such expressions of the Augustinian tradition as *The Cloud of Unknowing* and Kierkegaard. What is required of us is not so much actively willing the good but practicing an indifference to good and evil, giving our attention equally to both: If we do this, says Weil, "the good gains the day. . . . A divine inspiration operates infallibly, irresistibly, if we do not turn away our attention, if we do not refuse it. There is not a choice to be made in its favour, it is enough not to refuse to recognise that it exists" (107). Prayer itself is more accurately seen as "absolutely unmixed attention" (106) than as a kind of *willing*.

It is here that Weil finds a place for teaching and learning, which can serve as "a form of gymnastics of the attention" (108). The element of necessity in this is indicated when Weil remarks that although we are constantly seeking to "read" the world in terms of higher spiritual meanings, we can only do so through work in which, for example, we learn the alphabet of a foreign language by manually forming the letters (118). This element cannot be avoided. If the ultimate aim is knowledge of grace itself, "the relations between man and the supernatural," then it requires an accuracy more exact than mathematics or science (119), and a life of study is one form of preparing ourselves for this.

If study provides one method, art, and the beauty that we encounter in the world, provides another: When Weil writes "Beauty: a fruit which we look at without trying to seize it" (137), she seems to be echoing Schopenhauer's view that art provides a release from the otherwise endless hegemonic activity of the will. Yet unlike Schopenhauer, this is not understood so much as a movement away from the world but precisely as a movement of attention to the world. In beauty, she writes, "there is as it were an incarnation of God" (137). At the same time, truly to be able to see beauty for what it is, we have to be capable of renunciation: "This includes the renunciation of that which is most deep-seated, the imagination. We want to eat all the other objects of desire. The beautiful is that which we desire without wishing to eat it. We desire that it should be" (136).

Intellectual studies and art may provide two seemingly "humane" modes of attention, but Weil is no less insistent on what, for her, was perhaps the most decisive path to decreation: affliction. We have to allow the world of gravity, the world of necessity, to be what and as it is, even when it remorselessly grinds us between the cogs of its machinery. Or especially when it does so: Affliction in Weil's vocabulary is not merely a synonym for suffering; it is suffering that "is essentially a destruction of personality, a lapse into anonymity" (94). It is the suffering of the impoverished working classes of prewar Europe and of the death camps, both of which impinged upon Weil's own experience. One can have compassion with a fellow sufferer, but affliction implies an annihilation of the personality that makes any talk of compassion impossible. "Only Christ has done it," she writes (94). Even if we have experienced affliction in our own lives, it is not something we can ever "know," for it occupies a place at which no knowing subject can survive, a place where what was once a human being has become blind hunger, blind fear, blind pain. Could we consent to and love such affliction, letting it be no more than the object of a true attention, then it would become a baptism (95), a sure touch of the lightness of grace descending into the depths of necessity.

Augustine, Dionysius, *The Cloud of Unknowing*, and Kierkegaard gave us ancient, medieval, and modern testimony to how, in encountering the transcendence of God, the soul found itself both radically intensified, concentrated into a point of absolute intentionality, yet at the same time radically destabilized, as its conventional metaphysical, conceptual, and emotional supports are systematically destroyed or rendered questionable. Weil's testimony points in the same direction. Yet for all her own Platonic yearnings, Weil lived this side of Darwin and Marx and makes very clear that, for her, the way to God is not and cannot be a way out from the world but is inseparable from how we encounter the world, in its formal structures, in its beauty, and in the affliction we experience (but can never know).

These are the ways in which we learn to encounter and to love God. God is the wholly other and the wholly immanent and neither of these, since these, after all, are descriptions fetched from the world of knowledge and concepts. Our consciousness, in the encounter with God (which, of course, is not an "encounter"), is both our consciousness of the selves that we actually are in the lives we live yet at the same time the utter decreation of self-consciousness, so that in being conscious of ourselves we are seeing ourselves as if with the eyes of another, simply attending to and consenting to being what and as we are, an embodied intention that is no longer construed in terms of will but of simple attention to what is given us in our being and in this moment. Such attention is indeed a form of intentionality, but it is an intentionality in which we ourselves are intend*ed*. It is not the intention to be for-oneself but to appropriate the understanding of ourselves as being-for-another and from-another. For Weil, the most eloquent statement of this intention was, famously, found in George Herbert's poem "Love Bade Me Welcome."

> Love bade me welcome: yet my soul drew back,
> Guilty of dust and sin.
> But quick-eyed Love, observing me grow slack
> From my first entrance in,
> Drew nearer to me, sweetly questioning,
> If I lack'd anything.
>
> A guest, I answer'd, worthy to be here:
> Love said, You shall be he.
> I the unkind, ungrateful? Ah my dear,
> I cannot look on thee.
> Love took my hand, and smiling did reply,
> Who made the eyes but I?
>
> Truth, Lord, but I have marr'd them: let my shame
> Go where it doth deserve,
> And know you not, says Love, who bore the blame?
> My dear, then I will serve.
> You must sit down, says Love, and taste my meat:
> So I did sit and eat.[26]

Herbert's verses speak from within a culture in which the language and symbolism of Christian scripture and theology had become a kind of second nature. Kierkegaard's self-annihilating and Weil's decreating selves, however, indicate a path toward God that many—perhaps the majority—of their secular contemporaries are likely to have regarded as deluded, mad, or ill, a judgment sometimes extended to Kierkegaard and Weil themselves. A further example is Dostoevsky's fictional Prince Myshkin, the eponymous idiot of the novel *The Idiot*.

Sickness or the Vision of God?

Dostoevsky's way of setting the question up is very different from Kierkegaard's or Weil's, but he too, in his distinctively novelistic way, makes clear that the experience of divine transcendence (a problematic expression, of course, but used here in a merely indicative way) is an experience in which the usual rules of rational consciousness don't apply. Prince Myshkin is subject to epileptic fits, but these seem also to occasion experiences that are strangely akin to those reported by the mystics. In a key passage, Dostoevsky describes Prince Myshkin's attempts to understand these experiences.

> He remembered among other things that he always had one minute just before the epileptic fit (if it came on while he was awake), when suddenly in the midst of sadness, spiritual darkness and oppression, there seemed at moments, a flash of light in his brain, and with extraordinary impetus all his vital forces began working at their highest tension. The sense of life, the consciousness of self, were multiplied ten times at these moments which passed like a flash of lightning. His mind and his heart were flooded with extraordinary light; all his uneasiness, all his doubts, all his anxieties were relieved at once; they were all merged in a lofty calm, full of serene, harmonious joy and hope.[27]

A few lines on, these moments are described as "the acme of harmony and beauty, [giving] a feeling, unknown and undivined till then, of completeness, of proportion, or reconciliation, and of ecstatic devotional merging in the highest synthesis of life." For such moments, he thinks, "one might give one's whole life!" And yet he also cross-examines himself as to whether these moments "were nothing but disease, the interruption of the normal condition; and if so, it was not at all the highest form of being, but on the contrary must be reckoned the lowest."[28] Nevertheless, the point remains that if the person experiencing those moments feels that they are worth the whole of life, then maybe they *are*.

Admittedly, the language of the passage just cited and of what follows seems to say nothing of God, only of "the highest form of life," "existence," and "the highest synthesis of life." In those terms, they might seem to reflect something more like a philosophical than a religious vision.[29] However, there is a further dimension to these moments, as we learn when the prince reflects that "'at that moment I seem somehow to understand the extraordinary saying that *there shall be no more time*. Probably,' he added smiling, 'this is the very second which was not long enough for the water to be spilt out of Mahomet's pitcher, though the epileptic prophet had time to gaze at all the habitations of Allah'".[30] In the prism of the "smiling" reference to Mohammed, then, we are given to understand that this is not merely a matter of the highest forms of existence, in an idealist sense, but potentially of a vision of God. Nevertheless—or precisely for that reason—it is impossible to resolve the question as to whether the whole thing isn't, after all, the effect of sickness. Without the support of rational discourse, can human beings bear so much reality? Myshkin leaves us with an unresolved and irresolvable question, answerable, if at all, from a perspective beyond that of the human, a perspective we are, of course, unable to access—except in moments of sickness or madness.

The path indicated by such figures as Kierkegaard, Weil, and Dostoevsky not only scandalizes the intellectual sensibilities of Cartesian philosophers but affronts the deep-rooted demand for autonomy that permeates both popular and philosophical culture. Yet as we have seen in this chapter, the option for passivity is not straightforward. The desire that culminates in unknowing is very much the subject's own, a focused intentionality toward God that leads the one who prays beyond what are generally recognized as the proper limits of the self and therefore also beyond the limits of reason. At this point, terms such as "subject" and "self" seem only weakly applicable, yet both Christian and non-Christian traditions suggest that what we arrive at is not simply nothingness; that is to say, it is not simply *nothing*. The nothing reveals itself not only as negation but, in its own way, as a kind of paradoxical plenitude, something for which "one might give one's whole life," as Prince Myshkin thought to himself. One word for this fullness at the heart of the annihilation of the self is *mystery*. But what could this mean? It is with this question that we turn in the following chapters to three major figures of twentieth-century religious thought who each articulated a sense for the mystery of being experienced at the heart of human existence.

3

Mystery

Recollection

As we have been seeing, prayer leads the one who prays to acknowledge the limits of human knowledge of God, and since whatever exists beyond the limits of knowledge is assigned to the realm of the mysterious, it is unsurprising that mystery has been a defining feature of religious language. Religious teachings and practices are themselves sometimes referred to as "(the) mysteries." However, the apophatic moment of religious life does not emerge only in that moment when the human mind moves beyond itself to confront the reality of God. On the contrary, it begins with and within the human being him- or herself. Before we can engage the riddle of an apophatic knowing of God, we must therefore engage what have been called the apophatics of the human person.[1] Of course, these are intimately connected. A person who has a sense for the ineffable mystery of God is also likely to be alert to the dimension of mystery in each singular human life. And while not everyone who has a sense for the mystery of each singular human life will also put their faith in an equally ineffable God, they will understand something of why believers want to speak about God in that way.

To explore what is at issue here further, I want to start with a classic but now generally neglected text on Christian mysticism, Dom Cuthbert Butler's 1922 book *Western Mysticism*. The reasons for its neglect are not hard to fathom, since Butler talks about the *objectivity* of mystical experience in ways that subsequent generations have found hard to emulate. As Butler states it, the claim made by the mystics is that there is "a (conscious) direct contact of the soul with Transcendental Reality. A direct and objective intellectual intuition of Transcendental Reality. The establishing conscious relation with the Absolute. The soul's possible union in this life with Absolute Reality." In the language of Christian theology, this means "the experimental perception of God's Presence and Being" and even "union with God," a union that Butler insists is not merely psychological but ontological.[2]

Both philosophers and theologians will find much to quarrel with in these perhaps hopelessly ambitious formulations, and both might be amused by the abundance of capital letters with which Butler marks out his key terms. Kantians, for example, may think that "a direct and objective intuition of transcendental reality" is simply a contradiction in terms, while those familiar with Heidegger's critique of the ontotheological foundation of metaphysics will be uneasy at the apparently unproblematic transfer of terms such as Reality or the Absolute to God—and theologians of various kind will feel that this sounds too much like the god of the philosophers.

Nevertheless—and this is why I am citing him at this point—Butler insists with exceptional clarity that our approach to the objective and ontologically charged knowledge of God can only be through the inner experiences of the human subject. He discerns in each of the main figures he discusses a pattern of purgation, recollection, introversion, contemplation, and devotion. In other words, the mystic way, as he depicts it, is a process in which the self turns in on itself—as in Kierkegaard's formulation concerning the self's "self-relation that relates itself to itself." Here is what he says of Augustine: "For Augustine, as for all true mystics, the indispensable condition of contemplation is such a purification of the soul as will render it fit for the ascent to the contemplation of God."[3] To move from purgation to devotion requires refocusing the self away from the external world and toward itself. Even when it is nothing more demanding than giving up chocolate for Lent, the exercise is undertaken by the self for the sake of the self. This is all the more evident when it comes to recollection and introversion.

As Butler points out, "The word 'recollection' is taken, not in its present, secondary sense of remembering, but in its primary sense of gathering together and concentrating the mind.... Shutting off all external things from the mind, and emptying it of distracting thoughts ... is the object of 'recollection,'" and such recollection "is the prelude to that entering of the mind into itself which is effected by 'introversion,' which is a concentration of the mind on its own highest, or deepest, part."[4] A paradigmatic account of this kind of recollection is Augustine's meditation on the way to God through memory, as set out in book X of the *Confessions*. Starting from the assumption that all knowledge is a form of recollection and that we are never able to find anything unless in some sense we already know what we are looking for, Augustine examines the contents of his memory to find where in it he has, as it were, stored the knowledge of the God that his conscious mind has forgotten. But while he finds his memory replete with images of all manner of created beings, "God" is somehow not to be found. And so he concludes: "Where, then, did I find you so that I could learn of you? For you were not in my memory before I learned of you. Where else, then, did I find you, to learn of you, unless it was in yourself, above me?"[5] A paradoxical outcome, then, since in an important sense God turns out not to be "in" the memory or is "in" the memory only as a result of an encounter with God outside the memory and outside the human mind as such—"in yourself, above me." The process of introversion is radically inconclusive and discovers no "ground of being" immanent to consciousness but, rather, at the deepest (or highest) point of consciousness debouches onto that which cannot be contained in consciousness and is necessarily and intrinsically external to it, something that, in the next chapter, Augustine will variously describe as beauty, a call, a taste, and a touch.

Butler glosses this passage as affirming "the simultaneous truth of . . . the immanence and transcendence of God," invoking the well-known passage from the *Confessions* in which Augustine speaks of God as being more inward to him than he is to himself.[6] He finds the same in Gregory the Great, who comments that "often we desire to contemplate (*considerare*) the invisible nature of Almighty God, but we are by no means able; the soul, wearied by these difficulties, returns to itself and uses itself as a ladder by which it may mount up, that first it may consider itself, if it is able, and then may explore, as far as it can, that Nature which is above it."[7]

This is what Butler calls "an experimental perception of the presence of God in the soul, Who at all times is there."[8] He insists on the objectivity of this perception, but at the same time the logic of his argument suggests that the mystery of the divine already begins in the furthest reaches of self-knowledge. In such a perspective, the apophatic moment in the God-relationship is preceded or anticipated by a similarly apophatic moment in our self-relationship.[9] If unknowing is the way that we are to know God, learning to unknow ourselves or to know ourselves as unknowable is the primary preparation for such "knowledge." Although such an apophatic approach to human being finds testimony in ancient and modern mainstream Christian traditions, I believe that it is also a significant element in a number of radical post-Kantian Christian thinkers, including Nikolai Berdyaev, Gabriel Marcel, and Paul Tillich, who will be the focus of the remainder of this chapter.

Kant's emphasis on the noumenal and theoretically noncognizable character of human freedom was certainly bad news for any theological attempts to identify a substantive immortal soul as the hallmark of human being. However, this same emphasis also encouraged a recognition of the ultimate mystery of the human personality. Such a recognition appears in a first wave of personalist thinkers, among whom Schelling and I. H. Fichte may be mentioned. This line continues into the twentieth century, including Nikolai Berdyaev, Gabriel Marcel, and Paul Tillich, all of whom were significantly influenced by both Kant and Schelling. Their post-Kantian emphasis on freedom makes their discussions of the mystery of the self and of the way that this account frames the interpretation of the God-relationship decidedly modern and even modernist. Unlike Butler, they are not looking to the data of Christian spiritual experience as demonstrating the objectivity of God but, instead, approach their experience as ineluctably existential and, as such, inseparable from the self's self-experience of being in the world—and ultimately mysterious.

Berdyaev: Personality, Freedom, and Novelty

Berdyaev was highly conscious of not writing and not wanting to write in a rigorous or systematic way, and he rarely addresses in any detail what often look like inconsistencies or unargued leaps in his thought.[10] He regarded the systematic form and the kind of rigor that he saw in Husserlian phenomenology as unsuited to dealing with human spiritual freedom, and, it should be added, he was not a close reader of texts. Nevertheless, freedom is a constant and unifying theme running through all his writings. His understanding of freedom led him to oppose any account of the self that relies on a doctrine of being. "Freedom cannot have its source in being, nor be determined by being," he writes.[11] The depths of human personality, Berdyaev believes, are rooted and grounded in an abyssal freedom for which there can be no rational explication.

The limits of philosophy are frequently mentioned in Berdyaev's works. In *Spirit and Reality*, for example, he says of Fichte and the German Idealists that their ontology produces only "an objectified concept" and an understanding of being that is limited to being that is susceptible of conceptualization and rationalization.[12] In this sense, they perpetuate a tendency already found in the Greeks and in Thomism.[13] Hegel is praised for having attempted "to put life into numbed and ossified being" and for developing a dialectic that could do justice to "real life."[14] Nevertheless,

Hegel's fixation on objectivity proves ultimately limiting, and the outcome of his dialectic is a system that is monistic and impersonal.[15] Even the latest versions of ontology—Berdyaev mentions Heidegger—fail to give expression to "the depths of existence" and therefore end in nihilism and pessimism.[16] "The mystery of reality is not solved by concentrating on the object," Berdyaev writes, "but by reflecting on the subject."[17]

In his comments about the limitations of philosophy, Berdyaev closely associates philosophy and ontology. The error of philosophy is precisely a way of prioritizing being that fails to attend to certain features of real existence—and this, Berdyaev thinks, is especially fatal in the closely connected cases of God and Spirit. He therefore applauds apophatic theology for denying being to God. He writes, "Negative theology recognizes that there is something higher than being. God is not being. . . . Knowledge of being is not the last thing nor the first."[18] But what's wrong with being? As some of the comments we have already heard indicate, "being" privileges the unchangeable over what is dynamic and living. Typically it appears in philosophy in the "numbed" and "ossified" forms that Hegel criticized or, as Berdyaev elsewhere puts it, as "congealed" being.[19] Being is not something of which we have experience[20] but is a construct in which we impose our human limitations on a reality that is always richer, greater, and more vital than our words and concepts are able to grasp.[21] A science of being leads only to a concept of the Absolute, as "the boundary of abstract thought"—but the Absolute (which, incidentally, has no relation to any significant other) is not "the God of the Bible."[22]

Instead of seeking to ground ontology in objectivity, we would do better, Berdyaev says, to turn to subjectivity, existence, Spirit, freedom, and personality—terms he uses more or less synonymously. A philosophy that did this would no longer be a philosophy of being: "The philosophy of Spirit should not be a philosophy of being or an ontology, but a philosophy of existence."[23] And: "It would be an error to identify spirit and being. Spirit is freedom, creativeness. Spirit exercises a primacy over being, the primacy of freedom."[24] Consequently, "Existential philosophy is not ontological philosophy in the traditional sense of the word."[25] And because ontology is not primary, philosophy cannot and should not seek a foundation in knowledge of being. Spiritual (or personal, or existential) existence can be communicated only in myth and symbol, not in concepts.[26]

We are thus presented with two very different kinds of philosophy, "the philosophy which acknowledges the primacy of being over freedom and the philosophy which recognizes the supremacy of freedom over being."[27] Berdyaev, of course, chooses the latter. "Freedom," he says, "is without foundation; it is not determined by being nor born of it. There is no compact, uninterrupted being. There are breaks, fractions, abysses, paradoxes; there are transcensions. There exist, therefore, only freedom and personality."[28] And of personality, he adds that "personality is outside of all being. It stands in opposition to being . . . its principle is dissimilarity."[29] Personality is further characterized by creativeness, the concomitant possibility of genuine novelty, and the uniqueness of each personal existence. Each personal existence is "something new" in nature that never has been before and never will be again. "Personality is the exception, not the rule. The secret of the existence of personality lies in its absolute irreplaceability, its happening but once, its uniqueness, its incomparableness."[30] But personality is not only a "new thing" in itself; it is also possessed of the freedom to bring forth something new in the world, to act creatively. A personal existence is not simply a "new" phenomenon that has never been seen before but an existence that lives by being constantly productive of novelty. Yet, on the plane of our common experience of history it seems possible to find explanations for and to construct taxonomies for classifying human behavior, even if one does not go so far as to suppose the existence of unalterable historical or sociological laws (as, of course, communist theorists typically did). The "time" in which the creative novelty of each singular personal life exists is therefore not the "horizontal" or "objectified" time running from past to present to future, a sequence of events crying out for explanation. Rather, it is what, in his work *The Meaning of History* Berdyaev called "super-history" and that he later comes to call "existential time," time that "happens in the vertical and not the horizontal."[31] This is why the true time of existence is apocalyptic time, for "time is not the image of eternity . . . time is eternity that has collapsed in ruins."[32] Only in the prism of eschatological existence can contemporary existence become meaningful and fulfilled—a thought that, however differently argued, was concurrently being developed by, for example, Tillich and in a more secular key by Heidegger.

Three further features of Berdyaev's thought are important to note. The first is that the privileging of subjectivity is not to be equated with individualism. As opposed to the thinking "I" of Descartes or the universal "'I'" of Fichte that see the "other" only in terms of the non-I, personality is, from the beginning, open to the other, whom it also experiences as another I or as a "Thou."[33] "The vision of another person's countenance, the expression of his eyes" offers more than a set of data to be interpreted but is—or is potentially—"a spiritual experience."[34] But it is not only a question of a relationship of I and Thou as opposed to that of I and It. It is also, for Berdyaev, a "We," a communion in the Spirit, for which he invokes the Russian term *sobornost'*, a communion in which the uniqueness of each participant is not subordinated to any universal ontology or ethic.[35] This is precisely a community that belongs to super-history, to existential or apocalyptic time, a community of transhistorical memory that is always still-to-be-realized. As such it is the memory of what we shall be. This is both the open horizon into which the concrete encounter with the face of the other opens up and also that community that can only become actual in that same encounter.

The second, closely connected with this, is that although Berdyaev often adopts a highly dualistic rhetoric, it is not a dualism that requires rejecting or denigrating the body. The "flesh" to which the New Testament opposes the life of the Spirit is not to be equated with the physical body but with sin, a point that Berdyaev sees as especially clear in the assertion that the only unforgiveable sin is the sin against the Spirit.[36] Spirit is not only divine; "it is also divinely human, divinely worldly,"[37] and the process of theogony is inseparable from the concrete worldly existence of divine humanity. It is the face of the other and the light in the eyes of the other that calls me to assume the spiritual responsibility toward that face and that light in which I preeminently discover what it means to exist as freedom and as Spirit.[38]

The third point is that because or to the extent that what we are dealing with here is a matter of freedom, there can be no guarantees as to a happy ending. Berdyaev's thought is expressly tragic or potentially tragic. On the plane of historical time we will never see the Kingdom of God, although, in this same historical time, we are always free to begin, once more, to seek it.

Gabriel Marcel: The Mystery of Being

There is significant convergence between Berdyaev's thought and that of other contemporary personalist thinkers, especially Gabriel Marcel, a personal friend during the Russian's exile in Paris. For Marcel, however, it is not so much a matter of contrasting the realm of the personal with the realm of being as of deepening the realm of being until it opens out into the realm of the personal. Transcendence is integral to our experience of being: Experience is always more than mere experience. In varying degrees, experience is saturated with an intelligibility that exceeds what can be made into an object of empirical investigation, and it has a kind of purity that evokes a sense of transcendence.[39] But experience is always primarily self-experience. It is existence as manifesting itself in me, even in such simple cases as the child whose whole life seems to cry out "Here I am! What luck!,"[40] which Marcel calls "a kind of exclamatory awareness of oneself."[41] But this is also an experience of existing that is, at the same time, entirely bodily. This is not the body as a possession or an instrument of the self and still less the body that exists as the object of physiological investigation: It is the body that I myself am, the lived, mysterious, felt reality of my being in the world.

It is solely as embodied beings, as beings who do not exist otherwise than as embodied, that in, with, and under our experience of beings we also experience the exigency of being, which, conversely, requires us to attend to, to become open to, and to give ourselves to the other beings in which being is disclosed to us. We do not first experience being and then add to that the claims made upon us by other beings, but we first and foremost experience being in those very claims. For Marcel, this means that the claims of intersubjectivity are also the claims of love, the call to exist as other than a subjective being-for-itself. As he puts it: "Love is the active refusal to treat itself as subjective."[42] Our basic experience of being is therefore relational, or, in Marcel's preferred term, participatory. "I concern myself with being," he says, "only in so far as I have a more or less distinct consciousness of the unity which ties me to the other beings of whose reality I already have a preliminary notion."[43] It is in this spirit that he interprets contemplation not as an act of withdrawing the mind from the external world—as recommended in so many treatises in the Western mystical tradition—but as a kind of focusing of the lived reality of the world: "To contemplate is to ingather oneself in the presence of whatever is being contemplated, and this in such a fashion that the reality, confronting which one ingathers oneself, itself becomes a factor in the ingathering."[44]

Marcel nicely condenses the distinction between his approach and that of Sartre when he says that my being is disclosed to me primarily as *chez soi* rather than *pour soi*: I am not a being-for-myself who can only then problematically come into relation to other beings but a being that exists as a readiness "to receive [the other] in one's own prepared place of reception."[45] For Marcel it is further axiomatic that this ontological exigency of a basic openness to the other—of self-transcendence—is, at its deepest, properly experienced also as the exigency of God. "The exigency of God," he says, is "simply the exigency of transcendence disclosing its true face."[46]

Marcel thus offers a sequence of mutually participatory dimensions of being such that the basic possibility of experiencing myself at all—my basic feeling of myself as being here, in this body, as this body, now this moment—already involves me in an implicit relation to others and in that relation to others also exposes me to the exigency of love, which in turn is the human form of the exigency of God. To know myself as being in the fullest sense is therefore achievable only to the extent that I am able to affirm the presence of the other and the presence of God as integral to my presence to myself and my presence in the world. As Marcel says with specific reference to the other human person, "When somebody's presence does really make itself felt... it reveals me to myself, it makes me more fully myself than I should be if I were not to be exposed to this impact." As he immediately adds, "All of this, of course... is very difficult to express in words."[47] I cannot learn how to experience the presence of others by any kind of technique, and perhaps still less can I learn how to make my own presence present to others. For Marcel, there cannot be any question of learning how to charm. Presence is not reducible to a technique or an object. It can only be glimpsed, invoked, or evoked and is essentially magical.[48] Or, in a term that gives the lectures their title, it is experienceable only as mystery.

Where Berdyaev insists on the duality of spirit and world, Marcel sees the movement of transcendence that leads toward the presence of God as already implicit in our experience of the world. Yet there is also a significant congruence between their philosophies, a congruence that doubtless played a role in their friendship and intellectual collaboration. As I have noted, the influence of Marcel is especially discernible in Berdyaev's *Solitude and Society*. Here Berdyaev describes the personality as "immersed" in being, and religion is said to be "man's revealed life, his life in the depths of Being."[49] "We must affirm the primacy of integral man," Berdyaev now asserts, "of man rooted in the very heart of Being, as against the consciousness of the confrontation of subject and being."[50] The existential subject is not to be understood as opposed to but as a part of being, and Being itself is thereby shown to be internally differentiated, as when Berdyaev speaks of "a transcendence of being operative in the heart of being."[51]

As was the case for Berdyaev, our relation to the future is a defining element of Marcel's account of human existence. In some contexts, this is specifically defined in relation to the contemporary crises of European civilization, further deepened in an eschatological direction after 1945 and the possibility of a coming nuclear war. Elsewhere, the question of futurity is more focused on the individual's relation to death. In either case, it is a fundamental existential characteristic of the human condition, as appears in the rhetorical question that Marcel poses toward the end of *The Mystery of Being*: "But would it not be possible for hope to be another name for the exigence of transcendence" (that is, for what calls human beings toward God) "or for it to be that exigence itself, in as much as it is the driving force behind man the wayfarer?"[52] At the same time, he insists that "to hope is not essentially to hope that."[53] In other words, hope (religious hope) is not hope for something, not even for the granting of a prayer or eternal life, but a basic attitude toward existence, a distinction that Marcel makes by contrasting *espoir* with *espérance*, as in the subtitle of his 1945 collection *Homo viator*, where the English "a metaphysics of hope" translates Marcel's *espérance*.[54] Here too, this distinction indicates an apophatic limit to human existence. Hope is not directed toward a "what" that can be conceptualized or rendered in some defining and constant vision. It is what Marcel calls "an open thought" that, as such, is directed toward the unknown.[55]

Neither Marcel nor Berdyaev regards the question of God as a question to which an account of "what is the case"—metaphysically or historically—could ever give a satisfactory answer. Instead, it is a question that is only meaningful in the horizon of free, personal responsibility. As such, it is a question that only really arises for a subject who lives out of his or her spiritual possibilities, and it is only properly addressed when or to the extent that we understand it as requiring a free, personal response. Proof, evidence, and persuasion are not to the point. Berdyaev's polemic against philosophy—Greek, Latin, and German—is unambiguous: God is neither a possible object of knowledge in any philosophical system nor the object of any positive science. Even if myth and symbol may be regarded as appropriate forms for expressing the overflowing reality of the divine life—or, more precisely, the divinely human life that is the actual revelation of God—the interpretation of these is dependent on the free activity of the interpreter. Myth and symbol are suggestive rather than binding. Marcel, on the other hand, does see what he is doing as philosophy, yet it is a philosophy that culminates in mystery. And to repeat, it is in the domain of mystery from the beginning: The basic experience of the child's awakening to life in the world is already mysterious, and the mystery only deepens as we pass on to the freedom of responsible adult life and from there look out toward the mystery of God. It is therefore far from coincidental that Marcel was a dramatist as well as a philosopher and that his philosophical work frequently alludes to his own and to other works of literature. In their consistent attention to the limits of knowledge in relation to spiritual life, both therefore reenact the tropes of apophatic theology in the context of a post-Kantian tradition that sees mystery as already present in the existential life of the living human being. This sense that the mystery of God is somehow bound up with the mystery of the self, means that an apophatic theology is not only a response to the incomprehensibility of God. It is in the first instance a recognition of the mystery of personal life and, as such, an apophatics of the person.

Paul Tillich: System and Mystery

In grouping Paul Tillich with Berdyaev and Marcel, I am suggesting a basic convergence that overrides some of the more obvious differences between the systematic Protestant theologian and his more essayistic and aphoristic contemporaries.[56] Perhaps more than any other modern theologian, he is an inheritor and continuer of classical German philosophy, attempting to think through the problems it bequeathed in essentially its own terms—subject, object, dialectic, spirit, epistemology, ontology, etc. But although his *Systematic Theology* offers a constructive defense of the concepts and categories of university-based theology, he insists from the outset on the apophatic character of all fundamental theological thinking. At the same time, to some extent paralleling movements in Russian religious philosophy and to some extent anticipating postmodern messianism, Tillich attempts to reframe these questions in the light of biblical prophetic eschatology. Like Marcel, he also affirms the traditional naming of God as being itself. However, he develops this naming in a manner very different from what we find in, for example, Thomism. Let us see how.

Tillich starts his *Systematic Theology* by considering the well-established duality of reason and revelation. Asserting that epistemology demands ontological grounding, he also claims that reason cannot be limited to what he calls "technical reason," such as the reason or rationality exercised in puzzle solving. In its fullest development, reason is "ontological reason," that is, "the structure of the mind which enables it to grasp and to shape reality."[57] This is further unpacked in terms of "the *logos* structure of the grasping-and-shaping-self and the *logos* structure of the grasped-and-shaped-world," which is to say that in all its operations reason takes the form of a subject-object relationship.[58] "Subjective reason is the rational structure of the mind, while objective reason is the rational structure of reality which the mind can grasp and according to which it can shape reality. Reason in the philosopher grasps the reason in nature."[59]

This formulation can, of course, seem like an invitation to skepticism, for how can we be certain whether what we see in nature really is the reason in nature and not simply the projection into nature of the rational structure of our own minds? For Tillich, however (as also for phenomenology), this correlation leads to a rigorously antiskeptical conclusion. Whether there really is a tree out there, my experience of seeing the tree is indubitable, the tree-that-I-see, real or not, is the tree-that-I-see. This cannot be doubted. Similarly in logic, even the relativist "presupposes the validity of logic in argument" so that "the very concept of knowledge presupposes an absolute structure within the flux of relative knowledge."[60]

But if the structure of knowledge is in this way absolute, what does this mean for our knowledge of God? Doesn't it mean that God, like everything else, can become a legitimate object of knowledge? Or, if God is entirely outside the subject-object structure, doesn't it follow that, really, we can know nothing of God at all? This might seem to be the conclusion of those spiritual writers who favor unknowing over knowing. For his part, Tillich accepts that God is not, or not simply, an object, and it is in this sense that he can also say that God does not exist, since if God existed he would be an object among objects and therefore knowable in the same way that other objects are knowable. In fact, though, we don't even know the objects that we come to know in our living intercourse with the world simply as objects, since the knowledge we have of them will in any given case involve something more than an epistemological relationship. This is what Tillich refers to when he goes on to speak of "the depth of reason," which, he says, "is the expression of something that is not reason but which precedes reason and is manifest through it."[61] Precisely because it precedes reason, however, it can only be spoken of metaphorically, and among the metaphors he especially commends are those of "the 'substance' that appears in the rational structure or 'being-itself' which is the manifest logos of every being, or the 'ground' which is creative in every rational creation, or the 'abyss' which cannot be exhausted by any creation or by any totality of them, or the 'infinite potentiality of being and meaning' which pours into the rational structure of mind and actualising and transforming them."[62]

The mention of being-itself points forward to and contextualizes what Tillich will later say regarding the definition of God as being-itself, which, he says, "is a non-symbolic statement" and, as such, beyond any name, image, or essence we might possibly ascribe to God: "God is being-itself or the absolute."[63] Full stop. Although every concrete statement we might make about God is in some degree symbolic, ranging from full-blown anthropomorphism to subtler views of God as love or infinite mercy, these symbolic statements are fully meaningful only with regard to their power to communicate a relation to being-itself that they can never fully articulate, or, as Tillich puts it, "the religious symbol, the symbol which points to the divine, can be a true symbol only if it participates in the power of the divine to which it points."[64] That is to say, this power is more than symbolic, even though it is "knowable" only in its symbolic expression.

Just what this last statement regarding the participation of the symbol in the divine power to which it points actually means was, at one time, the focus of considerable debate between Tillich's critics and defenders. What I want to emphasize here is that while affirming some kind of continuity between the symbol and what it symbolizes (symbols, including symbols of God, *can* communicate substantial meaning), Tillich is also flagging an ineluctable element of distance or difference, relating precisely to the "mystery" of divine revelation. In this regard, he especially privileges the term "abyss," which, as we have heard, is one of the metaphorical ways he refers to what is beyond reason in every act of reason. Like Berdyaev and Marcel, he understands our relation to this abyss of being in terms of mysticism. As he puts it in *Systematic Theology*, "In mystical language the depth of the divine life, its inexhaustible and ineffable character, is called 'Abyss.'"[65] Although he thinks that classical mysticism lacks the resources to give a fully adequate response to the radical despair of meaninglessness characterizing the present age, he similarly insists that "mysticism is more than a special form of the relation to the ground of being. It is an element of every form of this relation," inclusive of what he calls "the person-to-person encounter with God."[66]

In all of this, we would misunderstand Tillich if we thought that he was attempting to speculate about a God who occupied a kind of metaphysical space outside the world of human experience. For Tillich, as for Berdyaev and Marcel, the way to God is a way that can only be found in and through humanity. Whether we are thinking in terms of spirit or being, we can only come to (non)knowledge of God in and through the human: It is human spirit that is our point of contact with divine Spirit, and it is human being that reveals divine being.

One way Tillich makes this point is by setting his favored metaphor of "depth" over against more traditional ideas of God "reigning" from "on high," ideas that could easily be fused with ideas of God as a supreme being outside and apart from the world of human experience. Against such views, it is in the depth of existence that Tillich thinks we are most likely to find God, and we are led to this depth by confronting existential questions about ourselves. As he puts it, the way to this depth leads "through confession, lonely self-scrutiny, internal or external catastrophes, prayer, [and] contemplation."[67] Those who have journeyed toward God on such a road, he continues, "have found that they were not what they believed themselves to be, even after a deeper level had appeared to them below the vanishing surface. That deeper level itself became surface, when a still deeper level was discovered, this happening again and again, as long as their very lives, as long as they kept on the road to their depth."[68] And, he concludes, "The name of this infinite and inexhaustible depth and ground of all being is God. That depth is what the word God means."[69]

At the same time, as for Berdyaev, the exploration of this depth is not a matter of going deeper and deeper in a continuous linear progression, since it happens in a way that engages our freedom and registers the irruption of nonbeing and negativity into our lives. Alongside the metaphor of depth, then, we must set Tillich's etymology of the word "existence" itself as meaning "standing out," that is, standing out from the continuum of being into the open and anxiety-inducing space of freedom.[70] As he puts it in explaining the relationship between divine and human spirit, "If the divine Spirit breaks into the human spirit, this does not mean that it rests there, but that it drives the human spirit out of itself. The 'in' of the divine Spirit is an 'out' for the human spirit"—a situation that he describes as the "ecstatic" element of the human being's religious situation.[71]

Tillich also shares with Berdyaev the view that the way to God is historical and eschatological. None of what has just been said is to be envisaged in terms of timeless or absolute structures but is to be parsed as historical and temporal. The God-relationship is no longer just a matter of what we as subjects can know about a given reality "out there" but about how we are to relate to the temporal character of our own existence, "the time of our lives," the time that, according to Hölderlin, we *are*; it is the time in which God came, comes, withdraws, becomes concealed, revealed, returns, and will be.[72] But if human beings' God-relationship is a relationship that has a history, then God can no longer be construed as an object who is there, whether we attend to it or not, or even, it would seem, as a ground or abyss of being that is in itself unchangeable. If God is God by virtue of being the one who acts in salvation history, God would seem ill-served by repeating the Thomist definition of God in terms of simple, timeless being. What can being-itself be without a history? But if it acquires a history, is it still possible or even helpful to speak of it as being-itself?

One response to this set of issues is that of process theology, which Tillich explicitly rejects.[73] Substituting "becoming" for "being" does not of itself do enough to engage the nub of what is at issue in eschatology, for eschatology is not the endpoint on a continuum of change. For Tillich as for Berdyaev, eschatology involves radical disruption, discontinuity, the end of the old, the coming of what is new, death, and resurrection. That also means that it points toward the possibility of radical novelty. In the words of Isaiah that preface the last sermon in *The Shaking of the Foundations*, eschatology requires us to "Remember not the former things, Neither consider the things of old. Behold I am doing a new thing. Even now it is springing to light. Do you not perceive it?"[74]

Tillich's own awakening to the importance of eschatology seems to have been existentially associated with his traumatic experience of the Battle of Verdun, writing back from the front that "I am an utter eschatologist. . . . I am experiencing the actual death of this our time. I preach almost exclusively 'the end.'"[75] He spoke of this as the "death of our time" but also as "the revelation of death," that is, the return of the medieval vision of death as the all-encompassing and decisive power in human life, as figured in the motif of the dance of death. But this in turn is the revelation of nonbeing and, as such, the revelation that most profoundly moves us to raise the question of being at all. As Tillich states in a radical formulation of the interdependence of being and nonbeing: "There can be no world unless there is a dialectical participation of non-being in being."[76] Does this mean that even God cannot be being-itself unless being-itself is also participated in by nonbeing and is therefore no longer simple being, *ipsum esse*, being-itself?

Reflecting on the eschatological dimension of Tillich's thought (and with Berdyaev and Marcel also in mind), we may extract three points of importance. First, the eschatological event is not part of a pattern or sequence. It has a character of once-ness or singularity that limits and undermines the capacity of any discursive attempts to articulate it. Second, to think philosophical questions in an eschatological perspective is from the beginning to forgo the prospect of these questions being resolved into simple or univocal answers. Eschatological thinking cannot absolve itself of the difference it marks in relation to every worldly configuration of events. Eschatological time is a time of radical inversions. The good man may prove to be bad, the bad man good, the king may become a beggar, and the beggar be clothed with a glory greater than Solomon's. We just do not know, and we can never delete the "not" from every eschatological "not yet."[77] And if, for us, God is who God will be in the final eschatological revelation, then God too is "not yet" all that He is or may be. Third, the logic of Tillich's argument suggests that what is perhaps most important is precisely the conjunction of absolute singularity and eschatological advent in God. There is no other like Him, and He comes at a time that is not computable in human time. Thus, as for Berdyaev, his coming is "a new thing," and if this coming is the revelation of being, it is, in Tillich's terms, the revelation of a new being, a being that has taken up into itself the difference that marks it out from the simplicity of being-itself.

In the interwar years, Tillich typically articulated his turn to eschatology in terms of the correlation between the Christian symbol of the Kingdom of God and the Marxist symbol of the coming classless society. On Tillich's interpretation of Marxism, this coming classless society would not result from a linear unfolding of historical laws, as in "scientific socialism." The classless society was a "transcendent symbol" as much as an "immanent fact" and, as such, could only be approached in an attitude of active expectation and enacted through fateful decisions that were not prescribed by existing historical conditions.[78] Only so could the anticipated revolution be a genuine Novum, a new event in historical life—and it is precisely in this regard that it can be, as it were, the incognito of the Christian hope for the coming Kingdom of God.

After the war, the symbol of the coming Kingdom of God is largely supplanted by the symbol of Jesus as the Christ, the once-for-all Kairos who, of course, has already come in historical time. He is indeed still to return, "the End" is still not yet, but, as the New Testament asserts, those who are in Christ have already overcome the world. Christ is the power of the new being appearing in, with, and under the conditions of the old being. At the same time, as the closing chapters of *Systematic Theology* make clear, whatever we experience or know of Christ "in" history must still be thought in an eschatological perspective that combines both "not yet" and singularity. As Tillich puts it: "In order to emphasize the qualitative connotation of *eschatos* I use the singular *eschaton*. The theological problem of eschatology is not constituted by the many things which will happen but by the one 'thing' which is not a thing but which is the symbolic expression of the relation of the temporal to the eternal. More specifically, it symbolizes the transition from the temporal to the eternal."[79] Interestingly, however, he immediately connects this to the transition from the eternal to the temporal in the doctrine of creation, perhaps implying that beginning and end share a trans- or non- or even supratemporal structural identity such that although the end is "not yet" it is also experienceable in "the eternal now," returning us, it may be, to the logic of mysticism.[80]

Tillich is clearly aware of the perils of saying too much and of saying too little. His philosophical commitment to maintaining the truth-bearing power of the logos, his religious awareness of the simultaneously abyssal and radically futural character of the God-relationship, and his theological insistence that God is not mere process but also blessed in Godself from and to all eternity make for complex and, it may be, ultimately unsatisfying discussions. Something of the tension he is attempting to negotiate may be gleaned from two sermons on the theme of the new.

The first is the sermon already cited from *The Shaking of the Foundations*, "Behold, I am doing a new thing.'" Here, the emphasis seems very much on the novelty of the new thing God will do: "The new does not appear from a collection of the elements of the old which are still alive. When the new comes, the old must disappear . . . the new is created not out of the old, not out of the best of the old, but out of the death of the old."[81] Whether with regard to individual or to social reality, "the new" "must break the power of the old. . . . Forgiveness means that the old is thrown into the past because the new has come."[82] This can happen, Tillich says, because the source of "the really new" is "that which is always old and always new, the Eternal," or, as he also puts it: "It is new, really new in the degree to which it is beyond old and new, in the degree to which it is eternal."[83] Do we here discern the difference of the *eschaton* merging into the simplicity of the eternally eternal? Perhaps, yet at least here, the moment of difference remains significantly underlined. To the extent that the eternal is beyond old and new, its difference from time is marked more appropriately by the *différand* of the new than by the evidence of the old, a point Tillich emphasizes by reflecting on the prophetic word "Remember not the things that are old."

The second sermon on the new is the eponymous sermon from the collection *The New Being*, this time focused on the text of Galatians 5.16, "For neither circumcision counts for anything nor uncircumcision, but a new creation." Here too Tillich gives time to expounding the "not" implied in the proclamation of a new creation. But having done so, and turning to the question "What is this New Being?" he answers: "The New Being is not something that simply takes the place of the Old Being. But it is the renewal of the Old which has been corrupted, distorted, split, and almost destroyed. But not wholly destroyed. Salvation does not destroy creation; but it transforms the old creation into a new one. Therefore we can speak of the New in terms of a *re*-newal: the threefold '*re*', namely, *re*-conciliation, *re*-union, and *re*-surrection."[84] The sermon concludes: "A new state of things has appeared, it still appears; it is hidden and visible, it is there and it is here. Accept it, enter into it, let it grasp you."[85]

There is a marked difference in emphasis in these two sermons. In the broadest terms, this can be seen in the shift from an eschatological difference symbolized in the coming Kingdom of God to an eternal being that, indeed, will be but will be not otherwise than it has been and already is, as in Marcel's "transhistoric depth of history." The difference is important, but it is not necessarily a matter of either/or. Instead, we may see here the indication of a multidimensional dynamic that permeates the human way of being. We exist in the world in tension with an abyssal depth within—and, at the same time, we are stretched out toward an unknown and unknowable future. In both cases, the quest for knowledge will only take us so far. Crucially, the limit to knowledge that is at issue is a limit we run up against in our own existence, not merely in terms of an unknowable dimension at the heart of our being but also in the ecstatic mystery of our relation to time and our thrownness toward a future that escapes the frame of every account of existence that limits itself to being. This is the mystery of who we are. Are we, then, reduced to silence in face of this mystery? What, at this point, can we say?

4

Words

Ineffability

Prayer enacts a mode of self-transcendence that reaches out into nothingness, into the radical unknowing and mystery at the heart of our abyssal and futural way of being. Here, knowledge fails—but what about words? After all, despite what some philosophers might think, words have many functions other than to convey knowledge. Nevertheless, there is widespread agreement among the practitioners of prayer and their commentators that prayer not only brings us to a state of unknowing but also reduces us to silence. William James famously declared "ineffability" to be a defining feature of religious experience, stating that the subject of a mystical state of mind will typically say "that it defies expression, that no adequate report of its contents can be given in words."[1] From an expressly theological position, Dom Cuthbert Butler's comments on the mystics whose writings he intends to present point in the same direction:

> It is well to warn the reader that much of the language used will appear hardly intelligible, and may even give rise to doubts as to the mental balance of some of the writers. . . . The obscurity and apparent extravagance of their language is due to their courage in struggling with the barriers and limitations of human thought and language in order to describe in some fashion what they experienced in the height of the mystic state.[2]

This kind of claim is well supported by classic texts of Christian and other mystical traditions. One such is Augustine's report of his last conversation with his mother.

> And while we spoke of the eternal Wisdom, longing for it and straining for it with all the strength of our hearts, for one fleeting instant we reached out and touched it. Then, with a sigh, leaving our spiritual harvest bound to it, we returned to the sound of our own speech in which each word has a beginning and an ending—far, far different from your Word, our Lord, who abides in himself for ever, yet never grows old and gives new life to all things.[3]

Other examples can be culled from every period of Christian literature, from the apophatic theology of Dionysius's *Mystical Theology*, through medieval texts such as *The Cloud of Unknowing*, on through the devout life school of the early modern era, and down via Schleiermacher's religious romanticism to contemporary spiritual writers such as Martin Laird and Maggie Ross.[4]

Despite the ineffability of mystical experience, James also claimed that some kind of noetic content, a certain *thought*, could be drawn out of the mystics' silence. An appropriately sensitive psychologist could learn to read whatever was to be found in that silence and interpret its contribution to a fundamental ontology of religious life. Against James, late-twentieth-century theories of mysticism underwent a kind of linguistic turn. An early paradigm of what has since become a near-consensus among philosophers of religion was the 1978 essay by Steven T. Katz, "Language, Epistemology, and Mysticism." Katz was by no means dismissive of the possibility of mystical experience, but he did object to some of the claims made by or on behalf of those who reported such experiences. Especially, he took issue with the then prevalent view (such as we have seen in Butler) that there was a single core "experience" underlying the dazzling variety of mystical writings, utterances, and phenomena. Such a view perpetuated a naïve understanding of the relationship between language and experience. Experiences are not something that go on in a kind of silent parallel universe and then get translated, more or less successfully, into words. Experiences only occur as experiences, as *human* experiences, as *our* experiences, because they occur in a context framed by the beliefs, values, and intentions embedded in the universal medium of self-conscious life: language. "Whereof we cannot speak, thereof we must keep silent"—these closing words of Wittgenstein's *Tractatus*, though often referred to as "mystical," can be taken in a sense provided by the later Wittgenstein himself as profoundly antimystical: for where language has nothing to contribute, then there is nothing for us to talk about. Only what has its place *within* language can be regarded as worthy of discussion.

Katz stated what he calls "the single epistemological assumption" behind his essay in the following terms:

> *There are* NO *pure (i.e. unmediated) experiences.* Neither mystical experience nor more ordinary forms of experience give any indication, or any grounds for believing that they are unmediated. That is to say, *all* experience is processed through, organized by, and makes itself available to us in extremely complex epistemological ways. The notion of unmediated experience seems, if not self-contradictory, at best empty.[5]

As becomes clear in the remainder of Katz's essay, the most important of the complex epistemological ways in which experience is always already mediated is language. As he goes on to say, "The Christian mystic *usually says* that what he experiences is 'union with God'. The Hindu mystic *says* that his experience is one in which his individual self is identical with Brahman or the Universal Self."[6] By this, Katz does not mean to say that mystical experiences don't happen: simply that they don't happen outside the structures of interpretation given in, with, and under linguistic form. If we want to understand what's going on in mystical experience, then, we should not try to familiarize ourselves with that ineffable prelinguistic dimension of which the mystic seems to speak; we should simply try to understand, precisely, what the mystic *says*. There is therefore not "a" mystic experience but a Hindu experience and a Christian experience and, within each of these, a multitude of more specific experiences that speak to and out of the more specific linguistic and cultural coordinates of the experiencer.

Although Katz says that he is "no great admirer" of phenomenology, he does find some value in what he takes to be the phenomenological concept of intentionality. In the context of language, this means that no word or linguistic unit is at any stage to be found floating around without any intended reference whatsoever: Consciousness is always to be found related to some "datum as meant," that is, an intentional aim at "some specific meaning or meaningful content."[7] Consequently, the mystics' words about the ineffability of what they have experienced are, despite appearances, always intended to say something and, we might guess, are understandable in terms of the total discourse within which the peak moments of their rhetorical self-presentation are set.[8]

In some respects, my argument here follows in the wake of Katz's linguistic turn, not least with regard to the need for caution regarding the grouping of widely diverse cultural and textual materials into catch-all categories such as "mystical experience." However, while I do not subscribe to the idea of "a" mystical experience, one outside and beyond all cultural relativity, I do wish to shift the emphasis of this linguistic turn. If the experiential dimension of religious experience will in every case be shaped by language, we do well to remember that language itself is never unrelated to what precedes or lies outside language ("precedes" and "outside" being, of course, very rough and ready terms). It is not a question of language versus silence but of language as the mode in which silence becomes humanly meaningful. What this means in the case of prayer, mystical or otherwise, is that what is experienced will always reflect the cultural and linguistic perspectives of any given language but will also bring a certain "more" to whatever is said. It is the difference between language that is full and language that merely intends, even if, in this case, what it is full of is—nothing. With regard to prayer, this nothing relates not only to the one who prays but also to the one to whom prayer is made and whose presence is the mystery disclosed in the self-annihilating unknowing endured in the extremities of prayer—in other words, God. But what kind of words might best articulate such God-revealing silence? And what do they tell us about the God-relationship? To help prepare for a further consideration of these questions, I turn now to Martin Heidegger and Martin Buber in order to help think further about the relationship between language and what is before, beyond, or outside "the word."

Heidegger and the Belonging Together of Language and Being

Language plays a pivotal role in both early and late Heidegger, and, at least in the later Heidegger, it would seem questionable whether there is or can be a genuinely *human* moment or experience that is not always already mediated by language. It is in the speaking of the word that the world is opened and that we, its speakers and auditors, are granted access to something that abides in the midst of what is otherwise a sheer meaningless flux of temporal becoming. We do not and cannot become human apart from the way in which our humanity is opened up to us in, by, and as language.

A convenient presentation of Heidegger's approach that relates well to the present discussion is found in his lecture "The Principle of Identity." Much of his argument has now been incorporated into the stock-in-trade of the philosophy of religion in the continental tradition. Nevertheless, precisely because many of his expressions are so extensively traded in the contemporary knowledge market, it is worthwhile reminding ourselves how Heidegger himself arrived at and used them.

In this lecture, Heidegger sets out to consider the contemporary significance of the principle of identity, conventionally summarized in the formula A=A. As he proceeds to interpret this formula, Heidegger discovers in it a further layer: that A is not understood here simply as A being equal or equivalent to A but as A *being* A. A=A means A *is* A. This doesn't seem to get us very much further, until Heidegger turns to a Parmenidean fragment, translated by Kirk and Raven as "for the same thing can be thought as can be."[9] Heidegger interprets this as a statement of the belonging together of the human being (the one who thinks) and being. He argues that for most of the Western philosophical tradition (inclusive of philosophical theism), this has been understood as meaning that the truth of thinking is determined by its sameness—its identity—with what is. To speak truthfully is to state what is the case. The truth of a *logos* is determined by its conformity to what is, that is, to being or, more precisely, to the particular being under consideration whose "being" is assumed to be comprised in and constituted by its identity with itself. Language is merely the instrument by which the selfsameness of the object being thought is enabled to appear in thought, as itself.

This assumption, Heidegger claims, is one of the basic principles of Western philosophy, science, and technology. If it did not presuppose the validity of the principle of identity, Heidegger says, "science could not be sure in advance of the identity of its object, it could not be what it is" (26). This also applies to humanistic science, as is illustrated by the approaches to mysticism that we have seen in James, Butler, and other early-twentieth-century theorists. These assume the principle of identity by presupposing that there was some "being"—even if this was only a psychological being or entity—that provided the determining and self-identical measure of theory. *The* mystical experience—irrespective of the objectivity of its deliverances about supernatural beings—was the "thing itself" that made any scientific study of the phenomenon of mysticism possible.

Heidegger does not directly reject this principle, but he does sketch an alternative, based on an examination of how human and being "belong" together in the writings of Parmenides. Where this leads us is not to a repudiation of philosophy, science, and technology, since the focus on *belonging* is even to be glimpsed in the enframing that Heidegger regards as the operative principle of technology (38). If this enframing sets up and disposes the world in such a way as to allow only what can be scientifically known and technologically acted upon to count as reality—thereby, however unknowingly, giving effect to the principle of identity—it too reveals that there is a fundamental belonging-together in the relationship between humankind and being. In terms of the modern world's scientific self-understanding, we cannot *be* (that is, live) otherwise than as denizens of the reality that science and technology enframe. We cannot escape the world, and there is nothing in the world that is not, in principle, knowable by us. Even in our modern alienation from the world, we recognize and, indeed, proclaim that we belong fundamentally to it. Yet by insisting that only what appears within the frame of science and technology can count as real, the modern world excludes other aspects of the belonging-together of humankind and being that also merit attention. So dominant is the frame of science and technology, however, that we can only get to see these other aspects by taking what, from the scientific point of view, must appear like a leap into the irrational dark. Heidegger, however, sees it as a leap "into the realm from which man and being have already reached each other in their active nature [*Wesen*], since both are mutually appropriated, extended as a gift, one to the other" (33).

In other words, where the representational thinking that is characteristic of philosophy, science, and technology sees being in terms of the "reality" to which thought and language have to conform (even when, as in the case of "the mystical experience," that reality is supposed to be something irrational or ineffable), the leap takes us into a realm where it is simply not necessary to worry about establishing a connection between thought and being because they are each given to us in their inalienable mutual coinherence. Thought never is without being; being never is without thought. The leap lands us in a place where we always already are. Heidegger speaks here of a "realm, vibrating within itself" (37)—"vibrating" in that there is no final fact, thing, or reality to which meaning could be reduced and, equally, no final logical requirement to which being would have to answer to count as true. In his idea of "the event of appropriation," he therefore seeks to stress both that this is an "event," something that happens, and an "act of appropriation" in which we, as human subjects, are fully engaged and active.[10]

Crucial here is the question of language.

> To think of appropriating as the event of appropriation means to contribute to this self-vibrating realm. Thinking receives the tools for this self-suspended structure from language. For language is the most delicate and thus the most susceptible vibration holding everything within the suspended structure of the appropriation. We dwell in the appropriation inasmuch as our active nature [*Wesen*] is given over to language.
>
> (37–38)

Language reveals being as being open to language. Being "is" as a linguistic "happening," and only as such is it thinkable. This may sound like, but it is very far from being, a repetition of the post-Wittgensteinian view that we have no access to being apart from language and that, therefore, being "is" *only* what it is in and as language. In a Heideggerian perspective, it would be more accurate to say instead that being "is" *also* as it is in language—and language "is" (that is to say, functions as meaningful discourse) *also* as revealing what is given us in and by Being.

Heidegger's emphasis on the "belonging" of humankind and being involves a striking acoustic metaphor, since the German "to belong" (*gehören*) incorporates the everyday word "to hear" (*hören*). What this suggests is that language users do not "construct" meaning but derive it from the manner in which they listen or attend to being. Language itself arises as the form that such listening and attention take in human existence. Moreover, even though all language is likely to contain some trace, however distorted or diminished, of its original belonging-together with Being, some forms of language express this in greater measure than others—and, for Heidegger, it is above all the poet who speaks the Word that most resonates with the vibrancy of this belonging-together. Where language is most true to its own essence, poetic attention to the resonance of being in language is certainly not undisciplined—but its discipline is that of poetic utterance rather than scientific statement.

I suggest that Heidegger's account of the intertwining of thought, language, and being and of the presence of a certain silence within language itself offers a better approach to what is going on in mystical speech about what is beyond language than either the Jamesian or the post-Wittgensteinian approaches. It is "better" both because it does justice to the claim that there is no simple unmediated or uninterpreted experience that can reappear as such in language and because it allows us to take seriously the mystical writers' own claim that they are writing "about" something that is more than language. The task is not simply to cut out one part of the lived and coimplicating reality of world, language, and understanding but to interpret what it all means in the how of its occurring. Here too, the literature of religious experience is already an interpretation that requires further interpretation—but both in the mystics' own self-interpretation and in our interpretation of their work, what matters is to arrive at an understanding of lived existence. This means both the lived experience of those whose work we now read and, through that reading, releasing possibilities for our own living experience in our own time and place.

Buber: Toward Dialogue

Before returning to the dynamic interplay of silence and language in the practice of spiritual life, I pause to take note of the discussion of just these themes in the early writings of Martin Buber.[11] These writings also adumbrate aspects of a complex of issues that were central to the problematic of *Being and Time*, including the interrelationship between the singularity of lived experience, being as a whole (to use Heidegger's, not Buber's, expression), language, and death.[12] In the essay "Ecstasy and Confession," Buber seems to favor a kind of wordless ecstasy as the ultimate possibility of human beings' self-experience. Like Heidegger, he starts with a sense of dissatisfaction with an everyday life characterized by busy absorption in the multiplicity of worldly tasks and roles, which Buber calls "*das Getriebe*." Liberation from this condition is only possible for the "I" that, through its own inner activity, is able to experience or live out (*erleben*) an experience of itself as essentially unified. In the past, Buber suggests, human beings called the power that was active in producing such experience "God," but now we realize that "God" is essentially the ecstatic projection of what is most pure and inward in human beings themselves. Yet "God" remains central to how Buber describes a kind of life experience in which self and world are no longer differentiated but that, by the same token, delivers the self, the I, over into "absolute solitude: the solitude of that which is without boundaries."[13] Such ecstasy is "Unification with God. Ecstasy is original; entrance into God, enthusiasm: being filled with God."[14] It is an *Urerlebnis* of the *Urselbst*.[15] As we might expect, all of this means that what is lived in this *Urerlebnis* is beyond language. "Language is a function of community, and cannot speak of anything outside communal life [but] ecstasy is beyond all common experience."[16] However, at the same time Buber acknowledges an inescapable human compulsion to speak: "We must speak [*reden*]," he writes, even though speech or discourse, despite offering us poetry, love, and a future, cannot speak of "the one thing needful."[17] The person who lives ecstatically is therefore compelled also to live out a paradox that, at the deepest level, is the paradox of existence as such. In pure ecstasy "there is no longer a You in the I." Such ecstasy is, so to speak, the I's pure immediate enjoyment of its own boundless being. But "as soon as they speak, they already speak the other."[18]

In this essay and other early writings, Buber makes a number of attempts to characterize the kind of speech that might be most faithful to the *Urerlebnis* of the *Urselbst*. In "Ecstasy and Confession," he writes of it as "the impossible message," thrown in the moment of ecstasy's passing into the stream of time;[19] it is "an utterly silent way of speaking that does not describe but limits itself to imparting Dasein."[20] In a postscript to a selection of sayings of the Taoist sage Chuang-Tzu, he writes of the specifically Taoist sense of teaching as a kind of speaking that speaks only of the unity of beings and only of what is "necessary," in the sense not of logical necessity but of what is experienced as necessary in being lived.[21]

Most famously, he will also speak of it as the "fire" of Hasidic discourse, in which ecstasy is no longer a matter of self-enjoyment but a calling or summons to pour itself out in words, albeit in words that he characterizes as "stammering" and that find their medium in the genre of legend. Like the experience of ecstasy, the joy of the Hasid is boundless, but within the boundlessness of life, it has found a way forward: "To find God means to find the way that is without limits," so that whereas "the angels rest in God . . . the holy spirits stride ever onward within God."[22] As one who is *called* to speak, the Hasid is no longer a pure I but an I bound to a Thou, both the Thou who calls him and the Thou to whom he must speak. Such a soul has moved from "the sanctuary of silence" to "the market-place of the word."[23] Those "who truly experience their life in the world, experience it as duality," that is, the duality inherent in the basic experience of existence as a basic word, what, in his most famous work, he will condense into the formula "the basic word I-Thou."[24] From here onward, Buber would no longer see language as a second-rate substitute for experience but as integral to human beings' original way of being.

Basic Words

With these reflections in mind, we come to the testimony of the spiritual writers themselves. I shall briefly examine three, each of whom has already appeared one or more times in this study, *The Cloud of Unknowing*, Kierkegaard, and Dostoevsky, and which, with certain qualifications, we could take as representing Catholic, Protestant, and Orthodox perspectives. From each I shall draw out a basic word, establishing the first steps toward a vocabulary of spiritual life that, at the same time, allows for the resonance within language of that to which language attends in speaking. These basic words are not to be understood as the kind of primitive names identified by Augustine as the building blocks from which language as a whole is gradually constructed, a theoretical approach referenced by Wittgenstein at the outset of his *Philosophical Investigations*—but rejected precisely because it reduces language to an accumulation of nominal references and does not take into account the whole form of life through which their use is regulated and socialized.[25] Instead, the basic words I shall focus on here are words that even in their simplest forms are meaningful solely through the context of what Franz Rosenzweig called vocativity, that is, the concrete situation of speaking and listening. They are not words intended to point to objects in the world but words that bring out the character of the relationship that is lived in a life of prayer.

I take a first word from *The Cloud of Unknowing*, which, as we have seen in Chapter 3, offers its readers a highly practical and readable guide to the contemplative life, starting with instructions about how to begin. How are they to pray? What are they to say? The author's answer is that the prayers of contemplatives, "if they are in words, as they seldom are," have "very few words; the fewer the better." And, he continues,

> If it is a little word of one syllable I think it is better than if it is of two, and more in accordance with the work of the Spirit. For a contemplative should always live at the highest, topmost peak spiritually.
>
> We can illustrate this by looking at nature. A man or woman, suddenly frightened by fire, or death, or what you will, is suddenly in the extremity of his spirit driven hastily and by necessity to cry or pray for help. And how does he do it? Not, surely, with a spate of words; not even in a single word of two syllables! Why? He thinks it wastes too much time to declare his urgent need and his agitation. So he bursts out in his terror with one little word, and that of a single syllable: "Fire!" it may be, or "Help!"[26]

Thus, he says, a single monosyllabic word "pierces the ears of Almighty God more quickly than any long psalm churned out unthinkingly."[27] Earlier in the work, he has given "God" and "Love" as other examples of such words.[28]

On a certain view of language, such isolated words are meaningless. What kind of understanding could they give of the God to whom they are addressed, the Love they invoke, or, for that matter, the life situation of the one who speaks them? Surely—as the Dionysian theology of *The Cloud of Unknowing* might be assumed to intend—this is language directed at breaking through the barrier of language into the wordless space of mystical ecstasy, rather like Miró's late canvases that the artist burned through with a blowtorch? If they do assume or involve a certain understanding of God, or of love, or of the self, surely this can only be found by applying the methods of historical reconstruction and systematic exposition in whatever ways we are accustomed to applying them.

But let us keep to what the text is actually saying rather than imposing or denying some preconceived doctrinal commitment. The author seems to think that any of "Help!," "God," or "Love" will do equally well. What follows? Surely that "Help!" interprets and shows what is at issue in "God" and "Love." If this seems overly simplistic, we should remind ourselves that the call for "help" is a call to be saved, and the one from whom help is sought is then a savior and the help that is given is salvation.

Although the author of *The Cloud of Unknowing* probably didn't have direct knowledge of the Jesus Prayer of Orthodox tradition, his advice points in a similar direction. The full form of this prayer is a plea for help, "Lord Jesus Christ, Son of God, have mercy on me a sinner," but in practice it may be reduced to the name "Jesus"—a name that literally means "God is salvation." As one expositor suggests, "The word 'Jesus' alone should be used," and "when we speak of the invocation of the Name, we mean the devout and frequent repetition of the name itself, of the word 'Jesus' without additions."[29] The practice of this prayer therefore reminds us that in its most intense articulation, the mystery of the call for help is bound up with the mystery of the name and that this call itself is most persuasive when it is directed by name to one who can and, in love, desires to help. Going further, if we are able to hear the resonance of this name in the cry for help, then we might also observe that for Christians, this name is the name of the one who comes as the word of God, calling us back into fellowship with God, as God's friends, children, and co-heirs of the Kingdom.[30]

At the most elementary level, then, the word "Help!" reveals a self that cannot live out the boundless experience of the "I" of Buber's ecstatic self; unlike the ecstatic "I," it is not infinite, unified in itself, and solitary; it is a self not sufficient unto itself, a self whose reality and being are radically unsettled and that is unable to be its own ground and therefore experiences itself as driven to look to a power not itself. If we then hear the word "God!" as further deepening what is implied in such a "Help!," then, to adopt Schleiermacher's expression, we hear God as the "whence" of such possible grounding: "from whence comes my help: my help comes even from the Lord" (Ps 121: 1–2); God is the One who helps or the One who may be looked to for help, a "help of the helpless" who might be called upon in such a moment of ontological destitution and unsettling.

Clearly, that power remains undefined in the word "Help!" itself, and maybe there is no one there to help—a point to which we shall return. No one is helping—or no one is seen to be helping—*now*. Help is what must come if I am to continue to be, to exist. "Help!" calls out not just to what is above (or, if one prefers, to a sustaining ground beneath)[31] but also in time, to what is to come. Let it come, may it come, may it come quickly! Such a praying self is, to use a Kierkegaardian expression, a self that knows its need of God not only in a passive sense but also in the active sense of "need" conveyed by Kierkegaard's Danish verb *at trænge*, to push forward, an idea known also to the author of *The Cloud of Unknowing*, who speaks of the self using its single monosyllabic word to hammer its way through the cloud and darkness that separate it from God.[32]

My second word comes from Kierkegaard, who, word-child as he was, had a good sense for the dimension of silence in devout prayer.

> And what happened then, if you did indeed pray with real inwardness? Something wonderful. For as you prayed more and more inwardly, you had less and less to say, and finally you became entirely silent. You became silent and, if it is possible that there is something even more opposed to speaking than silence, you became a listener. You had thought that praying was about speaking: you learned that praying is not merely keeping silent but is listening. That is how it is. Praying is not listening to oneself speak, but is about becoming silent and, in becoming silent, waiting, until the one who prays hears God.[33]

But if one succeeds in "hearing God," however we may understand this more precisely, how might we speak of what we have heard? Kierkegaard's answer is as simple as that of *The Cloud of Unknowing*. In the journal entry NB5:22 he writes:

> To be able without reservations to say Amen to a prayer, O how rarely, how awfully rarely this has happened even to someone who otherwise prays diligently and constantly! It is just as rare as that moment in love when the lovers are absolutely each other's ideal. To say Amen in such a way that one has not a single word more to add, but the only word that brings peace and satisfaction is precisely Amen; in this way after having prayed in such a way that the entire need of the soul has been satisfied in giving utterance to the prayer, that one has got said what lay on one's heart, said it entirely, i.e., that one has become transparent to oneself before God in all one's weakness but also in all one's hope! Ah, if there is a moment, and perhaps this has often been supposed, a moment in which the whole language wasn't sufficient to express what was causing one pain, wasn't sufficient to express what lay on one's heart—oh! such a moment would be the very opposite, the whole language is superfluous, it doesn't matter if one has forgotten every single word of the language, one has no use for it, no more than to add Amen![34]

Kierkegaard's words too evoke the scenario of a self that looks beyond itself for a help it cannot give itself. It is a self that, in prayer, has become transparent to itself before God in all its weakness and in all its hope. In concluding its prayer and speaking its "Amen," this self seems not yet to know whether help will or can arrive. Its "Amen" is, in the first instance, simply the affirmation that it has said all that it might say, that there is nothing further to say, and that even the resources of "the whole language" would not add one iota to what is said in "Amen." Thus, as Kierkegaard says, "Amen" itself says all that the entire language could possibly say with regard to what the self might ask of God. But the "Amen" is not simply a repetition of the cry for help. It is also the word of acceptance of whatever help may or could be given. "Amen" is the entire entrusting of the self, with all its articulated needs, to God and, in the context of the total act of prayer, the entire anticipatory acceptance of whatever is to be the outcome of that prayer. In relation to the cry for help, "Amen" signifies entire acceptance of whatever help will, in the event, be given—whether or not it is the help sought consciously by the praying mind. So be it—whatever "it" may be.

"Help!" and "Amen," then, reflect two aspects of what Schleiermacher described as the absolute dependence of the self on God, the one revealing this dependence as causing the self to look beyond itself for the help it needs to go on being, the other revealing the self as dependent on God for all it receives.

This, maybe, reveals much about the self. It shows us a certain comportment of the self toward God that is widely testified in religious literature, but what does it show us of God? We can see what the self might look to God for, but nothing that has been said can show us whether this is how God actually is or even whether God exists at all or is simply a projection of the needy self. There is a crucial gap between human asking and receiving, and it is, precisely, a God-shaped gap. Can we make any progress toward filling this gap and completing this unfinished picture?

We have noted that our basic words imply some notion of God as helper, savior, and giver of what is best suited to the needs of the soul. But isn't it then a case of mere wish fulfillment to say that there is one who corresponds to these desiderata? There is only one small step from Schleiermacher to Feuerbach. Yet the ontological need of the self, while disclosed to the conscious mind in and through a range of psychological and other needs, may be something other than—greater, higher, deeper, broader, more enduring than—simple psychological need. That the word in which our immediate personal need is articulated is addressed to God—*intends* God—also marks a kind of surrender on the part of the self to understand and to grasp its own good. It is not just a matter of calling God in to fix whatever is not functioning within a human lifeworld that is otherwise entirely at our disposal. Rather, it is a matter of acknowledging that the structure and development of our lifeworld as a whole is ordered and may need to be reordered according to a logic—a *logos*—that comes from outside the orbit of our subjectivity. And if we understand logos explicitly as word, then this means that our prayer is always response to a word that calls and that, in calling, transforms the whole life situation of the one who prays, inclusive of their needs, aspirations, and joys. In responding, we become—we have to become—different to how we were before.

In other words, it is not just psychological wish fulfillment that is at issue. It is what T. S. Eliot called "the purification of the motive in the ground of our beseeching," or what Kierkegaard described in terms of the heart becoming so purified as to will only one thing and become like a still and deep ocean, ready to receive the imprint of God's image.[35] In *The Cloud of Unknowing*, the author attributes the power of the monosyllabic prayer of need precisely to the fact that "it is prayed with a full heart, in the height and depth and length and breadth of the spirit of him that prays it."[36] In other words, the need that comes to expression in such a prayer is not a more or less accidental need for this or that but the need of the self as such, as a whole, in the concentrated center—the heart—of its life. Yet we may still say that none of this takes us beyond human subjectivity. Can we go any further?

A response—if not fully an answer—to this question is to note that, as many of the spiritual manuals also insist, the move from praying for accidental and extrinsic needs to prayer as expressive of the need of the self as such is itself a work of God in the soul. Again, of course, such a claim proves nothing, but what is at issue here is not the proof or demonstration of a fact or argument but trying to understand and see what is being said in the elementary words of religious life. In this regard, what the claim says is far-reaching. For while it remains a given that the self must look beyond itself for its ontological grounding and that it is what and as it is only as grounded in God, this "ground" is not related to the exigent self solely negatively. In theological parlance, that the soul turns to God and seeks God is made possible by God's own prevenient grace. When Kierkegaard says that the need of God is itself a gift of God, he is echoing a long spiritual tradition—Augustine too, for example, says that the longing for God is what the soul must most long for, while Baron von Hügel spoke of God's prevenience as "the root fact and root-truth" of all the beliefs about God necessary for prayer.[37] We might think again of Buber's "necessity" or "one thing needful": Turning to God in prayer is not an arbitrary or merely willful act on the part of the soul but an act elicited by a lived need. How else could it have the character of a genuinely urgent, genuinely focused cry for help? We pray truly only when we truly need to pray—and only when we are ready to receive all that is given and whatever is given in response to that prayer. When this is so, then "Help!" presupposes "Amen." Nevertheless, if the prayer for "Help!" discloses not only the need of the self but also, through the co-agency of God in the praying of that prayer, this same co-agent God, just what are we given to see of God in the word of prayer?

A short answer might (again!) be: "nothing." We see nothing of God in such a prayer because the prayer is what it is as a human prayer. If worked—ultimately—by God, all that can be seen of the prayer as prayer is the pray-er who prays it, the one who prays: their need, their expectation, and their hope, expressed or made visible in the word. If, then, we speak of God as agent or cause of the prayer, it is not as agent or cause in any mechanical sense such as could be brought to light by uncovering a longer or shorter chain of causal relationships. Is there, then, no word in which the power of God at work in the prayer might become more manifest?

It is in the light of this question that I come to my third keyword. "Alleluia." This is the word ascribed in scripture to the angels who behold the face of God, who see God as he is and who respond with a word that is the purest verbal reflection and revelation of the divine being. But we notice immediately that it is a word of a very different character from "Help!" and "Amen." This difference can be defined by saying that it is a word of song, a word that is scarcely a word at all, its combination of vowels and liquid consonants constantly on the verge of dissolving into a pure ululation. Even today there is no standard orthography in English. If "Help" and "Amen" can be deepened to reveal a determinate content—help for this, Amen to that—"Alleluia" is a word of pure praise, a word without content. Except that its content is the fullest of all: It is the word in which the radiance of the divine glory is most purely and fully reflected in verbal form. When Kierkegaard speaks of the divine light reflected without distortion in the deep calm heart of the soul or of the self that is transparent to and transfigured in God, "Alleluia" would be the word—perhaps the only word—that might best speak—by singing—such immediate divine presence.

The God-shaped gap between asking and receiving is, then, articulated in this ancient ululation. This is the word that says—that bespeaks—the glory of God manifest in the work of redemption that is the fulfillment in human life of the work of creation. As such it is more direct, more basic to the lived experience of religious life than even the words expressive of need, acceptance, and gratitude. This is no longer prayer. It is praise. It is what is to be said when God is seen as God is. It is the word that makes visible the invisible being of God.

It might be objected that, literally, Alleluia is a word of invocation rather than evocation: "Let us praise Jah" (something like "O come, let us adore Him," to borrow a phrase from a well-known English Christmas hymn). In this sense it would not be a word expressive of divine presence but only a summons to turn toward that presence. But these are not exclusive functions. The summons to turn toward the presence is made possible because of that presence itself. "Alleluia" is spoken or sung only when the summons can be fulfilled—as in the Christmas hymn, which assumes the presence of the child in the manger as making it possible for us to go to adore Him.[38] The longing for God *is* the gift of God and as such is the way God is present to us and among us, here.

This sounds good, but whatever progress we may have made or be making comes at a cost. If we have found a word that is more than the word of prayer, it is also a word that exceeds the limits of pure reason. It is not a word that can be sublated into concepts or given a determinate content or definition. In being thought, just as in being spoken, it seems constantly to dissolve into the lyrical flow of its own utterance. What can we say about "Alleluia" except to say "Alleluia"? Isn't this purest expression of doxology simply another way of surrendering all claims to speak meaningfully about God?

The question as to just what such a purely doxological "word" might possibly mean is nicely put in a story told, in *The Brothers Karamazov*, by the devil. It is the story of a Russian nihilist who, having "rejected everything, 'laws, conscience faith', and, above all, the future life, dies."[39] On dying, he wakes up in a future life where, as a punishment for his unbelief, he is sentenced to walk a quadrillion kilometers. Being an obstinate Russian nihilist, however, he refuses to budge and lies down on the road in protest. After a thousand years of lying there, he finally gets up and begins to walk, and, after walking for millions of years, the former nihilist finally arrives at paradise, where, the devil concludes,

> before he had been there two seconds, by his watch (though to my thinking his watch must have long dissolved into its elements on the way), he cried out that these two seconds were worth walking not a quadrillion kilometers, but a quadrillion of quadrillions, raised to the quadrillionth power! In fact he sang "hosannah" and overdid it so, that some persons there of lofty ideas wouldn't shake hands with him at first—he'd become too rapidly reactionary, they said.[40]

Like "Alleluia," "Hosanna" is a word of pure praise that cannot be explained, justified, or evoked other than by the pure presence of God; such words are the verbal correlates of divine light. The nihilist could never be *persuaded* into saying "Hosanna," but when he lives the experience of the divine presence, he can say nothing else.

Yet it is, still, a word. In Buber's terms, it is not the articulation of the pure self-enjoyment of the "I" but the pure welcome of the Thou into the life of the "I," loosed from the claim of any need and even from the need of gratitude for good and perfect gifts. It speaks—but, in being spoken, it too must go out into the marketplace and become subject to the dynamics identified in Heidegger's concept of *Gerede*. Once spoken in human tongues, it can be repeated and passed along without seeing what is being said in it. The disclosive word that, in its primordial utterance, brought the divine light out from unconcealment and translated it into human speech becomes a cliché, perhaps the stalest and most hackneyed of all the clichés in the vocabulary of religion. Merely saying "Alleluia" or even singing it—even singing it in a perfect rendition of a sublime musical setting (Handel, for example)—will not and cannot of itself bring to view what is being said in it. Here, at this crucial point, as we attempt to move beyond the revelation of the exigent human spirit so as to see the invisible God to whom that spirit addresses itself in the extreme need of its being, we discover that, as Hölderlin wrote, "holy names are lacking" and that the holy names we still have are lacking the power to move us. But, as Hölderlin also goes on to say, this "lack" is not just a matter of a certain epistemological deficit (we are finite, God is infinite, etc.). It is because "our joy is too small."[41] To speak of God in such a way that the divine presence becomes manifest in the spoken word requires not just the purifying focus of the heart on the one thing needful, not just hope in the divine good-will toward us, and not just gratitude for gifts bestowed. It requires also that all of these are taken up into the joy that is the only adequate and appropriate human way of being with God. It is therefore not coincidence when, later in *The Brothers Karamazov*, the Elder Zosima insists that joy must be the heartbeat of the monks' religious life.[42]

But, to repeat, we live in a cultural situation in which words that might express and convey such joy—were we ourselves to be capable of it—are lacking. The death of God indicates not just a metaphysical deficit but the advent of a joyless gray on gray. Where in the prose of average everyday bourgeois life, in the trivia of the workaday world, or in the myriad pointless and empty adventures that absorb our surplus energies but serve no greater human good, where might we still find words that could, once more, awaken the echoes of angelic song? Where, how, can we hear a word that calls us to such joy?

5

Preaching

The Sacrament of Preaching

We have been reflecting on the intertwining of language and silence in the basic words that articulate the intimacy of the prayer relationship. Precisely because this intimacy both seeks and finds expression in language, however, it cannot be pigeonholed as something purely inward or private. Even when it is a word breathed voicelessly in the hush of solitary devotion it belongs to language, meaning that it exists in a fluid and dynamic relation to the extroverted manifestation of the word—the energetic word, as Gustav Shpet would call it—spoken, written, printed, or digitalized in the public space of the believing community. The individual who prays alone prays with words belonging to a common vocabulary and even when individuals invent new words and combinations of words in which to pray, these new words are available to be taken up into the common speech of the wider human community. Equally, when the multiplicity of prayers learned from scripture, prayer books, or catechetical instruction are progressively discarded in order that prayer might be focused in the kind of basic words considered in the previous chapter, the communal forms remain the background that makes such focus possible. The basic vocabulary of prayer, then, lives in continuity with what we might call the extroverted language of ecclesial communities and does so in ways that are both complex and subject to constant transformation. Such forms include doctrinal teaching, ethical instruction, and—the focus of this chapter—preaching.

It is a cliché to see the difference between Catholic and Protestant Christian traditions in terms of the tension between sacrament and word, so that Catholicism embodies the sacramental dimension of Christian life while Protestantism favors the word—although, like many clichés, it contains a grain of truth. In the first instance, the Protestant emphasis on the word means the word of scripture as the source and criterion of what can and can't be said of God, but it also means the scriptural word as it is actualized, week by week, in preaching. In this perspective, prayer is not a basic and universal form of religious life, an anthropological "given," but a practice that is only made possible through the word of preaching. For whatever else it may be, the word of preaching is a call to prayer—as seems to be implied in Paul's letter to the Romans: "But how are they to call on one in whom they have not believed? And how are they to believe in one of whom they have never heard? And how are they to hear without someone to proclaim him?" (Rom. 10.4). In other words, prayer presupposes faith, but faith is itself a response to proclamation, specifically the proclamation of Christ as a savior who has power to save. Seen in this way, preaching and prayer are not two essentially diverse kinds of action or discourse but two modalities of relating to the one divine word, each requiring attention and interpretation.

Preaching has undeniably got a bad name outside the churches and even to some extent within them. Many now see preaching as epitomizing authoritarian and nondialogical communication, telling people what to think or do from a pulpit lifted ten feet above criticism. Others find it merely boring. Doubtless, those dysfunctional kinds of preaching exist—but then again, there are those, like Dostoevsky's fictional Elder Zosima, whose words are able to rouse hearers to the joy at the heart of Christian life. In this perspective, to recur to an image ventured at the end of the last chapter, preaching is the translation of the angels' joy in the presence of God into articulate human speech, in such a way as to make it effective in our average everyday prosaic existence and to give words to those seeking to pray.

That may seem a long way from many people's experience of church preaching. It would be good for the churches if things were otherwise, but it is not my aim here to offer practical hints as to how preachers might do better. That is a task for homiletics. Instead, I shall attempt to reenvisage the basic task of preaching by seeing preaching itself as, in a certain sense, sacramental. The intuition that lies behind this move is that the joylessness of much Christian preaching (Catholic and Protestant) has to do with an overemphasis on the cognitive content of what is preached and a corresponding loss of the tacit dimensions of verbal communication that have a certain affinity to sacramental experience. However, it is important to understand this in the right way. I am not arguing for making preaching more emotional, more pictorial, or even more lyrical, though each of these may reveal a sense for the sacramental. Equally, each on its own or all of them in combination may indicate nothing more than a well-practiced rhetorical technique. To see preaching as sacramental is not to call for it to become more emotional, etc. but to expand our sense of what properly belongs to the word as word. But first, some further brief reflections on what I mean by "sacraments."

According to the Catechism of the Book of Common Prayer of the Church of England, a sacrament is "an outward and visible sign of an inward and spiritual grace given unto us, ordained by Christ himself, as a means whereby we receive the same, and a pledge to assure us thereof." This invites the objection that a sermon is, in the first instance, a *sermo*, a word, a speech-act, and, as such, not a part of the realm of outward and visible signs. According to a long tradition that is deeply ingrained in Western thought, the Aristotelian definition of human beings as the living beings having logos is to be understood as meaning "the human being is a rational animal." That is to say, *logos* is equated with *ratio* or reason, and *ratio* or reason is in turn equated with a realm of ideas that is essentially inward and spiritual. On this view, it is precisely language that distinguishes us from all those other animals that live and move in the world of outward and visible things. It is against this background that Tillich, for example, spoke of the essential "silence" of sacraments as differentiating them from "the word," to which he added the comment that the sacrament is "older" than the Word, although the Word is nevertheless the primary form of revelation.[1]

Tillich wanted to develop thinking about the sacramental beyond Protestant theology's well-trodden debates about the two sacraments of baptism and Eucharist. A similar move away from the conventional theological focus on "sacraments" toward something like a sense of "sacramentality" has also been a feature of much modern Anglican theology since the nineteenth century. Drawing on Romantic aesthetics, a number of Anglican theologians have sought to extend the sacramental principle to the whole range of human beings' embodied life in the world.[2] In taking flesh, it is suggested, God made all forms of fleshly life potentially significative of the divine being-in-the-world. David Brown, for example, has written of the sacramental potential of landscape, sport, and dance, as well as of the visual arts and poetry.[3] In this perspective we might note that preaching, too, is, after all, a bodily performance and sometimes quite a dramatic and even balletic one, as in the series of silhouettes illustrating the extravagant gestures of the great early-nineteenth-century evangelical preacher Charles Simeon or the kind of revivalist preaching portrayed so memorably by Burt Lancaster in the movie *Elmer Gantry*. In this perspective, preaching is more than speaking a word: It is a whole-body performance art.

The case for expanding our vision of sacramentality often involves reference to the Incarnation, a reference that both parallels and often explicitly invokes arguments offered in defense of icons by ancient writers such as John of Damascus. If Christ had deigned to appear in the visible form of flesh, John wrote, we should be humble enough to accept the visible form of painted representation as an appropriate means of communicating the divine presence, comparable to that of the Word.[4] Alexander Schmemann, a modern Orthodox theologian, goes so far as to affirm the totality of human beings' embodied life in the world as "sacramental," as indicated by the title of his book *The Sacrament of the World*—although Schmemann begins not with the visual nature of worldly being but with human beings' basic need to eat, giving a theological twist to the Feuerbachian slogan "You are what you eat."[5] This turn to the sacramental need not exclude words (Brown explicitly thematizes "word" as one mode of the widened sacramental vision he is proposing). However, the attempt to generate a larger and broader sense of the sacramental tends to mean looking less at "the word" and more at the whole range of "outward and visible" bodily experiences. The emphasis is therefore generally on those experiences in which language and the rationality associated with language are absent or much reduced. Historic memory remains vigilant against the reduction of God to "three angry letters in a book," as the Scottish poet Edwin Muir put it in his poem "The Incarnate One," in which he reflects on the distortions of the "fleshless word" that he experienced in his Calvinist upbringing.[6]

Yet language is as much a manifestation of embodied life as any physical gesture. We could not speak at all if we were not beings endowed with vocal cords, and we could not hear without being endowed with ears, and we could not even think silently in words without the electrochemical activity of the brain. Language exists only as a function of embodied beings such as we are. At the same time, the expressive power of language relies essentially on what have been called the metaphors we live by, the presence of the body in the mind and in the symbols by which we communicate our thoughts to one another. This has been explored from the perspective of psychology in the influential work of Lakoff and Johnson, but a powerful theological account of the somatic character of language is already found in many historic figures of Christian thought, including the idiosyncratic but illuminating reflections of Kierkegaard's contemporary and adversary, the priest-poet-politician N. F. S. Grundtvig.[7]

As Kierkegaard complained, Grundtvig was by no means a rigorous thinker, and his ideas were often expressed allusively and poetically, making it difficult to extract a firmly defined teaching from what he wrote. Nevertheless, he had a powerful sense for the bodily character of language. As he wrote: "The word is revelation's body."[8] This remark pithily condenses a number of key theological affirmations. In Grundtvig's sense, "the word" is the word that, according to John the Evangelist, "was in the beginning with God . . . by whom all things were made" (Jn 1.2–3); it is the word that became incarnate in Jesus Christ and becomes present in spirit-filled preaching. But this last is only possible because it is also a human word. It is the word as we find it written in scripture, which Grundtvig identified with the original language of Eden. More importantly, he regarded this same word as present in and even shaping the mother tongues of all human communities. In all these senses, the word is not primarily a means of communicating ideas but of bringing to consciousness the spiritual and living reality that is God's creation. The presence of the creative divine Word in the humblest everyday human words is what makes it possible for these words to be the means of expressing divine truths, including the truth of the word incarnate. Importantly, Grundtvig sees the word as having an essentially pictorial character, corresponding to the sensuousness and materiality of human life in the world. The picture-thinking that takes place in and as language is therefore not something to be transcended in favor of a more conceptual form of thought (as Hegel supposed) but is precisely where we are to find the revelation that language makes possible. This is why the word is the *body* of revelation, the concrete living human form in which divine truth is made present.

Grundtvig's emphasis on the pictoriality of language points us to the power of language to help us to see. Kierkegaard several times quoted the saying *loquere ut videam*, "speak that I may see you." This supposes that language, the word, has the power to illuminate, to make visible, and so to make us *see*. Recalling the definition of a sacrament as an outward and visible sign, the word spoken in preaching is neither outward nor visible—but it may have power to make what is outward and visible become a sign, pointing us to a meaning that we do not see in mere seeing.

Letting Truth Be Seen

Again, it is Heidegger's reflections on language that offer further guidance, especially in the discussion of making-visible in the introduction to *Being and Time*. *Being and Time* presents itself as a phenomenological approach to the question of being, and Heidegger is sufficiently considerate of his readers to begin by spelling out just what he means by phenomenology, breaking the word down into its two parts, *phainomenon* and *logos*. Of the latter he says that "*Logos* as 'discourse' means . . . to make manifest what one is 'talking about' in one's discourse."[9] "The *logos* lets something be seen" (56/32)—which, as Heidegger indicates, puts in play the verb *phainesthai*, from which "phenomenon" itself is derived. Genuine discourse is apophantic, a phenomenologization in which we are enabled to see *what* is being said from the very process of talking and in such a way that what one person says is disclosed or made accessible to others.

Logos points us toward a certain something, toward "what" is being talked about. But precisely because it is not a dumb, gestural pointing, it "points" by letting what is being pointed to be seen "*as* something." It is therefore inherently articulated and has the character of a *synthēsis*, which, Heidegger notes, creates the possibility of what is being said being either true or false. However, as he understands it, the truth of *logos* is not to be understood in terms of its correspondence or agreement with things "out there" but as its capacity for making manifest and taking "the entities of which one is talking . . . out of their hiddenness . . . [and] let[ting] them be seen as something unhidden" (56/33).

This relates to Heidegger's distinctive idea of truth, namely, truth as *aletheia* or unconcealment. Of this he says that "to say that an assertion 'is true' signifies that it uncovers the entity as it is in itself. Such an assertion asserts, points out, 'lets' the entity 'be seen'" (*apophansis*) in its uncoveredness. The Being-true (truth) of the assertion must be understood as Being-uncovering" (261/218). Speaking truthfully is thus speaking in such a way as to draw what is being talked about out from concealment and letting it be seen for what it is as that which is being talked about. In this sense, every truthful speech-act is "phenomenological," since it shows what is being talked about and lets it be seen as what it is, as itself, as "the thing itself." Truth, however, is not what is said (truth is not a function or value of propositions) but of letting what is being spoken about appear. And, as Heidegger will also claim, it appears by becoming present, as actual—which, he says, is indicated by the Greek understanding of the meaning of Being as *ousia* and *parousia* (a choice of words to which I shall return).

Understood in this Heideggerian perspective, preaching, like any truth-revealing speech-act, aims at making manifest, bringing to appearance, or allowing to become visible that which it is "about": letting the truth of what it is about be seen in, from, and as itself. But, of course, what the sermon is about is not a subject like any other. As a word concerning the word of God, it must surely be subject to different demands and perhaps even to a different logic than a lecture about Heidegger (for example).

Probably. But let us first imagine listening to a lecture about Heidegger. If it was a good lecture, it would (on Heideggerian principles) not tell you what the lecturer thinks about Heidegger. It would first and foremost enable you to see for yourselves what Heidegger was about. Listening to the lecture, you would find yourself saying, "Ah! I see!" (or, if you had been reading Heidegger for many years but without gaining insight into what he was about, "Ah! *At last* I see!"). Such a lecture will have made present the essential thought of Martin Heidegger in a manner that makes that thought visible, as it were, and in that way present to the enquiring mind of the listener; that is, it will have made clear and have brought into the common light of day what would otherwise have remained locked in the obscurity of Heidegger's dense philosophical prose.

But Heidegger's philosophy, difficult as it is, is, after all, the philosophy of a fellow human being. Although his erudition and originality place him on a different level from most of his commentators, the differences are still only a matter of more or less, and it is therefore not impossible for his epigones to write and speak about his work in such a way as to see and to help others see the truth of that work, at least to some extent. But we surely cannot straightforwardly presume that this is the case when what is to be spoken about is the word of God, the word of creation, salvation, and judgment, a word spoken from the infinite and mysterious depths of a God who is concealed even as he is revealed—who, according to Christian faith, reveals himself supremely by appearing as an ordinary human being devoid of any supernatural attributes—"surely this is the carpenter's son" (Mt 13.55)! As Karl Barth, the most insistent advocate of the primacy of the Word of God acknowledged, even God's own self-revelation cannot mitigate the ambiguity of the secularity in which that revelation occurs. How then might a sermon, a human word composed of secular words and structured according to the common grammatical features of vernacular speech, make visible and in making visible constitute an outward and visible sign of the presence of this infinitely mysterious God?

In his characteristically subtle and provocative study *The Sacrament of Language*, Giorgio Agamben took the idea of sacrament back to the *sacramentum*, or oath of loyalty sworn by Roman soldiers. This is at the same time theological, since the oath is sworn in the name of God. Agamben argues that our modern experience of the oath is much weakened in comparison with that known to the ancient world, where the swearing of an oath revealed something absolutely decisive for human existence as such and for the role of language in constituting the human as human (unlike in such modern expressions such as "by God" or the once-ubiquitous "OMG"). Whether the more particular content of the oath is factual ("I swear to

God that what I have described really occurred") or promissory ("I swear that I will do what I have spoken"), the oath affirms the primordial unity of speaker, speech, and what is spoken. In this perspective, Agamben argues, the oath is the fundamental form of ontotheology: an invocation of the name and power of God as effecting the synthesis of language and being. To swear an oath is to commit ourselves to the belief that what we say is how things are. Historically, oath swearing played a central role in human beings' becoming capable of relating to one another ethically. In swearing to the truth of what is said, oath swearers put their own being on the line and do so totally. Nevertheless, attentive as he is to the culturally formative role of the oath, Agamben concludes his study with a brief eulogy of philosophy, which, he says, began in the moment when Heraclitus opposed *logos* to *epos*, discourse to "the word," and in the light of *logos* questioned the validity of the presumption in favor of the correspondence of words and things and thus also questioned the validity of the sacramental pledge that binds human beings and their world to the words they use. The *logos* of philosophy is, in this sense, essentially antisacramental.[10]

The warning is noted. A contemporary view of language as sacramental and a contemporary theology of preaching as sacramental cannot merely assert or claim that preaching makes present or reveals the Word of God and thereby remove what is said in the sermon from the kind of critical scrutiny that Agamben associates with the *logos* of philosophy. Even if we allow that what is said in the sermon, along with everything said, sung, or enacted in the liturgical happening, has a kind of performative validity that is experienceable only by those who participate in it, listeners' reports of hearing the sermon as making present the Word of God cannot protect the word of preaching from the intellectual, social, and cultural lifeworld to which preachers and worshippers return at the end of the service and that, in an important sense, they never really left. But this lifeworld, in its modern rendition, requires that everything said by humans to humans be open to scrutiny and question. In other words, if it is said that an authentically theological word, such as the word of preaching, speaks in the mode of doxology rather than philosophy, this cannot extinguish the question of how this mode and what is said in it may be related to other modes of discourse. The preacher may assure us that when preaching on the Epiphany (for example), historical claims regarding the wise men, the star, or Herod's murderous tantrums are not at issue. What is at issue is primarily or even solely the transformation of the story into a living word in which the power and promise of God are made present to the congregation. And it is probably true that the sermon itself is not the place to enter into a text-critical discussion of the purported historical events "behind" the text. Yet the sermon cannot, not even when it is directed toward and achieves its own proper end, preclude the historical, critical, and, in other contexts, moral, psychological, or political implications of *what* is said in the sermon from becoming the object of critical attention. Even if the outcome of such considerations is only to reinforce an original intuition as to the essential difference of such approaches from what is most at issue in preaching, they serve as an external defense against any naïve assumption that preaching is the kind of performative speech-act in which saying something is so makes it so. Even the pure word of praise, "Alleluia," must, it seems, be saying *something*, and, to that extent, we must be able to ask whether or how what it says is justifiable beyond the immediacy of its utterance. "Is God really present?" is always a valid question.

As we saw in the last chapter, Heidegger too critiqued the supposed identity of language and being, "the principle of identity" that, in his view, had been the basic presupposition of the entire philosophical tradition. At the same time, he also insisted that language and being belong together. In the present chapter, we have heard him argue that language or *logos* serves to bring to view, to draw out of concealment, how things actually are: to make them present to us as they are, showing themselves, as it were, in their true colors. "The salt is on the briar rose / The fog is in the fir trees," wrote the poet—simple words, but words that make us see a small aspect of the world differently, drawing it out of unconcealment and showing us what we would never otherwise have seen.[11] But, as *The Principle of Identity* suggests, the poet can only do this to the extent that he is himself able to listen or attend to that which his word will reveal.

Preaching as Listening

All of this must be preeminently true also of preachers as well as of poets: They must listen before they can speak, not just in the sense of first listening and then speaking but of being fundamentally disposed toward listening rather than speaking, an attitude for which Moses, afflicted by a speech impediment and therefore needing the vocal assistance of Aaron, provides a paradigmatic instance. Augustine too reported that because of having been in demand as an orator, first pagan then Christian, from his youth onward, he had insufficient opportunity to be what he most desired to be—a simple listener to God's Word.

But if language belongs (*gehört*) to being only to the exact extent that it listens or attends to and so hears (*hört*) the event of being, what, in language, are we listening to? If what we are to listen to is what grounds the possibility of language and therefore also thinking, then it seems that this must be something that addresses us from beyond language. If truth is a property of the self-manifestation of being and not of language, then to speak truly of what manifests itself from out of the realm of being requires us to direct our attention to what precedes any possible word. The poet must first learn *to see* and *smell* the salt on the briar rose and the fog in the fir trees before he can conjure the words in which his seeing becomes our seeing. This is why Heidegger suggested in another lecture that in order truly to speak—to speak truth—we must learn to listen to "*das Gelaüt der Stille*," the "peal," "sound," "sonance," or "sounding-forth" of silence.[12] On this basis, language becomes the re-sonance, the "sounding again," of silence, or, to recall Tillich's characterization of the sacraments as both silent and "older" than the word, language is the repetition, in words, of what *is* "silently" "before" the word. However, if, as I argued in the previous chapter, the primary context of the word is not to point to objects in the world but to articulate what is at issue in a relationship that is situated within the community of language use, then what is "before" the word is not an utterly silent thing but a silence that is already oriented toward a word.

Such Heideggerian reflections may be instructive for preachers, but there will also be a more particular kind of listening required of one who is to preach. Perhaps it is true that in becoming attuned to the dimension of silent being that the words of the sermon are to make present, the preacher too will be led both to become more silent, suspending the babble of words continuously bubbling up from within the mind and attentive to what precedes any particular configuration of words in English, French, German, or even Hebrew or Greek. Preachers must listen or be learning to listen to a certain silence, to what is incommensurable with any number or sequence of human words. Yet in this case, that which lies beyond the possibilities of human language—this silence—is itself a word or has the form of a word: the divine word, speaking, but from above, from beyond, from before, and continuing past all human possibilities of speech.

In his study *The Call and the Response*, Jean-Louis Chrétien contrasts the negative theology of Neoplatonic philosophy with the apophaticism of Christian theology in such a way as to highlight just this point: that the negations of the philosopher (even the mystical philosopher) aim at what is essentially alien to language and that the resulting silence therefore marks the end or absence of any language. But even in recognizing the limitations of all human words, what the preacher nevertheless seeks in the divine silence is a word, or, to put it otherwise, s/he seeks to hear the divine silence *as* a Word.[13] In a further study of Augustine and language, Chrétien reiterates this distinction before going on to show how for Augustine the Christian is obliged to speak of what is in itself unspeakable precisely because the biblical God to whom s/he listens and of whom s/he desires to speak in praise does not hesitate to self-describe in vulgar, anthropomorphic terms that many a philosopher would despise. Augustine suggests that God does not speak in this way as a kind of accommodation to the "primitive" worldview of the ancient Hebrews (as some Enlightenment and post-Enlightenment views would have it) but to demonstrate by a kind of *reductio ad absurdum* that even the most exalted words of the philosophers would have been inadequate to express the divine being.[14] And if our fear of speaking wrongly of God so overwhelms us that we end up by not speaking at all, this is in fact a sign that we have ceased to be listeners.

Of course, we do not and cannot listen to God in the manner of a stenographer. Listening to God as God speaks in "the ineffable voice of the heart,"[15] we constantly wrestle with the paradox that, precisely as a word written in the heart, God's word, God's being as word, comes from elsewhere: Written in and speaking in and to our hearts as a word "closer to us than we are to ourselves," it is utterly inward and interior to our self-identity[16]—yet it is a possibility given to us from beyond our own possibilities. The meaning of such a word is not simply a given. It is not simply "ours": It is a writing that we must learn to decipher and interpret. Perhaps, were we to be capable of truly listening, its meaning would require no further acts of interpretation, but, for now, we see in a glass darkly, and we must struggle to find the true meaning.

Those who stand within a living religious tradition do not imagine that this is a task they can undertake or accomplish on their own. Their attempts to hear what is spoken to them by God are typically focused on the human words of Moses, the prophets, apostles, evangelists, and the great figures of Christian tradition. But even Scripture, God's word becoming bodily present in human words, is not always so plain that Augustine would not welcome the opportunity to meet with Moses and question him as to what he really meant to say in one or other passage of his writings—although, as Augustine also somewhat humorously concedes, the conversation would not get very far, since he wouldn't be able to understand Moses's Hebrew.[17] Human words mediate the divine word, but the Augustinian version of the hermeneutical circle suggests that we will not be able to understand these human words aright, that is, as testimony to the divine word, unless we are also, in some measure, capable of listening to and, in listening, *seeing* that divine word for ourselves, becoming, as it were, seers of the Word. Augustine, who interprets the name "Israel" etymologically as "seer of God," thus translates the injunction "Hear, O Israel" as meaning "Hear, listen, in such a way as to become a seer of God."[18]

What is at issue here is a certain kind of attention. As Simone Weil taught us, even in its secular employment (as when we are attending to our work or listening to what our neighbor has to say about her day), attention, being attentive, is a kind of discipline of self-denial in which we let the other be or become manifest to us or speak to us in his, her, or even its own terms. Attention is an act, something we do, we must intend to attend if we are truly to attend, but, in attending, we hold ourselves or stretch ourselves out toward what is not ourselves and toward what we do not have power over. Attention is an act, but it is also a passivity, a waiting-upon, as is particularly clear in English, where "attending upon" someone involves being attentive to, ready to serve, and waiting for.[19]

The Temporality of Preaching

That the preacher's struggle to interpret the divine word spoken and written in heart and text is also a matter of attending to or waiting upon that word points us to the important and arguably decisive question as to the kind of temporality at issue here. As Agamben pointed out, the oath may be either constative ("it happened as I told you") or promissory ("I promise that it will be so"). Much contemporary preaching has followed modernity's hallmark historicism and therefore assumed that its task is to present or defend the constative truths attested in Scripture and in tradition. This is, for example, the case with the popular two-horizons hermeneutic, according to which the task of the interpreter is to say now, in our words, what was said then, in their words. Yet one of the great discoveries of modern historical research on the New Testament concerned the essentially eschatological orientation of early Christian thought. Fully thinking through the implications of this, I suggest, must end by bursting the old wineskins of historical criticism itself and dissolving both horizons of the two-horizon hermeneutic.

This "destruction" was the outcome of Heidegger's own 1921 lectures on the philosophy of religion, in which he attacked the historicism of Harnack and Troeltsch on the basis of the early Christian—that is Pauline— "factical life-experience" (as he called it) of living in expectation of the *parousia*, the future coming-to-presence of divine truth. Together with further input from Kierkegaard (among others), this fed into the argument of *Being and Time* that, with regard to the three time ecstases of past, present, and future, it is the relation to the future that is decisive and that grounds the human experience and understanding of what it means to be a temporal being.[20] Even when the theological word might seem to limit itself to the recitation of past acts of God or gratitude for gifts being received in the present, these are invariably accompanied by the desire for the continuation of those acts and gifts in time to come.

Waiting upon the word, then, is not simply a matter—difficult as that already is—of interrogating the texts of Scripture and Tradition so as to hear and see in them the re-sonance of a divine word spoken in a more or less remote past. Nor is it simply a matter—difficult as that already is—of ascending into the intellectual cloud of unknowing by the way of negation. The sacramentality of the Word of preaching is not won on the basis of work on texts nor in the intellectual ascesis of Platonic metaphysics. Both of these ways suppose that what is to be found is in some sense already there, unseen but fully present, like a precious mineral hidden inside some nondescript piece of rock. Even when the task encounters insuperable obstacles on the way, there may still be a hope that one might return with better equipment or renewed strength, but when the task is understood as waiting upon a word that still belongs essentially to the future, a word of which the essential character is *parousia*, then, surely, no preacher could imagine that he or she might attain mastery of such a word merely by waiting longer or trying harder.

Does this mean that in the face of God's essential futurity the preacher has nothing to say? If the meaning of the word is not fully given by its being a word that has been spoken and that is spoken in a timeless present but is only decisively fulfilled when it is grasped as a word to come, a word concerning what may yet be, how might we wait upon such a word and listen to it in such a way as to enable a truthful speaking in which what is heard is made present and comes to view?

The future is not a blank sheet. Even now the future is in some sense already meaningful by virtue of its anticipated relation to past and present. For our relation to the future, whether it is a matter of the imminent future (as in, what I am going to do tomorrow) or the absolute future (what my life will prove to have been about), is in play both in our present and in our present relation to the past. We do not and cannot know the future, but we always exist toward it in a certain way. Faith, it is said, is the assurance of things hoped for and a certain conviction regarding what is, as yet, unseen. But on the understanding of language we have drawn from Heidegger, the word of faith spoken in preaching would serve, precisely, to make what is unseen seen and to make that future a present and effective power in life. If we understand the category of "possibility" as intrinsically relating to the future, we might at this point apply Kierkegaard's beautiful and very concise saying: "By means of the possible, eternity is constantly near enough to be at hand and yet far enough away to keep a person moving forwards towards the eternal, on the way, moving forwards. It is in this way that, by means of possibility, eternity entices and draws human beings towards itself, from the cradle to the grave, if they thus choose to hope."[21]

Attending to the divine silence so as to hear in it the word to come, waiting upon the unseen future, the preacher may—if love and grace permit—speak a word that makes present or brings into view that which he waits upon: the word as word of promise and hope. That this is a word both unfinalized and unfinalizable in historical time will make the preacher sufficiently humble to listen also to the critical words of historians, philosophers, and people of common sense who in various ways warn against a rash or naïve identification of word and being, which in this case would amount to preachers confusing their own words with the word of God. But even before historians, philosophers, and others come to their aid, preachers will have their own reasons for understanding that the word to be spoken is not a word in which they exercise any kind of authority or power, even if it may also become a word powerful enough to move others to hope.

Having to wait upon a word that is not their own word and that, in all its fullness, is still to come, preachers know that, even if they have never read Kierkegaard, they need God precisely in the sense that he describes in the discourse "To Need God Is a Human Being's Highest Perfection." As noted in the last chapter, the verb translated into English as "need," *at traenge*, suggests forcefully pushing one's way forward, struggling against every manner of obstacle and hindrance and above all the obstacles and hindrances that lie in oneself. It is also, as Kierkegaard especially emphasizes, to be learning that we ourselves are nothing and that God is everything. This condition of absolute need, which is also and at the same time a condition of actively striving or stretching out toward the word of life that is to come, is integral to the kind of "listening" that makes possible the specific kind of "speaking" that we call "preaching." In this sense, the claim that praying is only possible in response to the call to prayer issued by the preacher is countered or, better, nuanced, by the recognition that the preacher can only preach by entering into the situation of the one who prays.

The weakness of the preacher is, of course, no new discovery. That the preacher is and must be a fool, afflicted, an earthen vessel, and weak—the scum of the earth (1 Cor 4.13)—was already known to one of the first great Christian preachers, and in this regard at least, Paul remains a model, so long as we do not also forget (which Paul did not) that the word in which God's word of creation, salvation, and judgment becomes present here and now is also and preeminently a word of joy.

Insistence that the preacher is "scum" is not said in order to encourage verbal self-flagellation on the part of the preacher, which would be just another way of drawing attention to the preacher's individual ego. Whatever is to be said by way of self-deprecation will more likely and better be said by way of irony and humor than by cataloguing afflictions and failings, since it is not the preacher or the preacher's own weakness or need that is ultimately at issue. As an individual, the preacher may well need God to the point of desperation, but the word that the preacher speaks is to be a word of hope even against hope, pointing out of and beyond any merely private need so as to awaken and sustain a living need of God in the congregation, so that in that need, in the nothingness it reveals, preacher and congregation may attend to and begin to hear the word that is word of life. At that point, the sermon becomes a call to prayer or, more precisely, a word in which preacher and congregation are enabled to pray together. For all of this is misunderstood if it is viewed as a purely individual process. If the preacher's words can guide the congregation to the spiritual depths where God becomes known in the sonance of silence, there is also a sociology of depth, as Marcel put it. I am never alone in my intimacy with God but always accompanied by the co-presence of all who share the gift of the word. It is for this reason that neither the word of prayer nor the word of preaching is complete unless or until it is extended to embrace the word that calls us to the need of the neighbor. We have heard Dostoevsky's insistence that the individual acknowledgment of guilt is a matter of responsibility for everything for which I could possibly be responsible and owning that responsibility in the presence of the whole human community. It is for this reason that, alongside preaching, the extrovert character of the word of prayer requires us also to turn our attention to the ethical demand, the word that calls us to the love and care of our neighbor.

6

Promise

Space, Time, and Covenant

We shall return to the relationship between prayer and the ethical demand, but I shall in this chapter first explore further the element of futurity that we have seen as integral to the word of Christian preaching. In doing so, I take my prompt from the words of the Eucharistic sacrament that, together with the word of Scripture preached, is basic to Christian worship. In each of Matthew, Mark, and Luke, Jesus speaks of the cup of wine he blessed and shared at the Last Supper as a sign of his covenant/testament—in Luke, explicitly *"the new covenant* in my blood" (Lk 22.20). These words are repeated in the Eucharistic liturgies of most major Christian traditions, indicating that despite its particular connotations in Reformed theology and history (I think, for example, of the Scottish Covenanters of the seventeenth century), "covenant" is just as "Catholic" as it is Calvinist. For Christianity, like Judaism, has at its heart the claim to be in a covenant with God. Nevertheless, outside the internal debates of theologians in the Reformed tradition, "covenant" is a term that has faded in theological prominence in modernity and even more so in postmodernity. Yet to overlook it would be premature. Even apart from its centrality in the Eucharist, it is preserved in the titles of Christianity's foundational texts, the "Old" and "New Testaments," where "testament" and "covenant" translate the same Greek term. It is, then, a term, an idea, that needs to be taken seriously—but how to approach it? In this chapter I shall sidestep some of the standard theological debates and consider instead the essential temporality of the covenant relationship. This will in turn bring us to a decisive moment of Christian prayer, condensed into the familiar petition of the prayer known as the Lord's Prayer: "Your Kingdom come."

For some years in the twentieth century, the study of religions made much of the distinction between religions that emphasize space at the expense of time and those that gave first place to time. Religions of space were religions that either had never known or had turned away from what Mircea Eliade, a leading proponent of this approach, called "the terror of history."[1] A primary characteristic of such religions was a cultic life centered on an annual liturgical return to the primordial time in which the gods made the earth and established human tribes and customs. Everything subsequent to that time was perceived in terms of decay and degeneration, a falling away from original purity and vigor. Such religions lay under the spell of what Eliade called "the myth of the eternal return." Religions that ventured outside this socially and cosmically reassuring myth and that confronted the terror of history accepted the linear movement of time and the ultimate impossibility of any kind of return. This, Eliade believed, was the case in Judaism and Christianity, although, as he also pointed out, elements of myth have continued to inform Jewish and Christian liturgical practice. Essentially, however, Judaism and Christianity look to history as the primary medium in which God is revealed to human beings and in which human beings are to work out the meaning of their God-relationship. Here it is not the past, the time of origins, that receives primary emphasis but the future, the time in which God's Kingdom is to come, whether through human works or divine intervention. We also find such a typology in Tillich, who sees this distinction as having a political edge, since the religions that privilege space were (he thought) likely to insist on ethnic purity and on the ontological link between people and sacred ancestral land. This was an especially urgent question for Tillich in the context of the Third Reich and its ideology of "blood and earth." Against this he set the prophetic, future-oriented message of the Hebrew Bible, restated in Christianity.[2]

Such taxonomies have declined in popularity over the last thirty years, not least because the complex lived reality of religious life makes it hard to find examples of the "pure" forms to which they ascribe normative status. At the same time, the kind of privileging of Jewish and Christian traditions in which time takes priority over space has had to respond to what has been called the spatial turn, a movement that has identified space and place as not only essential elements of human existence but also as contributing to a holistic view of being human.[3] This relates both to individuals needing to have a sense of their place in the world and also to the common task of caring for the earth, the place—the planet—where we live and without which we and all other inhabitants of the biosphere could not live. Nevertheless, the older taxonomies can still serve to focus significant questions. Not least, as stated by Eliade, they remind us that the historical, future-oriented dynamic of Judaism and Christianity entails an exposure to history as a condition of terror, unpredictability, and potentially tragedy. In this connection, it is striking that the covenant with Israel is inaugurated at a moment when the people are in flight from slavery in Egypt, stranded in the desert, with no possibility of return and no land to go to. Equally dark is the moment in which the Christian "new" covenant is inaugurated—"in the night in which he was betrayed." The very origins of these covenants are shot through with the terror of history. But how might a covenant, a compact agreed in, with, and under the conditions of historical life, be capable of assuaging this terror? Precisely because it is historical, doesn't the covenant too exist in such a way as to be exposed to the uncertainty and openness of life in time?

What, then, is the temporality of the covenant? At first glance it may seem to be essentially preterite. A covenant is a contract that has been signed, sealed, and delivered and now binds the covenant partners for all future time. Where in the idea of covenant is the possibility of the radical novelty of which Berdyaev and Tillich spoke? Both Old and New Testaments are written, complete, and John's Revelation, the final book in the Christian Bible, ends with a warning not to add to or subtract from anything that is written in it (Rev 22.18–19).

Yet the covenant is also always related to the future. Every covenant implies a promise relating to what will be. In each of the synoptic accounts of the Last Supper Jesus indicates this futural dimension when he forswears drinking again from the cup until he drinks it "new" in the kingdom of God (Mk 14.25). Although the Christian Eucharist is sometimes conceived of as primarily an act of remembrance (like drinking a toast to the memory of King William, as Samuel Taylor Coleridge put it), it also looks to the future of salvation in God's Kingdom, as signaled in the incorporation of the messianic verse "Blessed is he who comes in the name of the Lord" into many liturgies.[4] The new covenant looks to a good future that, in the dark and tragic night of its institution, is beyond all expectation and probability, a radical unknown. But perhaps the most concise statement of this future orientation of the promise is found in the revelation to Moses at the Burning Bush and God's self-naming as "I will be who I will be" (Ex 3.14). The promise that lies at the basis of the covenant with Israel is, from the beginning, a promise reaching out into time that is not yet. We can only know what it is and with whom it has been made through the experience of moving forward in time, into the unknown.[5]

Eschatology

The statement that promise and futurity are integral to the covenant-relationship may not be self-evident. Sometimes it seems that the historical foundations of covenantal communities function like the time of sacred origins in Eliade's account of mythical religions. Liturgical celebrations of Passover or the Christian Eucharist seem to involve just such an eternal return to their respective origins on the parts of Judaism and Christianity. But the past to which this return is made is not an immemorial past but a very specific, historical past. In this case, remembering is not escaping from the terror of history but finding orientation within it. And because remembering is itself an act or complex of acts firmly situated in our own present, what is remembered is remembered as relating to what must be done now, in the present. But because that present is itself lived in and through some orientation toward the future (whether that is next year in Jerusalem or the tasks that await the Sunday communicant in the week ahead), memory, even liturgical memory, is colored by the uncertainty inherent in any future.

The fact that the future has a defining role in the structure of covenantal thought generates a peculiar set of problems for imagination and symbolization. Hegel's dictum that the Owl of Minerva first flies at dusk and that a period of world history can only be understood from the point of view of its conclusion would seem also to apply to visual representation.[6] We can only depict what has been and even then only to the extent that it has a residual continuance in the present, in what "is." We cannot depict what has not yet come to pass, or if we do, we can do so only with images drawn from our experience of what has been and what is. Even though the apocalyptic fantasies of a Hieronymus Bosch or the elder Brueghel revel in producing images of creatures never seen on earth, they are, nevertheless, only recombinations of elements actually experienced and known in worldly life. In this regard, Bosch's paintings in particular reveal the connection between eschatology and protology, linking the promised future to a golden age in the past, a golden age that draws on both pagan and biblical forms. Other artistic examples of this tendency are the Northern Renaissance theme of the "land of Cockaigne" or the luminous pastoral sunsets of Claude Lorraine that so fascinated Dostoevsky.

Kierkegaard's widely quoted saying that life is lived forward but understood backward sums up what he saw as a fundamental epistemological challenge to German Idealism, which in his view was unable to account for the future-oriented freedom of the living human subject. This saying, in its own way, echoes Hegel's comment on the Owl of Minerva. However, Kierkegaard sees this situation of having-been (what Jankélévitch would call "passeity")[7] as defining the essential limitation of idealist thought. Why? Because in order to see the human subject as an object of "knowledge" it is necessary to imagine this subject as having reached a state of completion. Only so can we know "what" it is. Thus, the orientation of traditional philosophy toward the quiddity, the essence, the "what" (*to ti estin*) defines the identity of the subject under consideration in such a way that its temporality is rendered irrelevant, a mere accident that has no influence on what really matters. Kierkegaard illustrates this distinction with reference to the question as to whether human beings have an immortal soul. He argues that philosophy sees this question in the mirror of the past, that is, in terms of whether or not immortality belongs to the original endowment of human being and therefore whether it remains as a defining attribute of the human way of being throughout its history of temporal transformation. In other words, this is to treat immortality as if it were a naturally occurring element, a "given," as it were. But, as he saw it, the question of immortality cannot be solved by such a naturalizing movement, because immortality is an essentially existential question: Will *I* be immortal? What will my immortality mean to me? How can I live my life so as to attain a truly blessed immortality?[8] Furthermore, even if immortality *is* an essential attribute of human beings, it only becomes humanly meaningful in relation to the kind of immortality to be enjoyed—whether it will be the blessedness promised to the saints or something less good. The mere extension of life into an afterlife says nothing as to the meaning of that life, and neither preachers nor artists should waste their efforts on depicting it: The point is solely and exclusively the demand to do justly, love mercy, and perform the works of love that the Bible commands as the sole basis of blessedness—in time and in eternity.

Future and Possibility

Philosophically, Kierkegaard conceded (as he had to) that precisely because such a future life is not a given, we cannot *know* whether this is what awaits us. What is important, however, is that it can become an issue for us and, as such, an issue that has implications for the whole way in which we understand ourselves and our life in the world. A creature that is "like the beasts that perish" and a creature made for an eternal heavenly life are two very different kinds of creatures. The insolubility of the question thus throws a veil of ignorance over our basic possibilities of self-knowledge.

How can we know whether we are angels or monsters? At best, we see "in a glass darkly," but we are not yet what we shall be, and the truth of our being will only ever become manifest "in the end." Heidegger would criticize Kierkegaard for thinking time in relation to a premodern idea of eternity, but it is clear that for Kierkegaard, it is precisely the question of eternity that confronts us with the need to take seriously the thoroughgoing temporality of human life on earth.[9] At the same time, this also means that there will be a necessary limitation on our capacities for self-representation, that is, for conceptualizing, portraying, or even dramatizing the reality of human being. Our essential possibilities have a quality of "not-yet" that eludes all representation.

There is a moment in Alexander Sokurov's 2002 film *Russian Ark* that illustrates this well. The film follows the ghost of the Marquis de Custine through the Hermitage Museum in St. Petersburg. Each room or gallery he enters introduces a new historical era, from Catherine the Great down to the present. It is in the present that he comes across two teenage boys looking at an El Greco portrait of the apostles Peter and Paul. He asks them whether they read the Gospels, and when they admit that they do not, he asks how they can possibly understand the human possibilities revealed in El Greco's painting. I am perhaps overinterpreting at this point, but I take it that the point is that what the Gospels reveal is precisely how we shall be: that the Gospels reveal human being as essentially futural and therefore also essentially unknown and still-to-be-discovered. Looking back to these ancient texts, we are directed forward to life in a world to come.

Ancient pagan thought also understood that there might be limits to human knowledge, but there is a significant difference between the kind of apophatic anthropology that we find in, for example, the Platonic tradition and in existential thought. Plotinus knew that in relation to the One, everything we might say could only ever be a matter of "so to speak," while Plato's daring thought that the good was "beyond being" suggests also that it is beyond anything we might call knowledge or that if it is knowable it is knowable in a way distinct from all other ways of knowing. But as we have now several times seen, this limit relates to a cosmic and ontological hierarchy that maps onto the "upward" transition from mere matter to pure mind. Our inner journey indeed brings us to a point of unknowing, but in both the Platonic and Aristotelian paradigms, this unknowing is both inscribed in the cosmic world order and is a consequence of the inadequacy of any form of representation derived from sense-experience to show the truth of the divine mind. In existential thinking, however, the limit to our capacity for knowing God has to do neither with the overall structuring of the cosmic world order nor with the materiality of human existence.

Although Kierkegaard had his own issues with the physical aspects of life, the unanswerability of the question concerning an eternal happiness has primarily to do with the temporal structure of existence, and this structure is in turn generated by what Heidegger would call human beings' capacity for care, that is, the capacity to understand their lives by looking ahead into a near or more remote future and reflecting back onto their present decisions and past experiences in the light of that. In other words, the limits to our knowledge are internal to our own being, and it is in our self-relation that they come most urgently into view, as in Kierkegaard's concern for an eternal happiness that could not be assuaged by assurances about the immortality of the soul. Eternity is not external to the human being, but the human being is a synthesis of time and eternity in such a way that the difference goes right to the heart of human identity. In his account of the moment in which eternity becomes reflected in time, Kierkegaard alludes to Paul's anticipation of the final eschatological change that will come over human beings when they are summoned to the resurrection of the dead, "in the twinkling of an eye" (1 Cor 15.52).[10] As he argues the case, who we are is only ultimately decidable in such an absolute future, and in the meantime, all our judgments about ourselves and others cannot be more than provisional.

But is this right? Might there not be ways of thinking time that could allow for such representation? Where are we to look that we might see time, our time, the time of our lives?

Concealing Time

The challenge is considerable, and some might see it as more fruitful to proceed ex negativo and examine how dominant modes of representation have served to conceal the lived reality of time. This would be a case of what Heidegger called a destruction of the history of philosophy.[11] This destruction reveals how even in what philosophy has genuinely revealed about human life in time there is also always an accompanying distortion or concealment. In many respects, Heidegger's own thought can serve as an eminent training in such thinking. However, it is also arguable that even Heidegger perpetuates some of the most persistent assumptions about time that limit our insight into its true potential meaning, a point to which I shall return.

Examples of how time became concealed even in thinking about time can be seen in the cases of Aristotle, Plotinus, and Augustine. For Aristotle, the question of time is a question as to how time can be measured. But, he argues, time can best be measured by tracking the distance covered in the movements of the heavenly bodies. "A day" is a unit of time, but in the Aristotelian perspective, a day is the time taken for the sun to make a single circuit of its path through space. In this way it is ultimately space that becomes the measure of time, and time itself eludes observation. Indeed, the decision to set the question up in terms of cosmology already distances it from the lived human experience of time.[12]

For Plotinus, against Aristotle, the problem is precisely that time can't be measured and that temporality is a kind of rebellion against the eternal order of timeless mathematical relationships that is the standard of both being and knowledge. Time is therefore inherently marked by a tendency toward nonbeing and therefore escapes knowability.[13] Plotinus's argument is reformulated in more psychological terms and with a marked theological and soteriological interest in Augustine's meditation on time in book 11 of the *Confessions*. As he searches for traces of God in time and memory, Augustine is led to ponder whether time is indeed capable of revealing the presence of divine being. But what is time? As he quickly discovers, the past no longer is, the future is not yet. This is not just an epistemological problem, since for Augustine as for Plotinus and for the Platonic tradition generally, being and knowledge are two aspects of a single reality. Thus the unknowability of time reveals its ontological nullity. In psychological terms, to live in time is to be exposed to the constant possibility of annihilation. Our need, therefore, is not to "know" time but to be saved from time, and Augustine believes we can be saved from time because God is in himself timelessly eternal.

Heidegger acknowledges that various religious sources, including Augustine and Kierkegaard, were philosophically necessary in preparing for the phenomenological investigation of time that he undertakes in *Being and Time*. However, Heidegger did not believe that evaluating time by reference to eternity is either desirable or possible. Our human kind of being is being that exists in time as thrownness toward death. Our only recourse is not to appeal to a timeless God but, as Heidegger puts it, to "run towards" the nothingness of time as that is revealed in death. But it seems legitimate to ask whether, despite removing eternity from the analysis of time, Heidegger has really thought time in a manner that is true to its own proper temporality. Is nothingness the best that we can say about time?[14]

One Kierkegaardian term that Heidegger adopted was "the moment of vision" (*Augenblick*). In Kierkegaard, this is expressly related both to the New Testament idea of the *kairos*, the fulfillment of time in the coming of the Messiah, and the eschatological "moment," the "atom of time" or "twinkling of the eye" in which, as Paul puts it, we shall be "changed," putting on immortality (1 Cor 15.51–2).[15] Heidegger rejects the religious aspects of this concept, but he believes that we can nevertheless speak of a privileged moment that is able to give meaning to temporal life, namely, the moment in which we resolve to run toward death. This is a moment of truth, the revelation of pure temporality, which, on Heidegger's logic, is also—and solely—the revelation of what is in itself null.

The Other

There is something missing in Heidegger's account, and this, I believe, is connected with what many have seen as another missing or, at least, deficient element in *Being and Time*, namely, the role of the other. Heidegger certainly acknowledges *Mit-sein*, being-with, as a basic element of human being-in-the-world, and some of his commentators have taken his few remarks on this as nevertheless sufficient for the development of a robust account of ethical relationships. I am more skeptical and do not see anything in Heidegger's account that really requires us to look to ethical responsibility for and to the other as a defining element in human life.[16]

Among those philosophers inspired by Heidegger, the one who perhaps did most to revise Heidegger's phenomenology of existence by making the ethical demand central to his entire account of human existence was Emmanuel Levinas. We shall consider Levinas more fully in the next chapter, so for now I shall comment only on what the claim laid on us by the need of the other reveals about time, as when Levinas asserts that "time is not the fact of an isolated subject on its own" (which he sees as being the case with Heidegger's account of thrownness toward an always singular death as the measure of time) "but the relation of the subject to others."[17] In responding to the appeal of the other, I allow the time of the other to become the measure of my time.[18] When we realize the relation to the other, death, of course, remains as the end of our individual lives on earth, but we are not (Levinas says) obligated to see death as simply "annihilation." It is a mystery, indeed, but not of itself an annihilation.[19] Levinas does not spell this out at this point, but we might say, for example, that although I must die as a center of subjective self-consciousness, I will in some sense remain for a certain length of time in the memories of those with whom my life has been shared. Death is not simple, unqualified annihilation. That is a minimum.

At the same time as criticizing the lack of a significant other in Heideggerian ontology, Levinas also rejected Martin Buber's location of the relation to the other in the immediacy of the face-to-face I-Thou encounter. For Levinas, there must always be a third; being-with-one-another can never be just a matter of "two," since there will always have to be a third term through which the two are related, as when two people are united in a shared undertaking, the work in relation to which their relationship takes on its specific and actual form, or when two lovers attest their love to the wider community in what we call marriage (which Rosenzweig glossed as "the publication of the miracle"). Theologically, we might think of this in terms of being called by divine command to be responsible for the other, to be our brothers' and sisters' keepers, an interpretation Levinas would not reject. As we shall see further in the next chapter, he regarded the unqualifiedly "other" "height" from which we are commanded to care for the widow, orphan, and stranger as integral to ensuring that we recognize the other in terms of their actual need and not just as an occasion for us to extend our subjectivity. The other is really other, not me, and my obligation to the other is not a quality of my subjectivity but something in which I am, rather, an object, "accused," as Levinas put it, "me" rather than "I", "*Vous*" rather than "*Tu*."[20] This, I have noted, echoes the teaching of *The Brothers Karamazov*: "That we are all guilty of everything before everyone, and I most of all." But this is something very different from the ontological guilt described by Heidegger. It is a kind of guilt that places the other at the foundation of our self-constitution, rendering the final achievement of fully autonomous selfhood impossible—a point that is equally valid whether we think of the other in question as the human or the divine other (or, as both Christianity and Judaism tend to do, *both*: inseparably and unconfusedly).[21]

But how does this relate to the question of time? The remembrance of the dead that I briefly referred to earlier provides one hint. Another is that our experience of time is inseparable from how we experience our lives with others and therewith our experience of language. While you speak, I must wait until you have finished in order to understand and respond to what you say. While you are speaking, I am, in a certain sense and at a certain level, rendered passive, waiting, not coinciding with myself but extended beyond my-self in waiting on your words, your meaning, and your claim on me.

Time, Language, and Responsibility

Levinas learned much from Franz Rosenzweig, and for Rosenzweig it was characteristic of the "new thinking" that he sought to promote that it understood the intertwining of time and language.[22] Some analytic philosophers have attempted to understand propositions in ways that render their content timeless—if it is true that Napoleon lost the Battle of Waterloo, then it will always and in all possible circumstances be true that

Napoleon lost the battle of Waterloo. For such an approach, logic aspires to the timeless world of mathematics. For Rosenzweig, by way of contrast, there is no language that is not grounded in the relational structures of call and response, what he called the vocativity of language—and for which, he argued, the revelation of the divine name at the burning bush was a prime example.[23] We might for comparison think of Bakhtin's category of "answerability" as developed in his early writing, where he too insists on the irreducibility of the several "I"s involved in any speech-act.[24] Levinas would call this, or something like it, *le Dire*, the saying, as opposed to *le Dit*, where the latter refers to "what" is said, the quiddity. And this lived time of language, *le Dire*, is, precisely, the time in which I am engaged by what Levinas spoke of as "the face" of the other.[25]

And here we return to the themes of covenant and promise. For covenant is precisely a way of ordering time on the basis of responsibility for and toward the other. Equally, it is also a way of ordering our responsibility to the other in terms of time, since it involves a commitment that extends beyond the present into the unknowable future. And because the covenant must take some symbolic form, it is also, precisely, a way that our relation to both time and the other is woven together in the form of, normally, language. I am who I am because of what I have promised you and what you have promised me, and "what" we have promised is itself disclosed in the promise we have made. The word of promise reveals me to you and you to me, as we are, in time, coming together from separate pasts into a shared future, shared at least as far as the reach of the promise. In such an event, "the moment" is no longer just the moment in which I realize that I am a thrown nullity but, as for Kierkegaard and the biblical sources on which he drew, a real "fullness" of time.

But if time is taken to be a defining feature of human existence, this creates problems for the representation of human reality. Although the promise binds us together in time as we go toward a common future, this future itself is, for now, unknown. One or the other of us may break the promise, or circumstances beyond our control may make it impossible to keep. The meaning upon which I staked everything may unravel in time. To commit myself in a promise cannot therefore be a means of evading the intrinsic unknowability of the self. In point of fact, if we were not deeply unknowable to ourselves, we would have no need of promises; we would need only predictions. Versus Agamben, the oath is not the imposition of a restrictive ontology onto the flow of time: It is the recognition that our being together is a being in time.

In time, as long as I am in time, I know myself in the measure of my responsibility to and for you. I may have no control over the outcome of this responsibility, but the responsibility binds me to the life I am living. Levinas, as I have mentioned, spoke of the face of the other appealing for my help, although he by no means understood this literally. The face, in his sense, is only a "trace" of the claim that is laid on me by my being born into a community predicated on responsibility, a covenantal community. Yet the category of "face" does give us, perhaps, a hint as to how we might proceed to think about the kind of representation appropriate to representing a being whose life is hidden in the mystery of time. C. S. Lewis entitled one of his books (which had nothing to do with Levinas) *Until We Have Faces*, and this, I think, offers a suggestive program for understanding both our inherited and contemporary representations of human being.[26] Our philosophies, pictures, plays, songs, and poems are, at their best, sketches (again: "as in a glass, darkly") not of how human beings are or have been but of what we might yet be, the redeemable possibility that calls from beyond all distortions and failures of historical time.

This possibility cannot be known. Does this mean that, in the end, we must fall silent? I have now several times claimed that language remains relevant, belonging as it does to our human way of being. But when we speak of such possibilities we cannot speak as we do when we speak of what we can know through observation or research. Instead, we turn to parables, paradoxes, images, and stories. One such story is told by Dostoevsky, or, more precisely (and remarkably), by Ivan Karamazov in the preamble to his "poem of the Grand Inquisitor," a poem in which he denounces the apostasy of the Christian church and its denial of the freedom Christ came to bring. For most commentators, Ivan's argument suggests that this apostasy was inevitable and that the Grand Inquisitor was correct in thinking that human beings were not ready for that kind of freedom. In time, in history, we will inevitably fail to realize our best possibilities of existence and for that reason are chronically susceptible to the appeal of social, political, and religious regimes that will absolve us from the need to take responsibility for ourselves and for one another.

But before he comes to the Grand Inquisitor, Ivan alludes to a story that merits attention. This is the legend of the Virgin Mary's visit to hell and her encounter with those whom even God has forgotten. The notion that there might be a depth of hell so deep that those confined there have been forgotten even by the eternal memory of God is one of extraordinary terror. As Dostoevsky (via Ivan) tells the story, the Virgin is so moved by their plight that she recalls their fate to God, who grants an annual reprieve from their sufferings from Good Friday to Trinity Sunday.[27] Of course, as narrated, it is a tale told as if it were the chronicle of an event long past, what the Virgin did "once upon a time." But as a narrative set in eschatological time, the eternal time of heaven and hell, it is properly understood as a parable of our responsibility in time to work and to pray that all who labor in and under time may not be forgotten, indeed, that they may be remembered, and remembered according to the appeal of the face that they, beyond all knowing, turn to God and to us, their fellow human beings, crying "Let me be!" It is the cry that resonates equally in our call to God and in the call of the neighbor in need. Perhaps it may even be the cry that God too calls out to us, as envisaged in Bonhoeffer's late poem "Christians and Pagans," which speaks of a reciprocity of succor, mercy, and shared grieving for the world's suffering.[28] For our call, our prayer, our voice may be just what God needs in order to become the God whose rule of love is the true measure of human life. Without the prayer "Your Kingdom come," God's Kingdom couldn't be God's good Kingdom but only a new variant of heteronomous rule. If prayer articulates the human need of God, that same prayer testifies also to God's need of us. Why, indeed, would God enter into a covenant with us if God did not in some sense need us as covenant partners for the fulfillment of his divine purposes? In this perspective, the covenant-relationship becomes the opening up of a present that is exposed to and assaulted by the terrors of history to a future in which God might become the God in whose kingdom we might become as fully human as we can be.[29] In this perspective, "covenant" is not the hallmark of a faith that looks continually back toward its inaugural moments ("*in illud tempore*," as Eliade might have put it) but a faith grounded in promise and therefore also fundamentally and irreversibly hopeful. "The best is yet to come."

7

Height

If faith is shaped by promise and hope, we might well ask: promise for what? hope for what? I have spoken already of the ethical demand, and Christianity is surely more than the promise of "peace within." In the modern world, at least, even the cultivation of the inner life has been unable to avoid the claim of the other, as in the Trappist monk Thomas Merton's "confessions of a guilty bystander," in which he reflected on the problematic relationship between his life as a Trappist monk and a world that was being ravaged by war and injustice outside the monastery walls.[1]

I have said that of all those who were most profoundly shaped by Heidegger's existential phenomenology while at the same time transforming it, Levinas was the one who most decisively emphasized the need for an "ethical" rewriting of the Heideggerian inheritance. Certainly, Levinas's thought could seem to point us away from the kind of spiritual traditions that have been the main focus of this study. Nevertheless, as I hope to show, Levinas's ethical and even "worldly" turn has something vital to teach about what is at issue in prayer as well as about the dynamic role of futurity in the constitution of spiritual life.

Height in Levinas

We have been considering the spiritual life as a life fundamentally oriented toward the future, but how? What is the future that spiritual life proposes as the "end of all our striving"? Ernst Bloch was perhaps the most emphatic philosopher of hope in the twentieth century, and his three-volume *Philosophy of Hope* envisaged a utopian human future in a horizon shaped by his own Marxist commitment. But how far does Blochian hope extend? In a critical discussion of Bloch's treatment of death, Levinas calls attention to what he thinks is an unresolved tension in the Marxist philosopher's discussion. While Bloch interprets the entirety of human cultural development within the optic of hope, he also accepts the ineluctable animal mortality of the individual human being. Nevertheless (as presented by Levinas), Bloch argues that while the grave is indeed a limit to individual material existence, we can find a kind of redemption through working for the advent of a coming utopian society in which all positive human possibilities will be completely and adequately realized. In this way, Levinas comments, Marxism becomes "the truth, the way and the life" for human beings in search of self-realization—an allusion, I assume, to the words of Jesus from St. John's Gospel: "I am the way, the truth, and the life" (Jn 14.6). But if St. John also reports Jesus as saying "I am the resurrection and the life" (Jn 11.25), where, in Bloch's materialist perspective, can there be any resurrection?

Levinas's own way of putting this question is found in the concluding paragraph of his discussion, where he states that "the salvation of human beings and of being is thought [by Bloch] in terms of a two-dimensional ontology because it excludes all reference to height (*hauteur*), as if he had been afraid of confusing height and sky."[2] Bloch's avowed materialism allows him to think of the dimension of height as a mere leftover of supernaturalism, and he therefore wants nothing to do with it. But Levinas challenges the view that the supernatural meaning of height exhausts its philosophical significance, asking, "Wouldn't the evident elevation of the superlative notion of being [i.e., the being at which human beings arrive in the achievement of utopia] have to lead to the elaboration of a dimension of height less contestable than that of the pre-Copernican universe?"[3] In other words, Bloch is making the same error as the Soviet propagandists who proclaimed that Yuri Gagarin's journey into space proved the nonexistence of God.[4] That we can no longer credibly think of God as literally up in the sky or identify heaven with the star-filled heavens does not mean that the metaphysical and theological significance of height has been emptied of all meaning. The association of the metaphysical and theological sense of height with cosmological ideas that placed God (and other divine beings) "up there" is, in other words, a historic accident, and the falling-away of the cosmological scaffolding should not essentially affect the use of the term in philosophy and religion.

What, then, does Levinas mean by "height"?[5] In the paper "Transcendence and Height," he glosses "height" in terms of the encounter with the other human being as "infinitely" overflowing "the bounds of knowledge."[6] This offers a useful point of orientation for his usage as a whole, but it scarcely indicates its importance in the overall argument of his major work *Totality and Infinity* (1961), to which we now turn.[7]

In *Totality and Infinity*, the theme of height (*hauteur*—sometimes with a capital *H* in the French text) is developed in such a way as to suggest an implicit critique of Christian theology, a critique that, nevertheless, invites Christian theologians to rediscover elements of their own tradition that have been either lost or underemphasized. Precisely in drawing attention to what may be fundamental differences in the formative metaphors of Christianity and his own Jewish tradition, Levinas also opens up new possibilities for both philosophical and theological dialogue between them.

The Ascent of the Self

Although Descartes is a recurrent point of reference in *Totality and Infinity*, Levinas by no means identifies the self with the rational ego of Descartes's "I think therefore I am." Still less does he identify the self with what Sartre called an "upsurge of nothingness" in the world. Rather, the Levinasian self exists and knows itself as existing by virtue of what Levinas calls its *jouissance*, its simple enjoyment of living in the world. But such a self is also characterized by a desire for more—in fact, Levinas says, an infinite desire, which he also calls metaphysical. This desire, he insists, is not (as in Sartre) generated by any kind of lack. Instead, it is a spontaneous manifestation of life overflowing or exceeding any given state of the self. We are always reaching out for more. In these terms, our lives always give us enough to be going on with, enough to find happiness (*bonheur*), and to give us a sense of self that is fully autonomous and, he emphasizes, atheist—such a self does not need God to confirm its being: Its own life in the world is sufficient evidence of that.

Can such a desire ever find an object that would entirely satisfy it, an object that would, as it were, bring it to a halt? Indeed, it might seem that we exist in the paradoxical situation of being finite beings bearing within ourselves an infinite desire that is not satisfied with simple pleasure or happiness; indeed, this desire can even lead us to sacrifice significant pleasures. In doing so, we then find ourselves "above, or at the point of, the apex of being by virtue of enjoyment (pleasure) and desire (truth and justice). Above being" (57).

The Platonic echoes are clear.[8] As for Plato, the way to truth is an ascent. Whether it is the myth of the soul's ascent to the Elysian Fields in the *Phaedrus* or the images of the cave, the line, and the sun in the *Republic*,

Plato narrates the philosopher's search for truth along the axis below/above, that is, as systematically directed upward, a pattern repeated in the Christian Platonism of Augustine. And, as in a much-debated expression in the *Republic* (a sentence that, largely thanks to Levinas, became a commonplace of late-twentieth and early-twenty-first-century philosophy), Plato too could affirm that the ultimate object of the soul's desire (in Plato's case, the good), was "above being" (see 106, 241, 331).

In his *Symposium*, Plato also described metaphysical desire by reference to the myth of Eros having been the child of poverty and plenty and therefore, at least in part, as the desire for what we don't have or what we lack, a nostalgia for the sense of a plenitude of being that we have somehow lost (dovetailed in Christian readings of Plato into the haunting memory of a paradise lost through Adam's sin). This, as I have noted, is something Levinas is anxious to avoid, so he takes pains to offer an alternative reading. "Can this be interpreted," he asks, "as the poverty of richness itself, as the desire not just of what one has lost but as absolute desire, producing itself in a being in possession of itself and consequently already absolutely 'standing on its own feet'?" (58). The *Symposium*, it will be recalled, offers a series of speeches regarding the nature and origin of love, and Levinas reminds us that among the accounts rejected by Plato is the story told by Aristophanes that human beings were originally joined together with two heads, four arms, and four legs, etc., until the gods, fearing their power, cut them in two, making us as we are now. Love, on this view, is simply the search for the "other half." But, Levinas thinks, this is precisely to make love something negative. "In rejecting the myth of the androgyne that Aristophanes presents, didn't Plato glimpse the non-nostalgic character of desire and of philosophy as presupposing existence to be autochthonous and not a state of exile?" he asks (58).

However, Platonic desire is not (quite) the same as the desire that Levinas has been describing. The object of Platonic desire is the immortal life of the soul (extensively echoed in Christian ascetical theology), but Levinas's alternative is not the purely materialist alternative of Bloch and other Marxists. As he himself puts it, the ultimate object of our desire is "the Other, the stranger" (58), and it is precisely at this point that Levinas switches to a biblical register. The Platonic model, he suggests, implies that all beings participate in a shared fundamental being. In mythological language, the demiurge made them all out of the same original matter, and our philosophical nostalgia for the lost plenitude of being is precisely the desire to be reabsorbed into this original unity. According to the biblical creation narrative, however, creation is ex nihilo, out of nothing, which entails that the individual creature is not just an individuated manifestation of the one divine substance but a truly independent, self-sufficient being, entirely "other" both with regard to God and with regard to other human beings.[9] The philosophical account leads to supposing that the chief aim of political life is the mutual recognition by human beings of their common humanity and their essential equality, but religion supposes more. It is not that it rejects equality as a political goal or value, but it does not regard equality as sufficient to assuage our desire for a better social order. Religion, says Levinas, "is the surplus that is [still or nevertheless] possible in a society of equals" (equality is thus accepted as given). It is "that [surplus] of a glorious humility, of responsibility, and of sacrifice, the condition of equality itself" (58). Levinas doesn't mention but was clearly aware of the strong traditions of conservative French Catholicism that rejected equality in the name, precisely, of humility and self-sacrifice. These traditions found strong voices in writers contemporary with Levinas—Georges Bernanos, for example. By implication, Levinas is making clear that this is not his position. The point is not to launch a polemic against French Republican values of equality but to identify a firmer basis for those values than what is given in a mere constitutional prescription. Just fulfilling our civic duties in a purely formal way is not enough to guarantee the flourishing of the polis.

The Other: My Master—and My God?

A further implication that Levinas now draws from the structure of desire is that the absolute toward which desire is oriented is not something we merely have to discover. Unlike the philosophers' "being," it is not something of which we have innate (if mostly implicit) knowledge, as Socrates's practice of maieutic questioning seems to suppose; instead (and remembering that we don't lack anything necessary for our full human existence in the world), it has to come to us from outside. In other words, it is revelation—another religious-sounding category to which we should, again, avoid attaching supernaturalist connotations. Or (which, for Levinas, amounts to the same point), it comes to us as the expression, the articulated word, of another, that is, another who is as self-sufficient and as real in their own being as we are in ours. What I encounter at the limit of desire and what is alone capable of setting a limit to the infinity of my desire is therefore another human being, or, as Levinas memorably puts it, it is the revelation of the face of the other, a face that turns to me, addresses me, speaks to me from a place outwith the orbit of my own self-consciousness and thus having the character of what Levinas calls "exteriority."

Crucially, my encounter with the face of the other is not a matter of intuition: It is not that I simply "see" the other facing me and intuit their humanity along with the claim that their humanity has on me by virtue of—precisely—this shared humanity. Rather, I know the face of the other as a human face and not an animal face because it speaks to me, revealing that what I see in the face is the expression of another autonomous being who is not me but is able—by speaking—to make a claim on me. This may sound like but is not the kind of mutual revelation made famous in Buber's description of the I-Thou relationship. Levinas is respectful of this, but whereas the center of Buber's model of human relationship is the intimacy of the "thou" (or "*du*" or "*tu*"), Levinas prioritizes instead the formality of the "*Vous*." In other words, the primary revelation of the other is not given in a context of reciprocity but when I find myself (literally) faced with a demand that the other makes upon me. This involves a very different kind of recognition from that in which I recognize a brother, sister, lover, or friend. "To recognize the other is to recognize a hunger. To recognize the other—is to give. But it is to give to the master, to the Lord, to the one who confronts me as '*vous*' in a dimension of height (*hauteur*)" (73).

We might well ask how Levinas got here—and even in the full text of *Totality and Infinity* there seems to be a kind of leap that is scarcely explained by the unfolding of his description of human life in the world up to this point. One could argue that this is entirely appropriate, since he is now attempting to account for something that cannot be found through the self-analysis of our immanent, worldly consciousness. Nevertheless, even readers who have followed the argument up to and including the point at which Levinas says that the revelation of the other as other has to come from outside, as an appeal articulated in the expressive discourse of a human face, might wonder why he now glosses this in terms of the other being a "master" or even "Lord" (perhaps surprisingly, the term Levinas uses for the latter is "*seigneur*," the standard term used for addressing God in Catholic liturgy and corresponding to the English "Lord").[10]

In another thinker, we might assume that such a leap was deliberately theological. Levinas, however, claims otherwise. He certainly affirms that the relation to the other is a relation to the Transcendent (with, in the text, a capital *T*), a Transcendent that is "infinitely other, soliciting and calling upon us" (76). He also recognizes that this would appear to refer to God but still asserts that this reference is *not* theological and that he is not backtracking on his description of the human being living in the world as essentially atheistic. It is not theological because, he says, it is *ethical*. "Theology," as he understands it here, implies knowledge of God, as in Catholic theology's account of the attributes of the divine being. But, for Levinas, God cannot become an object of knowledge. God is as invisible to the mind's eye as to the physical eye. Only ethics brings us into relationship to such a

God. "The invisible God does not merely signify a God who cannot be imagined but a God who is accessible in justice. Ethics is the optic for spiritual life" (76).[11] "God" and the "other" are in this way inextricably linked yet not identical. Levinas writes: "Apart from the relation to human beings there cannot be any 'knowledge' of God. The other is the very place of metaphysical truth and indispensable in my relation to God. He does not play the role of a mediator. The other is not the incarnation of God, but precisely his face, in which he is disincarnated, the manifestation of the height at which God reveals himself" (TI, 77). These are dense sentences that need unpacking.

A first point is to ask why Levinas is determined to specify exteriority as height. We could even question whether precisely this specification doesn't in fact undermine the very point being made by his use of "exteriority." For if we are thinking of exteriority in the radical sense he proposes, it is not just a matter of such "external" objects as the tree outside my window but of an ontological exteriority, a difference in being between two beings separately created out of nothing and not participating in any common being. But saying that something is "above," "below," "alongside," or related to me in any other particular spatial relationship would seem to place it—whatever it is—within just the kind of shared ontological framework that exteriority is intended to exclude.

Clearly, Levinas is well aware that he is pushing language to its limits and cannot, perhaps, avoid paradox.[12] But despite the problems it generates, the emphasis on height can be seen to serve a number of fairly easily understandable purposes. To begin with, it continues the trajectory already sketched in the Platonic ascent. It goes beyond this, certainly, but in speaking of what happens in this "beyond being" as "height," Levinas retains the Platonic model as a point of reference. More immediately, as we have seen, it also serves to connect what he is saying to the biblical demand, that is, to the divine imperative to care for widows, orphans, and aliens and that Levinas regards as epitomizing the central ethical teaching of the revelation on Sinai.

The allusion to this biblical theme is at points explicit, as when Levinas writes that "the other qua other is situated in a dimension of height and abasement—a glorious abasement: it has the face of the poor, the stranger, the widow and the orphan" (281). Now we might take this last conjunction of "height and abasement" in a rather conventional way by ascribing the height to God and the abasement to the poor, as if God "on high" is commanding us to "do good" to our social inferiors, but this would be to misconstrue Levinas's point, which is that the poor, the stranger, the widow, and the orphan whose need I am called to attend to are not—or I am not to think of them as—in some way "below" me and to whom charity therefore obliges me to condescend.

That, of course, is how charity has sometimes been construed, both by those who practice it and those who receive it. But it is just this kind of charity that generates the resentment of those on the receiving end, since it effectively confirms their social subjugation and robs them of the respect due to all persons capable of moral agency. In such condescension they are treated as incapable of helping themselves and made into the entirely passive recipients of others' beneficence. This is perhaps an attitude with which we are familiar from literary and film treatments of Victorian charity, which is often depicted and mocked as a means by which the middle classes maintain a sense of self-righteousness in face of the suffering that the prevailing economic system (of which they were beneficiaries) inevitably brings about. Even if such portrayals are often caricatures, the point is clear. And despite our having learned to see such charity for what it is when it appears in Victorian guise, it might be considered a moot point as to whether we have entirely escaped the core problem, as contemporary discussions of the "White Savior" syndrome suggests. In a Levinasian perspective, what is going on here is the confusion of charity with what is ethically demanded and with the all-encompassing requirement of justice.[13]

On Levinas's account, what we owe to the poor (the widow, the orphan, and the alien) is precisely what, in justice, we *owe*—and is therefore not charity. On the contrary, in being confronted by the appeal of the poor I am being confronted with a voice that commands, the voice of one who is or is to be as a master to me, even my "Lord" (*seigneur*). Whatever I give to the poor, I "give" as one who is less than the one to whom I give—and here we may note the allusions made by Levinas on a number of occasions to the teaching of Dostoevsky's Elder Zosima that "each of us is guilty before everyone, for everyone and I most of all."[14] In other words, none of us are the good people (the "good guys") entitled to share our good with others, but each of us is in a situation of owing everything we have to others. As Levinas will say, we live "under accusation." In Zosima's "Talks and Homilies," Dostoevsky even extends this to judges, who are urged to know that they too are criminals, exactly like those who stand before them, and that the judge "perhaps is, more than all men, to blame for that crime."[15]

But why bring God into it? Is not the atheist who is confronted by the cry of the poor just as capable as the religious person of seeing that the demand being made is a demand of justice and not just, let us say, an emotional appeal that looks to play upon his or her sympathies?

Levinas would surely answer this question in the affirmative, but the grounding of the appeal in revelation, in the giving of the law, and in a recognition of the humanly unattainable height from which that law is promulgated forcefully underwrites the claim that this is not a matter of taking up a more or less voluntary moral stance. This is not a negotiable "extra" but a demand made upon me by virtue of my being the being that I am, simply as a human being, any human being, a being made ex nihilo living in a society of other beings likewise each made ex nihilo.

Again, we must be careful of supposing, Gagarin-like, that Levinas is inviting us to accept a literal understanding of the divine "height." Nevertheless, the biblical narrative does help identify what is at issue in the insistence on height. In the context of Levinas's Jewish faith, it should be emphasized that the point of divine revelation is not that it gives knowledge about God (and we have seen how Levinas rejects "theology" because it presumes the possibility of such knowledge) but that it sets out the law, the ensemble of commandments—the Torah—that human beings are to obey if, as the Bible puts it, they are to live well in the land.

This giving of the law is placed in the biblical history at the point at which the Hebrew people have escaped from slavery in Egypt and have gathered at the foot of Mount Sinai. Moses alone ascends into the "thick cloud" that covers the mountain (Ex 19.16), and the people are repeatedly warned not to try to "break through" so as to "gaze" on the Lord (Ex 19.21). God speaks to Moses "in thunder" (Ex 19.19) and remains throughout veiled in "thick darkness" (Ex 20.21). From this darkness He promulgates the Law that the people are to obey, of which the Christian "ten commandments" are only the beginning of what, for the pious Jew, are 613 commandments—and although these include many that relate to ritual, dietary practices, and sexual morality, they also include those concerning the duty to the widow, the orphan, and the stranger, as at Exodus 22.21–23: "'You shall not wrong a stranger or oppress him, for you were strangers in the land of Egypt. You shall not afflict any widow or orphan. If you do afflict them, and they cry out to me, I will surely hear their cry.'"[16]

This is a commandment given from "on high," and the notion that God is, as it were, "on high" continues as an abiding trope in biblical theology. Just as it is on the mountain of Sinai that the law is given, so, later, it is to Mount Zion that the Israelite tribes are summoned to "go up" (Ps 122.4) to worship the God who "rides upon the clouds" (Ps 68.4) and is "enthroned in the heavens" (Ps 123.1), whose glory is praised even "above the heavens" (Ps 8.1).[17] God knows us as we cannot know ourselves, and "such knowledge," writes the psalmist, "is too wonderful for me; it is high, I cannot attain it" (Ps 139.6). In Isaiah, God himself declares "'Heaven is my throne and the earth is my footstool'" (Isa 66.1). But God's being "on high" is not to be read simply as a hangover of mythical beliefs about mountain deities. Rather, it is to be read as the nonconvertibility of the divine-human relationship. God is God because God is somewhere ("on high") where we can never be, and while God may call on Zion to "arise" (Isa 60.1), the attempt to build a tower reaching all the way to heaven—the tower of Babel—epitomizes misjudged hubris (Gen 11.1–9). As the preacher of Ecclesiastes cautioned, "God is in heaven and you upon earth, therefore let your words be few" (Eccl 5.2). Statements about divine elevation are equally well read as statements about human finitude, about the limits of our powers, and about the limits of our self-knowledge. But the claim that God speaks to us from above, from beyond the limits of what we ourselves can be, know, or do, implies that we have obligations that are, simply, inescapable. There are things we cannot know, but there are also things that we must do.

Again, it must be conceded that this doesn't mean that the atheist can't also do justice for the widow, the orphan, and the stranger. It does, however, remove a misconception as to how the religious person understands what it is to be religious. For on this basis, being religious cannot involve the attainment of knowledge of God (God remains clothed "in thick darkness"), nor can it involve the achievement of a stable state of moral goodness—no matter how often I have helped the widow, the orphan, and the stranger, the commandment remains insistent that I go on doing so. Obligation is never exhausted.

At the same time, "height" could seem to introduce a new misunderstanding in that it confronts the supposedly autonomous and even atheist self with what is likely to be experienced as a heteronomous command. In this sense, the implications of locating the origin of the command in some inaccessible height run against everything that the modern mistrust of hierarchies and moral authorities who preach from secure positions twelve feet above criticism has taught us. But it would also run against Levinas's own insistence on the legitimacy of both autonomy and atheism. As Michael Morgan has put it, "God cannot enter Levinas's thinking as a divine commander."[18] Levinas's God is not reducible to an authoritarian sovereign still less a metaphysical tyrant, but nevertheless, "command" there is. Just what is going on here?

Three points may help clarify this further "apparent paradox." The first is that if "height" is introduced as a qualification of exteriority, exteriority in turn qualifies "height" because where I encounter what is entirely *exterior* in Levinas's sense cannot be "above" or "below," "behind" or "in front." God, in other words, is not to be found in the top tier of a hierarchy of relationships. Biblically, he is not just in heaven but above the heavens or, Platonically, beyond being and therefore beyond all relative location. The second is that, as we have seen, it is precisely in relation to the poor, the orphan, and the widow that I encounter the divine command, which, as we have been seeing, means that it comes from a source that I might be tempted to think of as below me, a source that is relatively powerless in relation to me and that needs my assistance, my intervention, in order to attain its justice—as if I were a White Savior, perhaps. As Levinas put it in an interview, "There is a commandment in the appearance of the face, as if a master spoke to me. However, at the same time, the face of the Other is destitute; it is the poor for whom I can do all and to whom I owe all."[19] But, third, the command reaches me specifically as discourse, as a word, as what the one imploring my help *says*. But in being spoken the command comes as something that I must interpret, on which I can think, and in relation to which I can and must make a free decision as to how I am to respond. I may not be able to escape being put on the spot by the beggar who asks for help, but I am nevertheless free to decide how I am to respond to that appeal. If the request comes with the force of obligation, it is up to me to decide what that obligation actually means for me, here and now. The power that the weak exert over me is not emotional blackmail but an appeal to the justice I am obliged to serve and that engages me as a person capable of moral reflection and autonomous action.

Height and Depth

If we allow that Levinas is deliberately invoking the biblical God (and some of his secular readers may want to resist this connection), then it seems not far-fetched to suggest that he is also making an implied distinction between Judaism and Christianity in favor of the former. As we have seen, the theme of God being "on high" runs virtually throughout the Hebrew Bible. It is continued in the Christian New Testament, where Jesus ascends the mountain to give teaching (Mt 5.1),[20] is transfigured on a mountain (Mark 9.2–8), and even his crucifixion is referred to as being "lifted up from the earth" on the cross (Jn 12.32), located on the hill Golgotha. After rising or being raised from the dead, he ascends into heaven, traditionally represented in Christian iconography as happening from the top of a hill, though this is not explicit in the text.

Yet Christianity seems also to emphasize images of descent. As it says in the Nicene Creed (a definitive statement of Christian doctrine), "He [Christ] came down from heaven and was made man" or, as one popular Christmas hymn puts it, "love came down at Christmas." Paul's Letter to the Philippians even more radically sees this as Christ emptying out his divine nature, writing that "being in the form of God, [he] did not consider it robbery to be equal with God, but emptied himself [Greek: *ekenōsen*], taking the form of a bondservant, *and* coming in the likeness of men. And being found in appearance as a man, He humbled Himself and became obedient to *the point of* death, even the death of the cross" (Phil 2.5–8). Following the Greek *ekenōsen*, this passage has inspired what are known as kenotic theologies that emphasize the thorough emptying-out of the divine attributes in the Incarnation and, in effect, God's complete abandonment of divine height (what Protestant theologies have called the *status exinanitionis*, the state of abasement). In A. N. Whitehead's much-cited phrase, God is no longer "up there" but has become "a fellow sufferer who understands."[21]

As a model for Christian behavior, this pattern of descent would seem to encourage views of charity as involving giving up what we have for the benefit of those who have less, that is, as a matter of condescension. But this is exactly what Levinas is asking us to supplant with the idea of the other as my destitute "master." Yet if Levinas's account of the "height" from which the destitute "master" speaks to me can be taken as implicitly critical of Christianity, it could also be read as summoning Christianity back to a more nuanced view of its own version of the relationship between height and lowliness. In describing the crucifixion, John's Gospel in particular emphasizes that Jesus is "raised" on the cross, and the evangelist draws a parallel with the story of the bronze serpent (John 3.14).[22] On the basis of the Johannine text, this incident then becomes a standard trope of Christian iconography and is often to be seen in the background of the crucifixion, as in Lucas Cranach's Reformation altarpiece in Weimar. This (and similar works) often emphasize the height of the cross, stretching it vertically beyond any historical verisimilitude. The cross is thus less a symbol of Christ's descent to the ultimate misery of suffering and death but of his elevation. The passage from Philippians just cited continues: "Therefore God also highly exalted him and gave him the name that is above every name, so that at the name of Jesus every knee should bend, in heaven and on earth and under the earth" (Phil 2.9–10). The *status exinanitionis* is transformed into the *status exaltationis*. Is this a piece of divine legerdemain, or are we to see the two states as mutually interpreting such that Christ's elevation is his humiliation and his humiliation his elevation?

There is no doubt that in the many variations played on these themes of ascent and descent in Christian tradition the interrelatedness of humiliation and elevation are made to perform very different tasks. Some of these involve a too easy and too rapid switch from abasement to elevation. And of course, because Jesus Christ is for most Christians an object of worship, he cannot easily or exactly be put in the same place as the poor, the widows, the orphans, and aliens of Levinasian ethics. Or not obviously. Nevertheless, as Jesus's own parable of the sheep and the goats suggests, the poor are indeed those through whom and in whom Christ is present in the world. Feeding the hungry, welcoming and clothing the stranger, and visiting the prisoner thereby become the litmus test for how human beings actually relate to Christ—rather than whatever they say about this relation. In the words with which Jesus ends the parable: "Inasmuch as you did it to the least of these, you did it to me" (Mt 25.40). Read in the light of these words, it would seem that Christianity too requires us to see the poor as the visible representatives of the Christ who is raised high on the cross of suffering and therefore as commanding justice and not just begging for charity.[23]

Inverting the Hierarchy of Prayer

Levinas's argument has significant implications for a philosophy of prayer. Not least, it invites us to question the traditional hierarchy of forms of prayer. This typically identifies intercession as the lowest rung of prayer, from which we ascend toward increasing intimacy with God until, finally, we reach the height of wordless contemplation. Here, however, it seems that the extroversion of the intimacy of the God-relationship means allowing ourselves to be turned inside out and, in our prayer, literally to put the other first. Of course, Levinasian ethics, like much Christian teaching (remember Kierkegaard's insistence on *works* of love), reminds us that action and not only prayer is required. But are height and depth, contemplation and intercession, prayer and action really mutually exclusive? Didn't everything that Marcel, Berdyaev, and Tillich said about the internally dialectical and paradoxical character of existence point instead to seeing these polarities as aspects of one dynamic and complex movement, namely, the movement from egoity toward God? With specific regard to prayer, we note that both Levinas's account of heeding the call of the other and Buber's discussion of mystical language coincide in placing the word of another at the heart of our own human and individual capacity for language. And, with Simone Weil in mind, the discipline of self-decreating attention to this word is as applicable in the case of the word addressed to us by the neighbor as it is in the case of God. In praying for the other (rather than single-mindedly pursuing our own ascent toward God), prayer and ethics converge—not, of course, when praying for the other means no more than reading through the intercession list but, perhaps, praying for the other as placing ourselves at their disposal and, even more fundamentally, finding that place from which our common human need proceeds. Of course, it is clear that the interior self-giving movement of prayer and the exterior self-giving for the neighbor ("in deeds") are not "the same," but they each call for the suspension of our drive for autonomous self-affirmation for the sake of a reality that engages us from outside the circle of our own self-interest and that, at the same time, we are compelled to see as foundational for our own existence in the world. In these terms, it is the enactment of a basic solidarity that (I suggest) is the presupposition of charity and justice alike. "Your Kingdom come" is never, or never solely, a prayer for me alone but for us all.

We began this chapter by considering Levinas's criticism of Ernst Bloch's purely horizontal and materialist utopianism. Yet as we have seen, Levinas's justice is also a utopian possibility that we are to strive for, a future possibility still to be realized within history. The ethical demand is not just about rearranging the present world order but aims to bring about a new and even messianic order, a rule of justice. But does this mean a complete break with all that we have been and all preceding history? Shouldn't it rather be an affirmation—the ultimate affirmation—of all that has mattered most to us, individually and collectively, in the past? To explore further what this might mean, I turn now to see how a messianic hope may also be figured as homecoming, again taking the Marxist philosopher Ernst Bloch as a point of departure but pursuing the question in dialogue with Heidegger, a more or less constant companion in these reflections.

8

Homecoming

Heidegger—a Thinker of Place?

In the petition "Your Kingdom come," Christians pray, in Rosenzweig's evocative expression, to "hasten the Kingdom." The essentially future-oriented and messianic character of this prayer seems to be shared equally by a Jewish thinker such as Levinas and Christian thinkers such as Berdyaev and Tillich, who, despite Levinas's equation of (Christian) theology with untenable claims to a speculative knowledge of God, exemplify modern renditions of the ancient view that theology is less about knowing and more about unknowing and acting.

The contrast between a biblically inspired, future-oriented conception of human existence and a Platonic view that privileges the remembrance or recollection (*anamnesis*) of eternal and unchanging forms is a commonplace way of narrating the distinction between the Hebrew and Greek elements of Western culture. Like all such distinctions, however, a closer examination reveals a more complex picture. Past, future, and present are deeply coimplicated in the structure of human time-experience, even if certain contexts suggest that one has primacy over the others. The idea that the past too is deeply implicated in the basic shape of messianic thought is nicely expressed in the closing pages of Ernst Bloch's *Philosophy of Hope*, where he writes that utopia is a memory that has shone into the childhood of all but where no one has ever been, "homeland" as he puts it—a memory, but a memory of something unknown and unknowable, something both lost and something that has never been.[1]

The idea of messianic striving as a kind of homecoming is familiar to both Christian and Jewish traditions, as in the figuring of the New Jerusalem as the eternal home to which we return after our earthly exile, a return to the lost paradise in which we walked and talked in deep intimacy with God. In the specific context of a philosophy of prayer, the pathos of exile and homecoming is deeply inscribed in the movement of spiritual desire that is both a desire to return to the source of our being and, at the same time, a longing to hasten the coming of the Kingdom. We shall later see this illustrated in one of the founding texts of philosophical theology in the Western tradition. First, however, we turn to Heidegger, whose analysis of the time-structure of human existence is, in Levinas's words, an "obligatory passage" for modern philosophy.[2]

In *Being and Time*, Heidegger too drew attention to the priority of the future while also paying close attention to the coimplication of all three temporal "ecstasies" of past, present, and future. It has often been claimed that at some point after *Being and Time* his thought underwent a major "turning." Whether this was a shift of focus or a real change of direction has been much debated, but it does seem to be the case that while the future never ceases to play a vital role, he increasingly places more value on origins than destinations. Or to be more precise, he more and more emphasizes how the way in which we envisage and anticipate the future is shaped by our memory of the past. Ultimately, this means that our journey into a future that cannot be anticipated or imagined is also a journey home. However, whereas Bloch drew extensively on Jewish and Christian eschatology in order to articulate the tension between futurity and homecoming, Heidegger looked more to a poetically transfigured return of the gods of mythology rather than the advent of a new and incoming reign of justice. This return, moreover, was especially focused on a national and even local utopia. Time is in this way folded back into the experience of place, perhaps suggesting that the philosophy of the later Heidegger is a philosophy of space, to use Eliade's taxonomy. If that is so, is this, then, inherently opposed to the hopeful eschatology of Levinas, Berdyaev, Marcel, and Tillich? Has the call of the other been subordinated to the call of hearth and home?

Even if we hesitate to categorize the later Heidegger as exclusively or predominantly a thinker of space rather than time, metaphors of place (and more than metaphors, perhaps) pervade his later writings, which seem to describe a path leading from the "Mount of Olives" that had engaged the imagination of the young seminarist he had once been to the Black

Forest, where the mature philosopher pursued the rigorous path of thinking in the solitude of his mountain retreat, in solidarity with the sempiternal toil of the farmer, building, dwelling, and thinking. Is this path, from priestly vocation to sylvan wanderings, a path *away* from the God of Christianity and away from theology? Is it a path toward a *new* God? Or perhaps even back to the old God, but "otherwise"?

For many readers, Heidegger's valorization of the forest has unfortunate associations with the "blood and soil" rhetoric of Nazism, and his philosophy is irretrievably devalued by his membership of the Nazi Party and his very public support for Hitler. We have already noted Tillich's suspicion that the prioritization of space over time is characteristic of antiprogressive political values. As Simon Schama has explained, citing Wilhelm Heinrich Riehl's 1861 *Natural History of the German People*, the opposition between city and forest was a defining feature of German nationalist imagination, one that acquired a hard political edge, such that "in this scheme, the rootless Jew was the purveyor of this corrupted, citified society, while the forester was his antithesis—the embodiment of ethnic authenticity, rooted like his trees in the ancient earth of the Fatherland."[3]

An overall accounting of Heidegger's philosophy cannot ultimately ignore his politics, but, at the same time, not everything is reducible to this.[4] Even in relation to the concepts of home and homeland that are (shall we say?) politically sensitive, what Heidegger has to say is rich with references to the histories of philosophy and (I shall argue) faith that cannot be reduced to their political abuse in nationalist ideologies. These references invite us to a kind of questioning and listening that is, I suggest, illuminating for a philosophy of prayer.

The Way Home

"Where do we come from?" and "Where are we going to?" have been among the most basic questions that humans have asked themselves for millennia. One way of answering both questions is: home. Home is where we all begin, in the home that saw our birth, our infant joys and tears, our acquisition of what Heidegger at least does not regard as accidentally named: our mother tongue. But history itself, the common history of us all, can also be portrayed, in Schelling's phrase, as the Odyssey of the spirit, a perpetual homecoming. "Home" not only evokes the aura with which memory surrounds the people, places, and things of childhood and youth; it also speaks of the end of all our exploring, as in Novalis's saying that our journey in life is ever homeward or in Bloch's evocation of home as the ultimate term of radical social thought.

If both these senses of home, as beginning and as end, are now distant from us—perhaps because we ourselves are far from home, no longer children but not yet declining toward our end—this all the more underlines the hidden unity of beginning and end. But where we are now is neither beginning nor end. Where, then, can a thinker be said to be at home? This is a question we can still ask even if we meet the thinker when, like us, he is far from home, wayfaring, homeless, en route into an ever more uncertain future.

Such a question, asked of Martin Heidegger, is not, of course, plucked out of thin air, and its relevance to the interpretation of Heidegger does not require any great familiarity with his texts. Perhaps one of the first things students learn about Heidegger is how, in *Being and Time*, he describes the human condition as being thrown into a world that is experienced as "uncanny," *un-heimlich*, un-homely: This is the determining content of that most characteristically Kierkegaardian/Heideggerian term: "angst." Angst-full existence is essentially un-homely, the experience of ourselves as not being at home. But it doesn't end there. For if we read further into Heidegger we discover that our experience of being far from home enters into the very constitution of philosophy. In *The Fundamental Concepts of Metaphysics* (lectures from the winter semester of 1929–1930), he begins by asking about the essence of philosophy. Having, very briefly, considered and discarded several forms of intellectual life with which philosophy might be confused—science, worldview, religion, and art—Heidegger attempts to determine philosophy "out of itself," "taking [a] lead from a word of Novalis." This "word" is akin to, though not identical with, the word we have already heard from *Heinrich von Ofterdingen*. It runs: "Philosophy is really homesickness, an urge to be at home everywhere."[5] Heidegger immediately acknowledges that such a saying is easily dismissed as a piece of romanticism, though he clearly also knows that Novalis is himself playing a variation upon a theme that reaches back through Western philosophy at least as far as Plato. But whatever its lineage, Novalis's "word" prompts a further question. "Homesickness—does such a thing still exist today at all? Has it not become an incomprehensible word in everyday life? Has not contemporary city man, the ape of civilization, long since eradicated homesickness? And homesickness as the very determination of philosophy!"[6] Things look unpromising, but in a matter of minutes, seconds even, Heidegger has expounded Novalis's saying in terms of philosophy's concern for the wholeness of the world and thus for being as a whole, while our alienation from such being as a whole, the home-*sickness*, "the unrest of this 'not,'" simultaneously directs philosophy to the finitude, individuation, and solitariness of Dasein, which is said to be "something quite other" than "man: the animal, the dupe [!] of civilization, guardian of culture and even personality."[7] The awakening of philosophy in this sense, Heidegger adds, "in each case happens in a fundamental attunement" such as the experience of homesickness itself, an experience that befalls us in, for example, the boredom that is characteristic of modern life.[8]

By the time of the lectures on the *Fundamental Concepts of Metaphysics*, Heidegger had made his home in the Black Forest, a geographical location that seems not irrelevant, given Heidegger's own dismissal of the "city man" as one who is closed off from the experience of homesickness. This is not because the city man knows what home is but, on the contrary, because he has no sense whatever for any possible meaning of home. By way of contrast, Heidegger is now learning that his solitary life in the mountain hut where he goes to devote himself to his philosophical work is not simply the "lonely hobby of an eccentric" but work that "belongs in the midst of the work of the farmers." My work, he asserts in his essay "Schöpferische Landschaft: Warum bleiben wir in der Provinz?" ("Creative Landscape: Why Do I Stay in the Provinces?"), written in 1933, a few years after he gave his *Fundamental Concepts* course, is "*of the same kind*" as theirs. Whereas "the city man believes that he is going 'among the people' the moment he condescends to have a long conversation with a farmer," Heidegger is happy just to sit there with them in the evenings, saying nothing, silently smoking his pipe, and listening to someone occasionally mentioning a cow that's about to calve or commenting on the weather.[9] The climax of such monosyllabic communings comes at the close of the essay, when a seventy-five-year-old farmer, who has read in the papers about Heidegger's call to Berlin, looks the Herr Professor in the eye, places his hand, his "*treu-bedächtige*" hand, on Heidegger's shoulder, and shakes his head: No! Which Heidegger takes as confirmation that the farmers too recognize that he belongs with them, as one of them.[10]

For all the unfortunate political resonances of Heidegger's decision to make his home in the Black Forest, this decision has many parallels elsewhere in the modern cultural landscape. From the English Lake Poets, through Thoreau's Walden, George Mackay Brown's Orkney, and Charles de Foucauld's explicitly religious choice of the North African desert, inner emigration has repeatedly taken the form of a retreat to places experienced as remote and solitary. But such removals are not solely a matter of retreating from everything associated with urban civilization. They are or can be a rediscovery of the meaning of home (and, no less importantly, a rediscovery of the profound connections between landscape and thinking, but that is a topic for another occasion).

In a lecture of June 6, 1943, marking the centenary of Hölderlin's death, Heidegger offered an interpretation of the poem "Homecoming." Not surprisingly, the meaning of "home/land" is central to this interpretation, and this, for Heidegger, is tied up with the identity of the poet whose "homecoming" across the Lake of Constance to Swabia is the subject of the poem. The "essence of home" is said to consist in preserving "the homely" (*das Heimische*, meaning what is home-bred, native, indigenous). What this involves is then explored by means of a close-knit complex of terms, among which "origin," "joy," "brightness," "healing," "the holy," "mystery," and "nearness" are particularly striking. Homecoming, we learn, is not simply the theme of Hölderlin's poem. Homecoming is at the very center of poetic vocation as such: "The vocation of the poet is homecoming, and through it the homeland is first made ready as the land of nearness to the origin."[11] The poetic word is the word that speaks "the mystery of the nearness [to the origin] to those who are near," and it does so by poetically speaking "what is most joyous," and "what is most joyous" is itself nothing other than "coming to be at home (*Heimischwerden*) in nearness to the origin."[12] The note of joy is decisive, for it is joy that makes the power of origin to be both a healing and a holy power. Heidegger speaks of this also as "*Die Heitere*" (translated by Richardson as "the Glad-some"), which he interprets (uncharacteristically!) by means of the Latin terms *claritas*, *serenitas*, and *hilaritas*. The joyous, *Der Freudige*, is also identified with the *Äther*, the Father, the heaven that overarches the land, making it the Father-Land, a joy heralded, in Hölderlin's poem, by angels and poets.

Being at home in nearness to the origin, being awake to this joy, is not, however, an attribute of all the people who happen to be native to a certain land in any direct or straightforward way. Not all of those among whom and to whom the poet speaks his mysterious word hear what is spoken in it: We only truly come home when we hear the poetic word of homecoming, the poetic word as homecoming. Fatherland and home are not primarily geographical or even geopolitical entities. Naming the joyous mystery of home is the privilege of the poetic word. Moreover, the very condition of this poetic word is the poet's own experience of exile, for it is only as a returning exile, as one who is coming home, that he fulfils his vocation to bring home the message of home. This, then, would seem to preclude or at least to qualify the kind of immediate identification between the thinker and his geopolitical particularity that was evidenced in "Creative Landscape."[13]

However, we cannot be sure that this poetizing of home/land means that Heidegger has abandoned the domain of the social and the political altogether. Note, for example, Heidegger's rhetorical question: "Are not the sons of the homeland, who far from the soil of their homeland but looking towards the brightness beamed towards them from the homeland, spend their lives and expend them in sacrifice for the treasure it still holds intact—are not these sons of the homeland the nearest relatives of the poet?"[14] This suggests that Hölderlin's poetic spirit best lives on "today" among the soldiers dying (and, as he omits to say, killing) on the Eastern Front to protect their homeland. If we think of this homeland as Germany rather than the Reich, and bearing in mind the catastrophically accelerating casualty rate among German forces, we should hesitate before sneering at Heidegger's sentiment at this point—it is, after all, a sentiment shared by the majority of people in a time of war, whatever the cause. But we should also be careful to note that the poetizing of home/land cannot simply be interpreted as a retreat into some kind of inwardness. Even if we don't like Heidegger's particular social application, it does make clear that the poetic word belongs very much to this world.

If Heidegger came to make his home in the Black Forest, his "real" home, the home of his birth and childhood, lay elsewhere, in the large village of Meßkirch, further to the south and east, where his ancestors had lived for many generations and where his father was sexton of the Church of St. Martin's. It was to Meßkirch that the philosopher "went home" on July 22, 1961, to give an address at a special Heimatabend, an "At Home," in the context of festivities marking the seven hundredth anniversary of its foundation.

Heidegger's thoughts in this address turn first to the historical nature of the occasion and the fact that his audience has gathered to think about the Meßkirch of yesterday and of today—but what, he asks, of "Meßkirch tomorrow? In the future?"[15] The future is not, of course, something of which we can "have" knowledge, but there are many signs of what is in store, most conspicuously the radio and television aerials springing from every rooftop. These, Heidegger asserts, "show that human beings are, strictly speaking, no longer 'at home'[*zuhause*] where, seen from outside, they 'live.'"[16] Television is the most immediate and visible sign of the dominion of technology over our lives, and we have every reason to suppose that this dominion will grow rather than diminish in the future (a point on which Heidegger was, surely, right). In the world represented by telecommunications there is no "abiding city," the new is rapidly succeeded by the even newer, modernism by postmodernism, postmodernism by postsecularism, and postsecularism, doubtless, by something already waiting in the wings: If a movement in ideas once lasted a generation, then a decade, it is likely that today it might last scarcely a year.

Spellbound and pulled onward by all this, humanity is, as it were, in a process of emigration. It is emigrating from what is *Heimisch* to the *Unheimisch* [the alien, the unfamiliar, the uncanny]. There is a danger that what was once called home [*Heimat*], will dissolve and disappear. The power of the *Unheimisch* seems to have so overpowered humanity that it can no longer pit itself against it. How can we defend ourselves against the pressure of the *Unheimisch*? Only by this: that we continually arouse the bestowing and healing and preserving strength of the *Heimisch*, that we enable the strengthening springs of the *Heimisch* to flow, and create proper channels in which they can flow and so exert their influence.[17]

Then, perhaps predictably, he continues: "This remains most possible and most consistently effective in places where the powers of the natural environment and the resonance of historical tradition remain alongside each other, where the ancestry and the customs maintained from of yore determine human existence [*Dasein*]"—in other words, places just like Meßkirch, protected from the "life of the big cities and the monstrous domain of modern industry."[18]

In order to effectively "redeem and care for" the *Heimisch*, however, we have to know exactly what it is that threatens it. In the first instance, we can call this "technology," with its law of ceaseless innovation. And at one level, Heidegger says, we have to acknowledge that this is irresistible. We really do live in the age of technology. Even Meßkirch cannot escape it, as the television aerials testify. Perhaps, then, "home" in the deepest sense is a thing of the past: "Perhaps humanity is migrating to a condition of homelessness," Heidegger muses. Perhaps the relation to home and the pull of home is disappearing from the Dasein of modern humanity.[19] Perhaps. Or "Perhaps," Heidegger continues, "a new relation to the *Heimisch* is preparing itself even in the midst of the pressure exerted by the *Unheimisch*."[20]

The pull of home, Heidegger goes on, is what we call homesickness, a phenomenon that has far from vanished. On the contrary, homesickness is the true meaning of that most modern of moods, boredom, the boredom that pervades a world shaped by technology and the technological consciousness. Boredom is "hidden homesickness."[21] But at this point, Heidegger's talk takes a curious twist. The question is this: How are we to recognize the "sought-for home" postulated in the phenomenon of homesickness? By preserving that from which we have come and staying near to the mystery of the origin, in the language of the Hölderlin lecture. But *where* to do so? A preliminary answer seems obvious: the graveyard, "God's acre."[22] Here is the place for the remembrance of what has been, the parental home, and the time of youth; it is a place where the noise and frenzy of modernity are matched by stillness and restraint. The encounter with the *Unheimisch* thus itself occasions reflective remembrance, *Besinnung*, upon the *Heimisch*, the quiet but festive remembrance that enables us to maintain a countermovement, a *Heimkehr*, over against the power of the *Unheimisch*.

> By reflecting upon tomorrow, we arouse the healing power of yesterday, understood correctly and appropriated aright. On such ways we first attain the Today that we must live through [endure] between the past and the future. Such living through helps us to become earnest [*inständig*] in what holds its position against all change.[23]

All of this may simply reinforce our worst fears about Heidegger's folksy conservatism. Yet he is careful not to endow Meßkirch with any absolute privilege over against the world of technology, the city. There is much more chiaroscuro here than in the simple confrontation between Berlin and the world of the mountain hut. For Meßkirch too is caught up in the onward movement of technologization and change. In other words, Heidegger is saying that we cannot simply stop, still less bail out of, technologization. What we have to do instead is to find a way of being at home, even in the midst of the confrontation with the *Unheimisch*. No less important, second, is the fact that Heidegger turns the question of homecoming and of the relationship between villager and city man into an issue of historicity. It is not simply a matter of here versus there but of the interconnectedness of past, present, and future as resolved in those acts of festive, reflective remembrance in and through which we recall our lineage and come to an understanding of who we are.

One of those whom Heidegger called to mind on the occasion of another return to Meßkirch was Johann Ulrich Megerle, better known by his religious name of Abraham à Sancta Clara, a late-seventeenth-century court preacher in Vienna who had attended the Latin School in Meßkirch. Let us briefly examine two of these "words" that Heidegger selected for comment.

The first is his summary definition of the human being: "The human being—this five foot long nothing." As Heidegger points out, this seems contradictory, for how can something that is five foot long be "nothing"? But, he adds, "it is precisely this contradiction between the nothing and the length of five foot that expresses the truth: earthly magnitude and the nothingness of its meaning belong together."[24] The other "word" is, at first glance, somewhat less accessible: "Come, you silver-white swans that, defying the snow, swim around upon the water."[25] To understand this saying, Heidegger says, we need to know that, for Abraham, "snow" is an image of human life in its transitoriness, here today, tomorrow melted away. Snow, of course, also melts in water. "The plumage of the swans, on the other hand, preserves a pure whiteness, thus bearing 'snow,' as it were, across the surface of the water. Swimming, they prevent it from dissolving. The movement of the white swans across the water is thus an image of what abides in the midst of transitoriness."[26]

In the mirror of this "word," the return home to Meßkirch and the reflective remembrance it provokes confront us with the Heraclitean issue at the heart of the common human experience of temporality, the issue of permanence in the midst of change and finding meaning in the midst of nothingness. The question, then, is not how the provincial village can defend its native values against the world of the city; it is how we can experience, understand, and work out these interdependent complementarities that are simultaneously spatial and temporal. How do we preserve the values of the provincial village in the global village? The intimacy of the neighborhood in the megapolis of a linked-in world? The heritage of the past in the midst of the uprooting onrush of the future? Heidegger's way, I am suggesting, is not reducible to a way back. Rather, it is a search for ways of inhabiting the world that now is and for ways of making our home in the midst of the *Unheimisch*. If planetary homelessness is a threat to our sense of being, it may nevertheless offer its own unexpected gifts. It is paradoxically the experience of the fallen world itself, that is, the experience of the world as fallen, that first stimulates the memory of a paradise that is always already lost. In this sense, the *Unheimisch* is itself the abiding condition of our homesickness and of the meaning of the home toward which we are always traveling but where we have never been. The point is well put by the poetic word of Edwin Muir: "What had Eden ever to say / Of hope and faith and pity and love / Until was buried all its day / And memory found its treasure trove?"[27] The same thought is already implied in the Christian motif of the happy fault (*felix culpa*): "happy the fault that led to such a great redemption," or, in the words of the Old English hymn, "Ne'r had the apple taken been, ne'er had our Lady a-been heavene's Queen." Or, in a line from Hölderlin that Heidegger several times quotes, "Where danger is, grows the saving power."

However, this is not yet the most important point. This is that home/land is not simply a matter of place, the site of our historical rootedness. It is both of these, but as imagined in the poetic word it is both of these *in and as language*.

This is already implicit in Heidegger's homage to the poet in his Hölderlin lecture, and it is very much in his words and in the images figured in his words that he discerns the importance of Abraham à Sancta Clara.

The point is further underlined in a lecture of July 2, 1960, delivered by Heidegger to the annual meeting of the Hebbel society, an address subsequently published twice, under two mutually interpreting titles: "Persistence in the Midst of Change" and "Language and Home." Here it is particularly the poetry that Johan Peter Hebbel wrote in the Alemannic dialect that provides the focus for Heidegger's reflections.

The exegesis of these poems gives Heidegger an opportunity to air some general comments of a kind to which we are, by now, accustomed. "Humanity," he says, "is homeless," adding that the threat posed by this homelessness drives us to seek a saving power, a power that would preserve both language and home in what is most proper to them.[28] Stressing the "and" of his title, Heidegger defends the apparent provinciality of the Alemannic dialect. For "the essence of language is rooted in dialect (*Dialekt*). Here too, if the spoken language (*Mundart*) is the mother tongue, we find the roots of the homeliness (*das Heimische*) of home (*Zuhaus*), home (*Heimat*) itself. Our spoken language is not only the language of our mothers but first and foremost the mother of language."[29] Thus, although home and language are alike threatened by the homelessness of our age, these dialect poems use the most homely of all forms of language to open up what Heidegger calls the "fourfold" (the articulated interconnectedness of earth and heaven, man and the "still spirits"), the silent presence of which pervades all that is said.[30] Thus "it is poetic saying that first lets mortals dwell on earth, under heaven and before the divine." Yet "language, by virtue of its poeticizing essence, is the most hidden—but also for precisely that reason—the most adequate, the earnest, bountiful, bringing forth of home," and, Heidegger concludes, we should not so much say "Language and Home" but "Language as Home."[31] That is to say, it is not the return to some mystical or mythical time or space that we learn what it is to be "at home" in the world: It is in and through the language into which our mothers first inducted us. Acceptance of the world in its articulated complexity, a complexity in which the advent of the *Unheimische*, the future that threatens to devour past and present and to dissolve poetic depth and the idiom of the mother tongue into the uniformity of the technological age, is inseparable from the struggle to discover and to maintain the values of homeliness. For the postwar Heidegger at least, this is not a struggle between nations or worldviews but a struggle within language itself. For Heidegger, this means within the German language, but the argument is equally well extended to any language. The issue of the struggle is not the simple privileging of "home" against the impersonal it-world of the anonymous "they" of the technological age but concerns how we can rightly speak of what is happening to us and who we are becoming.[32]

Prayer, Exile, Homecoming

Obviously, much of Heidegger's rhetoric and metaphoric is richly paralleled in the Judeo-Christian and other religious traditions. The language of devotion is pervaded by a sense of exile, of existential homelessness, a longing for an abiding city not made with human hands, an eternal home. A classic example is the first chapter of Anselm's *Proslogion*, where Anselm describes himself as "expelled . . . from our homeland into exile," and it is the anguished nothingness of this experience of exile and the consequent "bitterness and horror of death" that drives him to seek God and, in the following chapters, to develop his ontological argument for the existence of God. If we take this seriously, it suggests not only that Christian ontology itself derives from the dynamic of exile and homecoming but also that it is in the prayed articulation of this dynamic that the way is opened from faith to philosophy.[33]

Interestingly, it was to just this chapter of the *Proslogion* that Heinrich Ott appealed in his 1958 article "Theology as Prayer and as Science," in which he illustrated his view that the kind of dynamic of faith seeking understanding developed on the basis of the tension between exile and homecoming, as expressed by Anselm, corresponds to the relationship between thinking and being as conceived by Heidegger.[34] This suggests that being is both deliverance from exile and the ultimate form of homecoming.

In postulating the envisaged homecoming as eschatological, however, Christian theology puts down a marker warning against understanding this in a sentimental or nostalgic way and simultaneously asserts that it is ultimately the future that is decisive with regard to the truth of who we are. In historical time, our time, the time of exile, we are hard-hearted if we do not experience the pathos of homecoming, but the futurity of the coming rule of justice means that our homecoming is also a journey into a new world. Neither exactly "back to the future" nor "forward to the past," it is more a relation to what is both "once and future," that is, forward to possibilities of fulfillment that were there in our beginning but that have been neglected, discarded, or crushed in all that has happened since. In other words, it will be a humanly recognizable and meaningful world, a life that resonates with all that we most value in being human, all the way back to our collective and individual times of innocence.

For both Hebrew and Christian biblical writers, one of the most significant figures of the eschatological event is Jerusalem, the new Jerusalem, "our mother." This too identifies the promised future as a homecoming, even if we moderns hesitate to make the identification of motherhood and home that seemed unquestionable to the ancient authors. It also connects what we have been saying to Heidegger's reflections on the connections between homecoming and poetic language, for it suggests that learning to pray and, in prayer, initiating the advent of a life with God mean neither more nor less than learning or relearning the mother tongue of Christian existence, the first articulation of words that supervene on the babbling of infancy. In this perspective, the emergence of our capacity for words in which to speak with and to God reflects an essentially maternal relationship between God and the one who prays.

In ways we examined in chapter 5, speaking with God in the intimacy of prayer generates a basic vocabulary by which to illuminate the inner mystery of our being-with-God-in-the-world. This, as we have also seen, involves accepting that the word of another stands at the foundation of any possible self-understanding—a statement that applies both to the other's demand for justice and our inner exposure to what we experience as the divine call. Yet if this word comes to us not as instruction from a transcendent patriarch but in, with, and under our mother tongue, the language into which we are inducted from or even from before birth onward, then it should not come as an affront to our autonomy. And for the most part, we don't learn language any other way. Language is not something we each of us invent independently to express the content of our unique subjectivity. No matter how intensely individuated we become, the words in which we understand ourselves are only rarely words we have invented for ourselves—and if they are, we must anticipate that few if any will understand us. Learning to speak means receiving our words from others, from the community that, in language (and primarily in the language spoken by mother to child), inducts us into a shared humanity. As such it is a continuation of the process of generation that brought us into our life in the world, a continuing overflow of the movement of life. Speaking with God and speaking with one another, called by and calling upon God, and calling upon one another: This is how our need of mutual help becomes actual and effective in the world. It is the medium in which all can come to meet, each in their passage through and out of the world. It is a necessary condition of learning to be at home, here together, in this place, on this planet, and learning what justice requires. It is how love works.

9

Humility

If my account of what prayer teaches us about our humanity is accurate, one conclusion to be drawn is that the virtue most suited to expressing a deep personal prayerfulness is humility. This is hardly surprising. Humility was long counted as the chief Christian virtue, yet it has become widely downgraded in the modern world. This is partly a result of various abuses of humility but also reflects modernity's culture of maximal autonomy. One consequence of this situation is that we today are often unable to distinguish authentic Christian humility either from its pathological variants or from the proper self-regard of Aristotelian virtue. For while an authentic humility incorporates a realism lacking from pathological cases of abjection and equally injurious cases of excessive self-assertion, it also involves more than sensible modesty. The main thrust of this chapter is therefore to see what humility might mean in the contemporary situation of Christian existence in the world. In doing this, we shall also discover that the issue of humility opens up a range of fundamental issues regarding what it is to be a human person and, especially, a human person who believes that life is given and directed by God. In this way, humility is the moral aspect or enactment of all we have been learning about the self-annihilation of the one who prays.

I shall begin by offering a brief summary of classic Christian teaching regarding humility and its connection to the theological virtues of faith, hope, and love before looking at the reasons for its cultural eclipse over the course of modernity and, finally, sketching a context for its rediscovery.

Humility: The Foundation of Virtue and the Imitation of Christ

Although it is not listed among the three theological virtues of faith, hope, and love (1 Cor 13), humility long had a leading role in Christian ideas of the virtuous or holy life. Thomas Aquinas argues that humility is not the highest but it is the first of virtues, in the sense that it is the foundation on which the other virtues build.[1] For Thomas, it is a virtue of an especially theological kind, since it primarily concerns our relation to God, "for whose sake," as he puts it, "[the Christian] humbles himself by subjecting himself to others."[2] Moreover, and importantly, Thomas notes that it is not counted among the Aristotelian virtues, which, he says, has to do with the fact that "the philosopher" treats only of virtues that pertain to "civic life" and not to the relation to God.[3]

In these definitions, Thomas is effectively summarizing widespread teaching about humility in Christian spiritual practice. *The Imitation of Christ* by Thomas à Kempis was written several hundred years after Thomas's *Summa*, but it too testifies to the ongoing value placed on humility in what we refer to as "medieval" thought. It is particularly important to note that this was a work produced for the instruction of lay Christians, a kind of do-it-yourself manual of Christian living for those who were living not in a cloister but in the world.

After an opening chapter in which he sets out the imitation of Christ as the foremost aim of Christian life, à Kempis immediately turns in chapter 2 to humility. Here he states that "a true understanding and humble estimate of oneself is the highest and most valuable of all lessons. To take no account of oneself, but always to think well and highly of others is the highest wisdom and perfection. . . . We are all frail; consider none more frail than yourself."[4] He especially associates lack of humility with intellectuals: "A humble countryman who serves God is more pleasing to Him than a conceited intellectual who knows the course of the stars, but neglects his own soul." Indeed, "an inordinate desire for knowledge" involves "much anxiety and deception."[5] Knowledge that is not self-knowledge is at best secondary, but self-knowledge will teach us that we are, really, worthless. This lesson is repeated many times over the course of the book, as in the chapter "On Self-Denial and Renunciation of Our Desires." Christ here speaks to the disciple: "My son, complete self-denial is the only road to perfect liberty. . . . Forsake all, and you shall find all."[6]

As à Kempis's reference suggests, humility is important within Christianity because it is enjoined by the biblical writers and is paradigmatically manifested in Jesus. Two texts are paramount. The first is from Paul's

Letter to the Philippians, where the apostle describes the Incarnation as exemplifying Christ's own humility: "Let this mind be in you which was also in Christ Jesus, who, being in the form of God, did not consider it robbery to be equal with God, but made Himself of no reputation, taking the form of a bondservant, *and* coming in the likeness of men. And being found in appearance as a man, He humbled (*etapeinōsen*) Himself and became obedient to *the point of* death, even the death of the cross" (Phil 2.5–8). The second is from Matthew's Gospel, in words that are ascribed to Jesus: "Come to me, all you that are weary and are carrying heavy burdens, and I will give you rest. Take my yoke upon you, and learn from me; for I am gentle and humble in heart (*tapeinos tē kardia*), and you will find rest for your souls. For my yoke is easy, and my burden is light" (Mt 11.28–30).

In such texts humility becomes key not only to the character of the man Jesus but also to the character of God, as reflected in the later Christian doctrine of divine condescension, according to which God lowers himself to human level in order to raise human beings up to his own divine level. Kierkegaard would beautifully illustrate this doctrine in his parable of the king who falls in love with a lowly maiden and puts aside his kingly attributes in order that she might fall in love with him and not with the outward appurtenances of kingly power—wealth, robes, splendor. God is not only a God of heights but also of the depths, and to know God we too must be ready to enter the depths.

The promotion of humility remained a salient feature of Christian teaching into the modern era and arguably achieved its most striking development in the spirituality of what has been called the French School of the seventeenth century, including such figures as Pierre de Bérulle, François de Sales, Jean-Jacques Olier, and Archbishop Fénelon. In briefly surveying some of the teaching on humility offered by these figures, we shall also see that humility is not simply regarded as a virtue but also seen as revelatory of a fundamental aspect of the human condition. This survey will in turn help us see something of the context in which the rejection of humility became a defining feature of emergent modernity.

The Introduction to the Devout Life (1609) by François de Sales, bishop of Geneva, has been among the most widely used works of Christian devotion in the modern period. After books 1 and 2, which respectively deal with "Attaining a Firm Resolution to Live a Devout Life" and "Prayer and the Sacraments," book 3 turns to the actual practice of the devout life, and in chapter 4 of book 3, he addresses humility, which he divides into external and internal forms.

De Sales writes that

> in order to receive God's Grace in our hearts, they must be as empty vessels—not filled with self-esteem. The swallow with its sharp cry and keen glance has the power of frightening away birds of prey, and for that reason the dove prefers it to all other birds, and lives surely beside it—even so humility drives Satan away, and cherishes the gifts and graces of the Holy Spirit within us, and for that reason all the Saints—and especially the King of Saints and His Blessed Mother—have always esteemed the grace of humility above all other virtues.[7]

Integral to such humility is remaining vigilant to the danger of taking worldly success too seriously: "When the peacock opens his showy tail, he exhibits the ugliness of his body beneath; and many flowers which are beautiful while growing, wither directly we gather them," de Sales remarks.[8]

More important, however, is inner humility. In order to achieve such inner humility, de Sales recommends a twofold strategy: "Nothing so tends to humble us before the Mercy of God as the multitude of His gifts to us; just as nothing so tends to humble us before His Justice as the multitude of our misdeeds."[9] The first part of this strategy brings to mind that everything we have we have from God and not through our own merits or actions. However, de Sales notes that reflecting on our gifts *could* lead us to become rather pleased with ourselves, perhaps in the manner of a spoiled child who thinks it entirely natural that he should have the best of everything. Here, then, we need the second part, the meditation on our unworthiness for receiving these gifts or our misuse of them. Crucial, of course, is that this really is inner humility. "True humility does not affect to be humble and is not given to make a display in lowly words. It seeks not only to conceal other virtues, but above all it seeks and desires to conceal itself," writes the bishop. "Take my advice, my child," he adds, "and either use no professions of humility, or else use them with a real mind corresponding to your outward expressions; never cast down your eyes without humbling your heart; and do not pretend to wish to be last and least, unless you really and sincerely mean it."[10] This is, of course, important—not least with regard to the fact that the revolt against humility takes particular aim at just such outward professions of humility as de Sales is here warning against.

Thus far, we might think that humility means no more than modesty, but de Sales goes further. Humility, he says, makes us rejoice in abjection. What is the difference? "Abjection," he says, is the poverty, vileness, and littleness which exist in us, without our taking heed to them; but humility implies a real knowledge and voluntary recognition of that abjection. And the highest point of humility consists in not merely acknowledging one's abjection, but in taking pleasure therein, not from any want of breadth or courage, but to give the more glory to God's Divine Majesty, and to esteem one's neighbor more highly than one's self.[11]

As an example, and a rather challenging one, he invites us to think about two forms of cancer, one in the arm, the other in the face. The person who suffers from the former has only the pain to bear, but the latter also has to bear the abjection and ignominy that comes from not being able to conceal his disease, which becomes a cause of social shame. De Sales, of course, is *not* saying that we *should* be ashamed by it, simply that, in his society, most people probably would be, and, if that is the case, then, he says, the shame is not only to be accepted but, even against the judgment of society, be made a cause for rejoicing. Take away the flowery rhetoric of seventeenth-century French spirituality, and the logic is that of contemporary movements that have rethought and empowered the social experience of sickness and disability. Do not be ashamed—own who you are.

Later representatives of the French school promoted humility in even stronger terms, if possible. They also connect humility to a more extensive theological-philosophical account of human existence than does the very practically oriented de Sales. In writers such as Olier and Fénelon, humility reveals that we are entirely dependent on God and have no substantial being apart from the being with which God continues to endow us. Here we can also, I think, see a shift that distinguishes this early modern discourse on humility from that of medieval writers. Although there may be a continuity of practice, the context has in the meantime undergone a radical change, not least because of the cosmological revolution of the sixteenth century. We are no longer in a universe seen in Aristotelian-Ptolemaic terms but in the post-Copernican universe of Pascal's silent infinite spaces. Those who are becoming keenly aware of this new world no longer feel that they are an integral element within an ordered cosmos but are rather exposed to the constant possibility of their radical contingency. In this situation, humility becomes the practical recognition of the nothingness that haunts human reality as such.

Take this passage from Olier. Much of Olier's advice on humility concerns humility in the context of human relationships. Here, however, he spells out the fundamental reason why humility is so important.

> All being, goodness, and truth exist in God and, through participation in creatures, whose depth and intrinsic reality is nothing. Flowing from the nothingness that we are as creatures, our proper activity is a tendency towards nothingness. The essence of nothing is to tend toward nothing. This is what man is and how he should want to appear. Otherwise he is robbing and stealing from the supreme Being, desiring to take his place and to claim for himself what belongs to God.[12]

In such passages, humility is no longer just a virtue in a purely moral sense but has acquired ontological significance: It is a state that reveals who we essentially and fundamentally *are*. Such an ontological account of humility is further developed by Fénelon, who gives it a more explicit philosophical basis. This appears particularly clearly in part 2 of his treatise *A Demonstration of the Existence of God*, "The Existence of God and His Attributes Drawn from Purely Intellectual Proofs and the Idea of Infinity Itself."[13]

Fénelon's argument reads like a pastiche of Descartes's discourse *On Method*, which indeed it is. Like Descartes, he begins by resolving to doubt everything that can possibly be doubted.

> It seems to me that the only way of avoiding error entirely is to doubt without exception all the things in which I do not find clear evidence. Thus I oppose myself to all my own prejudices. The clearness with which I have until now seen various things is no reason for supposing them to be true. I oppose myself to everything that people call sense impressions, conventional principles, probabilities. If there is nothing that is not perfectly certain I am not willing to believe anything. I am willing to acquiesce only when I am forced to do so by evidence and the entire certitude of [the] things [I am considering], apart from which I leave them to be counted as things doubtful.[14]

However, if Fénelon's opening is Cartesian, his conclusion is Pascalian. Dissatisfied with Descartes's conclusion that it is impossible to doubt one's own existence as long as one is thinking, he is, unlike Descartes, prepared to think even what seems impossible. "Perhaps nothing [*néant*] is capable of thinking and, in thinking, I am nothing [*rien*]. Perhaps the same thing can altogether exist and not exist."[15] Although it would be "the universal shipwreck of human reason" to think that an all-powerful spirit that had created everything out of nothing could actually make a being that both was and was not, "that thinks and is nothing and that thinks nothing," this seems to be the conclusion to which he is eventually driven.[16]

Yet this also means that, qua nothing, he cannot have been the source of his own being—he cannot have made himself. A being that was able to bring another being into being out of nothingness would have to be a being that existed by and through itself; this is the being we call God, and for us to know God is precisely to know him as this being who calls us into being out of nothingness. Such a God is necessarily incomprehensible to us, his infinity "astonishes" and "overwhelms" us, and "it is through this infinity that I recognize you as the being that has drawn me forth out of nothingness." "This infinity," he argues, is an idea

> that is in me, that is more than me; it seems to be everything and I nothing. I cannot efface it or obscure it or diminish it or contradict it. It is in me but I didn't place it there, I found it there and I couldn't have found it there unless it had been there prior to my seeking it. . . . It doesn't depend on me, but I on it. . . . Behold the prodigy that I always carry within me. I myself am a prodigy. Being nothing . . . I am a nothing that knows the infinite.[17]

We may seem to have come a long way from the concrete abjection of humility in bearing with instances of concrete physical pain and social shame. But the logic of humility is precisely the logic of divine being and human nothingness. As Fénelon writes in a letter on humility: "There are only two truths in the world, that concerning God being all and that concerning the creature being nothing [*rien*]; for humility to be genuine, it is necessary for us . . . to remain in our place, which is to love and to be nothing."[18]

Here, in ontological terms, is the point at which divine being and human nothingness find their most exact point of identity. Being the creature that I am, I am a nothing dependent in everything on the God who is absolute being in and through himself. Humility, in other words, is the appropriate way to be of a being that lacks the basis of substantial being in its own constitution and that lives, to the extent that it lives, only through its relation to, in the first instance, the source from which its provisional, contingent being is derived. And here it must be stressed that the point—the practical point—of this analysis is not to direct the self to the cultivation of a low self-regard but is, precisely, to direct it toward the God who is imagined as the source or ground of all the being that it has. Negatively, humility is surrendering our pretension to be as God and to be the ground if our own being; positively it is to restore to God what is God's and, as Olier puts it, to take God's side against its own ultimately illusory claims.[19] Or, most simply, to live lives marked by a basic attitude of unqualified gratitude for being. Fénelon's and Olier's formulations may raise the kinds of worries about a theological elevation of God matched by a corresponding diminishment of the human that we shall examine in the next section.

Rejecting Humility

But if humility was embedded so deeply in models of Christian practice, spanning many centuries, what happened to it?

One factor is the change of manners that happened over the seventeenth and eighteenth centuries. This is an extremely large subject and covers a vast range of currents and countercurrents. Nevertheless, we can see that between François de Sales at the start of the seventeenth century and Kant at the end of the eighteenth, an extraordinary cultural change has taken place. I shall return to Kant but first will note some key elements of this change.

The first is the increasing association of humility with false humility and hypocrisy. Of course, older writers had been fully aware that a show of humility can mask a secret pride. We have already heard de Sales comment on this, and many earlier religious writers had too. Indeed, several of the best-known sayings of Jesus draw attention to just this kind of religious immorality, as had prophetic writers before him, such as Isaiah, whom he quotes: "This people honors me with their lips, but their hearts are far from me" (Mt 15.8, cf. Isa 29.13). Yet in the early modern period, this increasingly comes to be seen not as a defective mode of religious life but as typifying religious behavior as such. Any show of devotion becomes suspect, as in Molière's classic exposure of religious hypocrisy in the comedy *Tartuffe*. The eponymous Tartuffe is described in the dramatis personae as "a hypocrite." The image he projects is that of a model of religious humility.

> He came to church each day, with contrite mien,
> Kneeled, on both knees, right opposite my place,
> And drew the eyes of all the congregation,
> To watch the fervour of his prayers to heaven;
> With deep-drawn sighs and great ejaculations,
> He humbly kissed the earth at every moment;
> And when I left the church, he ran before me
> To give me holy water at the door.
> I learned his poverty, and who he was,
> By questioning his servant, who is like him,
> And gave him gifts; but in his modesty
> He always wanted to return a part.
> "It is too much," he'd say, "too much by half;
> I am not worthy of your pity." Then,
> When I refused to take it back, he'd go,
> Before my eyes, and give it to the poor.[20]

Of course, we soon learn that it is all a sham. As Tartuffe, who is plotting to seduce his host's husband, says, "The public scandal is what brings offence, / And secret sinning is not sin at all."[21]

This same period also saw the emergence of alternative accounts of virtue, such as Hume's reduction of moral categories to passions shared with animals. In these terms, humility is represented as the product of what we might call social pain. As Hume puts it in his *Treatise on Human Nature* (1739–1740): "By pride I understand that agreeable impression, which arises in the mind, when the view either of our virtue, beauty, riches, or power, makes us satisfied with ourselves; and . . . by humility I mean the opposite impression. It is evident the former impression is not always vicious, nor the latter virtuous."[22] With regard to this last remark, we must assume that Hume was very well aware that, in a Christian perspective, pride is indeed always vicious and humility virtuous. The provocation is deliberate.

Twenty years later, Adam Smith still recalled enough of traditional Christian teaching to comment that "this disposition to admire, and almost to worship, the rich and powerful, and to despise, or, at least, to neglect persons of poor and mean condition . . . is . . . the great and most universal cause of the corruption of our moral sentiments." Yet, in the same sentence, he can also say that it is "necessary both to establish and to maintain the distinction of ranks and the order of society."[23] That social utility could thus become the measure of virtue and vice is plainly stated in Voltaire's *Dictionary*: "We live in society; there is therefore nothing truly good for us but that which does good to society. An hermit will be sober, pious, and dressed in sackcloth: very well, he will be holy; but I will not call him virtuous until he shall have done some act of virtue by which men may have profited."[24] In this perspective, humility would seem to fail the standard of virtue. As we have heard Thomas argue, it is not a virtue relating to human beings' social relationships but primarily and even solely to their relation to God.

Of course, Kant is a moral thinker of a very different stamp from either Hume or Voltaire. Yet it would be Kant who perhaps delivered the most decisive blow of all to humility in his account of autonomy, which he takes as the ultimate principle of enlightenment:

> Enlightenment is man's emergence from his self-imposed immaturity. Immaturity is the inability to use one's understanding without guidance from another. This immaturity is self-imposed when its cause lies not in lack of understanding, but in lack of resolve and courage to use it without guidance from another. *Sapere Aude!* [dare to know] "Have courage to use your own understanding!"—that is

> the motto of enlightenment. . . . Nothing is required for this enlightenment, however, except freedom; and the freedom in question is the least harmful of all, namely, the freedom to use reason publicly in all matters.[25]

This is a, perhaps *the*, classic statement of the principle of autonomy: Each must take responsibility for their own intellectual, moral, and political judgments. Morality is not submission to a given set of laws or to the will of another but the free resolve to act in accordance with the law of reason. As we saw in Chapter 1, Kant did not absolutize autonomy. He understood that human beings are limited with regard to bodily freedom and social roles. Moreover, moral freedom consists precisely in choosing to act in accordance with *universal* laws. The exercise of my individual autonomy is further limited by the obligation of respect for the autonomy of others: We must never treat others as a means to our end, but each other is an end in himself, says Kant, and the idea of moral being is only fulfillable in a community of moral beings practicing mutual respect.

Nevertheless, Kant's privileging of autonomy would be taken up and developed in manifold ways in the course of the nineteenth century. Via German idealism it inspired Ralph Waldo Emerson, who fused the Kantian idea of moral autonomy of moral reason with the American conviction that each individual has the right to "life, liberty, and the pursuit of happiness." As Emerson put it when speaking to the Harvard Divinity School in 1838:

> Let me admonish you, first of all, to go alone; to refuse the good models, even those which are sacred in the imagination of men, and dare to love God without mediator or veil. Friends enough you shall find who will hold up to your emulation Wesleys and Oberlins, Saints and Prophets. Thank God for these good men, but say, "I also am a man." Imitation cannot go above its model. The imitator dooms himself to hopeless mediocrity. The inventor did it, because it was natural to him, and so in him it has a charm. In the imitator, something else is natural, and he bereaves himself of his own beauty, to come short of another man's.[26]

In his 1842 essay "On Self-Reliance," he sums up his argument with the assertion that "the only right is what is after my constitution, the only wrong what is against it."[27]

One of Emerson's readers was Friedrich Nietzsche, whose own insistence on the will to power as a defining feature of human being can be read as the ultimate rejection of an ethics of humility. Indeed, as explored in a number of his works, Nietzsche sees the passivity and humility of the religious self as a veiled manifestation of the will to power. The religiously humble person or the religious community that valorizes humility and lowliness is in reality using humility as an instrument of domination. Internalized powerlessness takes root as self-hatred, which in turn breeds hatred of others, and the passivity of such hatred makes it no less aggressive. In this way, Nietzsche prepares the way for the now widely recognized phenomenon of passive aggression. Crucially, Nietzsche's atheism is not predicated on God's nonexistence (though he almost certainly didn't believe that anything like the theist's God did actually exist) but on God's moral inadequacy and even, as here, perversity. The rejection of God is precisely the rejection of the value system that requires us to subordinate our self-affirmation to an alien being. Consequently, such a rejection paves the way to a life of self-creation—not just "become who you are" but "become who you will to be."

Two paths go from here. The one is toward the interpretation of the will to power in terms of humanity's technocratic dominion over the world. This will be especially marked in Heidegger's reading of the history of Western metaphysics, which sees Nietzsche as the ultimate spokesman for the will to power manifested in modern technology. The other is toward a transformation of the culture of selfhood. Pedagogy and care of the soul are no longer to be dedicated to instruction and discipline but to enabling the self to find, invent, and be itself. Along a line that runs from Emerson through Nietzsche, Freud, and Jung, this enters via Carl Rogers into the commonplace assumptions of contemporary psychotherapy. As Rogers puts it: "To be the self which one truly is" means moving "away from façades," "away from 'oughts,'" "away from meeting expectations," "away from pleasing others," and *toward* "self-direction," "toward being-process," "toward being complexity," "toward openness to experience," "toward acceptance of others," and "toward trust of self."[28] Of course, not all of these movements are incompatible with humility: Openness to experience and acceptance of others might seem to be attitudes available and even integral to a genuinely humble self, too. But the general thrust of Rogers's program seems radically to undermine the promotion of humility that we encountered in the Christian tradition. And in this regard, Rogers is programmatic for the broad stream of currently popular therapies and self-help movements.

We might ask: What's wrong with this? Hasn't this strategy of encouraging and enabling self-affirmation contributed to the increase of human happiness and all-round flourishing by helping us break with all the negatives associated with a religious culture that systematically inculcated self-hatred? This may be so. Nevertheless, there are ways of promoting autonomy and self-affirmation that seem to generate a new set of psychological and societal ills. It is not just that, to borrow Dostoevsky's language, they install a Man-God in the place of God and, as it turns out, a Man-God who has many of the worst features of the older metaphysical God. The problem is that this Man-God is likely to be and often is a kind of self-centered being that is unable or unwilling to accept any limitations on its own power. Forgetting the Kantian imperative of respect, this (usually self-appointed) Man-God sees no need to recognize the moral or emotional claims of others, while its world as a whole is radically "disenchanted." Such a self may rise to a certain stoicism, but it is a self that is poor in its relations to others and in its relation to its world. Its power is limited to the power of self-assertion; it is a gratuitous freedom without ultimate aim or purpose. In such Dostoevskian characters as Raskolnikov (*Crime and Punishment*) and the nihilist Kirillov (*Demons*), it is a freedom that asserts itself in, respectively, murder and suicide, while Dostoevsky, following Pushkin and like Kierkegaard, also sees boredom as a likely fate awaiting the fully autonomous self. Philosophically, it is probably Jean-Paul Sartre who provided the most brilliantly consistent account of such a self, a self that, as Sartre's account makes clear, seems incapable of all that normally counts as making for happiness. It is a self constantly threatened by loneliness, boredom, and absurdity. Others are a threat rather than a comfort. Irony becomes the accompaniment of every pleasure and every discomfort. Such a self does what it does simply because it does it, and it can do no other because it acknowledges no external goal to which it might or ought to submit. Yet as Sartre also makes clear, it will consistently and necessarily fail in its attempt to be as good, condemning itself to a life that is "a useless passion."

How, then, are we to limit the pretensions of this self, how are we to induce it to become humble, without reverting to the kind of heteronomy that seems implicit in older models of humility? How are we to find a humility that is not predicated on self-hatred?

Retrieving Humility

A contemporary retrieval of humility need not mean engaging in some culture war aimed at pushing back the inroads of modern Prometheanism. Precisely to the extent that a consistent prioritization of autonomy is experienced as leading to the impoverishment of the self and its world, humility might be shown as offering a constructive way forward that would enable the self to reach a point at which it might see its life as the occasion for gratitude, for acknowledgment of the infinite debt that it doesn't just owe to God but is happy to owe to God. This would not in every case—and perhaps in most cases would not—require such a self to surrender any particular one or any particular ensemble of the freely chosen undertakings to which it was already committed.

The dialectic of autonomy was well analyzed by Paul Tillich in the mid-twentieth century. For Tillich, as for Kant, autonomy was always to be affirmed in its struggle against the heteronomous authority of church and state. Nothing should count as good, true, or just simply because scripture, or the church, or the state says it is so. We must have the freedom to think and to judge for ourselves. But Tillich was no less clear that, of itself, autonomy was unable to produce any positive content. God might be able to create out of nothing, but the human being cannot. Consequently, the movement of autonomy needed to be completed by a further movement that Tillich called theonomy, allowing one's autonomy to be directed by God. Now it is clear that, on Tillich's account, God is not to be thought of as some external power, otherwise we would be back in the situation of heteronomy. God, as he put it, is the ground of being, closer to us than we are to ourselves, to use Augustine's phrase; God is being and the power of being, beyond every word, image, or symbol with which we might attempt to identify it/him. In submitting to God, I am not submitting to another being, divine or human, but to being itself.[29]

There is much that is controversial in Tillich's account, and we don't need to accept every detail of it, simply—and essentially—that autonomy needs something *more* if it is to provide a basis for human flourishing, something that (I have suggested) comes to the self from outside the orbit of its own self-concern. Attention to this "more" is key to humility, since it is in and through humility that we are able to experience life as the gift of a power, not ourselves, that makes for gratitude.

However, we have to acknowledge both the power of the present culture of autonomy and the forcefulness of the reasons that led to the turning away from humility. Any rehabilitation of humility will therefore need to proceed very cautiously, and I therefore want to finish by sketching a sequence of stages with which to counter the ideology of autonomy, proceeding from the least to the most controversial: modesty, responsiveness, accusation, and self-emptying.

The first step (modesty) is to recall the pre-Christian Greek warning against hubris. Humans cannot do what is reserved to the gods, or, as Pindar put it, "what is mortal befits mortals."[30] Heidegger is only one among many critics of a certain kind of technological thinking who portray modern human beings as having collectively made themselves into lords of creation and reduced the world to a mere resource to be used (or perhaps better plundered) at will. But in reality, we are not above nature; we are a part of it and in manifold ways dependent on it. Furthermore, after a period of maybe two centuries in which we had simply ignored the limits to growth inherent in the material finitude of earthly life, we are now, as in a Greek tragedy, faced with potentially catastrophic global warming as the punishment for our hubris, for overstepping our boundaries. Recalling that the root meaning of the Latin *humilis*, *humilitas*, and the Greek *chtamalos* mean "near the ground," "humility" might seem an exceptionally well-chosen word for the kind of reorientation we need in this respect.[31]

As regards the self-relationship of the human self and its relation to other human selves, contemporary life offers a range of morality tales that might seem to echo the warnings of Greek tragedy, as with the notorious "Wolves of Wall Street" and "Masters of the Universe" widely seen as responsible for the global financial crisis of 2008. Similarly, the sphere of personal life and relationships provides extensive evidence of malfunctions resulting from the refusal or abandonment of long-term commitments or the prioritizing of self-fulfillment over, for example, loyalty or duties of care. Bernard Williams's example of the moral luck of a Gauguin, whose abandonment of his wife and family for the sake of his art proves to be vindicated by the value of his art, seems an exception to the more likely rule.

However, the Greek sensitivity to the dangers of hubris did not lead to humility in the Christian sense but to what we might call a modest self-estimation, recommended by Aristotle as the mean between shyness and shamelessness. This is not contemptible, and it is certainly a step that many of our nonreligious contemporaries might be prepared to endorse, but I suggest it is only a first step.

In a second step, resistance to hubris can be extended to Friedrich Heinemann's *respondeo ergo sum*, "I respond, therefore I am."[32] In other words, we are who and what and as we are by virtue of our participation in a network of relationships to other human beings and to nonhuman environmental elements, the web of life. As we saw in the last chapter, even the language in which we are now considering these questions is something we did not invent but have inherited; "my language" is not "my" language but language shaped by millennia of development—even if it can also become the medium in which I articulate my own life projects and perhaps even make some small contribution to its continual transformation.

In a third step, the principle of *respondeo ergo sum* is radically extended in Levinas's insight that we exist "under accusation," that what is primary is not the "I" but the "me," that is, that the primary mode of self-knowledge is to know myself as commanded to care for the orphan, the widow, and the alien, or, in Kierkegaard's Christian version of a similar idea, to the commanded love of neighbor. To become a moral self is not a way of fulfilling the project of achieving maximum autonomy but to know my autonomy as always already limited from the outset by a demand that comes from outside, from a transcendence I can never encompass. Here, Fénelon's account of how radical introspection reveals an infinity that the self can never encompass seems to anticipate Levinas's own account of the, as it were, interior otherness of the infinite (both, of course, responding specifically to Descartes).

Levinas's articulation of this idea connects to and is in part inspired by the teaching of Dostoevsky's Elder Zosima in *The Brothers Karamazov*—"that we are all guilty of everything and before everyone and I most of all." In Russian (as Levinas, born in the Russian empire, would have known), there is a close etymological link between the word "guilt" and the grammatical "accusative" case. But Zosima's emphasis is not on moral guilt, in the narrow sense; rather, it is something like an ontological guilt, the coimplication of my very being in the suffering endured by others in their being. The threefold acknowledgment of guilt ("we all," "before everyone," and "I most of all") is thus more than an act of mea culpa ("I am to blame"). In fact, it is not really about the imputation of guilt in any familiar forensic sense. Instead, it is more like an act of self-emptying, the renunciation of any claim to moral virtue or moral rights. It is not the self-accusation involved in saying "I have sinned" but, in its way, strangely parallels Nietzsche's hope for a way of existing "beyond good and evil." But, *pace* Nietzsche, while a nonreligious view might be able to endorse both the necessity of responsiveness and the infinity of moral demand, it is perhaps at the point of self-emptying that a radically religious position starts to distinguish itself. Where the post-Enlightenment Man-God is who he is by elevating himself above the herd, the distinctive character of the Christian God is revealed in Christ's self-abasement before human beings, humbling himself under their suffering and shame.

This is dramatically illustrated in two episodes of the novel. In the very first scene, Zosima bows down to Dmitri, the hard-drinking, brawling, womanizing soldier, and, in the second, he prostrates himself before God in the moment of death. There is clearly a connection here, but what is it? Let us look more closely at these two moments. When Zosima bows to Dmitri, he is bowing to the suffering that he sees Dmitri must undergo. His bow makes a space for Dmitri to become aware of this and to take responsibility for it, since, for Zosima as for Dostoevsky, a readiness to suffer and to take suffering upon oneself is a preeminent path to redemption. Of course, Dostoevsky needed no lessons in the horrendousness of suffering.

It is in *The Brothers Karamazov* that Ivan Karamazov sets out one of literature's most harrowing accounts of human suffering as part of an argument leading to the rejection of God's world and, by implication, of God. What Dostoevsky offers us in Zosima and in his disciple Alyosha is not a counterargument to the fact of suffering but a counterexample to Ivan's attitude to it. The best response to horrors is not intellectual argument but humble service of the other grounded on a constant and unrelenting consciousness of obligation to the other and the impossibility of achieving my own happiness unless or until the other is delivered from their suffering. But this means being able to believe that neither suffering nor the death to which Zosima also prostrates himself negates the presence or the love of God. Self-emptying, the spiritual stance correlative to the act of prostration, is becoming open to this presence; it is radical prayer, making space for God in relation to the other and in relation to the self.

In many respects, Dostoevsky here repeats in novelistic form the basic assumptions of Christian teaching on humility, namely, that our dependence on God will also determine our relation to the neighbor as one of humility. But there is one point that perhaps comes out more clearly and that may, arguably, be innovative in his account. And this is a more direct connection between humility and love. Humility is not the practice of a solitary virtue. Fénelon was by no means a solipsistic personality, but his anti-Cartesian meditation on self's nothingness before God is Cartesian in the sense that it is presented as a solitary reflection on the self abstracted from its social context. Zosima's life and teaching, by way of contrast, centers on the affirmation of solidarity, solidarity in suffering and in shared dependence on God.

This is connected with a further feature of Dostoevskian self-emptying, namely, Zosima's teaching that we are to kiss the earth and water it with tears of joy.[33] We are to bow down not only to God and to others but to the earth, as we have seen Alyosha doing in his own moment of ecstasy in the garden. Not only does this teaching resonate with the root meaning of the word humility; it also connects directly to other teachings of Zosima:

> Brothers, have no fear of men's sin. Love a man even in his sin, for that is the semblance of Divine Love and is the highest love on earth. Love all God's creation, the whole and every grain of sand in it. Love every leaf, every ray of God's light. Love the animals, love the plants, love everything. If you love everything, you will perceive the divine mystery in things. Once you perceive it, you will begin to comprehend it better every day. And you will come at last to love the whole world with an all-embracing love . . . for all is like an ocean, all is flowing

and blending; a touch in one place sets up movement at the other end of the earth. . . . Treasure this ecstasy, however senseless it may seem to men.[34]

This, I suggest, is the ecstasy of humility, and for Dostoevsky in his way, as for Thomas and de Sales in theirs, it is the foundation of virtue. Perhaps the final sentence gives Dostoevsky's version a Russian twist by virtue of a likely allusion to Russian traditions of holy foolishness. We cannot presume that the humble will be faceless, gray nonentities. They might seem altogether outlandish to good bourgeois citizens. Though not necessarily. Like Kierkegaard's knight of faith, they might look just like an average everyday person who works in any average everyday employment. They might even *be* average everyday people in average everyday employment.

But is any of this enough to make someone *want* to become humble? Given that becoming humble seems to involve relinquishing most of what we are used to regarding as essential to our personal and social identity, is this in any way a possible object of desire? Such questions return us to the earlier chapters of this book where we encountered persons such as Kierkegaard, Weil, and Dostoevsky, for whom becoming nothing really was something like a life aim, however that was more closely understood. But in the end, there is and can be no *reason* to want to engage in self-humbling to the point at which one becomes (as) nothing—unless one sees such nothingness as the truth of the human condition. Echoing her much-quoted remark that "the only genuine way to be good is to be good 'for nothing,'" Iris Murdoch extends the same logic to humility, saying that the humble man (*sic*) "who sees himself as nothing . . . sees the pointlessness of virtue and its unique value and the endless extent of its demand."[35] Likewise, there is no reason to love God apart from the love of God. Indeed, for some significant figures in the Christian tradition, the love of God and the desire to become (as) nothing are, as we have been learning, two facets of one human reality. Their testimony is that strange, foolish, and inexplicable as it is, and knowing that many will dismiss it as pathological, it is a chance worth taking, since, beyond the logic of "why?" it is as nothing that they will be best fitted to find the self-emptying God who, renouncing the attributes of divinity, became as nothing to live among us as one who serves.

Postscript

When, as a young adult, I first started experimenting with what is now called spirituality, I was much influenced by the "Ten Ox-Herding Pictures," which were included in D. T. Suzuki's *Manual of Zen Buddhism*. These told the story of a herdsman taming his ox, which provided a parable of the spiritual attempt to bring the wild and passionate side of human nature under control. After many struggles, the ox is pacified and eventually vanishes, leaving the man alone. But this is not the end, since the next picture shows a blank circle, indicating that ox and man have both vanished into the void.

Suzuki's book presents two versions of these pictures. In one, this really was the end: emptiness, nirvana, nothingness. The other version pointed to a new beginning, showing the enlightened man "entering the city with bliss-bestowing hands." This had a great influence in deciding me to seek a path that required engagement with society rather than pursuing what I found to be the naturally attractive option of withdrawal into some spiritual haven "out of the swell of the storm." However, I'm sorry to say that that, back then, I imagined myself as the enlightened one, coming to bring good news of spiritual awakening to those city dwellers who, as I imagined, lay in deep darkness. Needless to say, this was back to front. Time and experience, often hard and unwelcome experience, have shown what I should have known to be the case: that in reality it is from the "bliss-bestowing" hands of others that we receive all good things, including the very desire for spiritual truth. In the nameless and wordless world of a solitary individual there is no call, no promise, no response, and no prayer. The possibility of spiritual life is to be found only in the adventure of being for one another, which is to say: the possibility of love.

Notes

1. Annihilation

1. Immanuel Kant, "Religion within the Boundaries of Mere Reason" (1793), in *Religion and Rational Theology*, ed. and trans. Allen Wood and George di Giovanni (Cambridge: Cambridge University Press, 1996), 210.

2. Kant, "Religion within the Boundaries of Mere Reason," 212.

3. J. G. Fichte, *Die Schriften zu J. G. Fichtes Atheismus-Streit*, ed. H. R. D. Lindau (Munich: Georg Müller, 1912), 26.

4. Fichte, *Die Schriften zu J. G. Fichtes Atheismus-Streit*, 116.

5. Fichte, *Die Schriften zu J. G. Fichtes Atheismus-Streit*, 31.

6. Fichte, *Die Schriften zu J. G. Fichtes Atheismus-Streit*, 32.

7. The closest we come to such an experience is dealt with by Kant in terms of the sublime. For discussion, see Paul Guyer, *Kant and the Experience of Freedom* (Cambridge: Cambridge University Press, 1996); and Jean-Luc Nancy, *The Experience of Freedom*, trans. Bridget McDonald (Stanford, CA: Stanford University Press, 1993).

8. A nuanced systematic approach to the interrelationship between passivity and freedom can be found in the work of Ingolf U. Dalferth. See, e.g., Ingolf U. Dalferth, *Creatures of Possibility: The Theological Basis of Human Freedom* (Grand Rapids, MI: Baker Academic, 2016).

9. F. D. E. Schleiermacher, *Speeches on Religion to Its Cultured Despisers*, trans. R. Crouter (Cambridge: Cambridge University Press, 1988), 103.

10. Schleiermacher, *Speeches on Religion to Its Cultured Despisers*, 102.

11. F. D. E. Schleiermacher, *The Christian Faith*, trans. and ed. H. R. Mackintosh and J. S. Stewart (Edinburgh: T. & T. Clark, 1989), 12.

12. Schleiermacher, *The Christian Faith*, 15.

13. Schleiermacher, *The Christian Faith*, 16.

14. Schleiermacher, *The Christian Faith*, 16.

15. Cf. Jean-Louis Chrétien, *The Ark of Speech*, trans. Andrew Brown (London: Routledge, 2014), 21–2.

16. Søren Kierkegaard, *The Sickness unto Death*, trans. E. H. Hong and H. V. Hong (Princeton, NJ: Princeton University Press, 1980), 13; N. J. Cappelørn et al., eds., *Søren Kierkegaards Skrifter* (Copenhagen: Gad, 2006), 11:129. Further references to volumes in this edition will be given as SKS followed by volume and page number.

17. Kierkegaard, *Sickness unto Death*, 14 (SKS 15:130).

18. Cf. Schleiermacher: "To feel oneself absolutely dependent and to be conscious of being in relation with God are one and the same thing; and the reason is that absolute dependence is the fundamental relation which must include all others in itself. This last expression includes the God-consciousness in the self-consciousness in such a way that . . . the two cannot be separated from each other." *The Christian Faith*, 17.

19. Chrétien applies Kierkegaard's discourse to illustrate the dependence on God of the one who prays even for the mere possibility of being able to pray: "But it is part and parcel of prayer itself that in it alone the person praying learns that he does not know how to pray. . . . Such is the circularity of prayer: the person praying prays so as to learn how to pray, and first and foremost to learn that he does not know, and he gives thanks for his prayer as a gift from God." *The Ark of Speech*, 24. To which he adds that this circle "is not absurdly circular: it leads us to the event of an encounter" (25).

20. Søren Kierkegaard, *Eighteen Upbuilding Discourses*, trans. H. V. Hong and E. H. Hong (Princeton, NJ: Princeton University Press, 1990), 378 (SKS 5:362).

21. Kierkegaard, *Eighteen Upbuilding Discourses*, 382–83 (SKS 5:366).

22. Kierkegaard, *Eighteen Upbuilding Discourses*, 383 (SKS 5:366).

23. Kierkegaard, *Eighteen Upbuilding Discourses*, 384 (SKS 5:367).

24. Kierkegaard, *Eighteen Upbuilding Discourses*, 388 (SKS 5:371).

25. Kierkegaard, *Eighteen Upbuilding Discourses*, 390 (SKS 5:373).

26. Kierkegaard, *Eighteen Upbuilding Discourses*, 391 (SKS 5:373).

27. Kierkegaard, *Eighteen Upbuilding Discourses*, 392 (SKS 5:374).

28. I don't comment on whether this is good pedagogical practice.

29. Kierkegaard makes a similar point regarding the shift in prayer from speaking to being silent. See Chapter 4 in this volume for further discussion.

30. Kierkegaard, *Eighteen Upbuilding Discourses*, 399–400, translation adapted (SKS 5:380).

31. Kierkegaard, *Eighteen Upbuilding Discourses*, 400 (SKS 5:380).

32. Kierkegaard, *Eighteen Upbuilding Discourses*, 134 (SKS 5:137).

33. Søren Kierkegaard, *Purity of Heart Is to Will One Thing*, trans. Douglas Steere (1938; London: Fontana, 1961). The Danish text is the first part of the collection *Upbuilding Discourses in Various Spirits* (SKS 8).

34. F. M. Dostoevsky, *The Brothers Karamazov*, trans. Constance Garnett (London: Heinemann, 1912), 378–79.

35. We shall consider aspects of these later and in subsequent chapters.

36. See, e.g., Malcolm Jones, *Dostoevsky and the Dynamics of Religious Experience* (London: Anthem, 2005).

37. Dostoevsky, *The Brothers Karamazov*, 334.

38. See, e.g., my article "'Water the Earth': Dostoevsky on Tears," in *Litteraria Pragensia: Studies in Literature and Culture* 22, no. 43 (July 2012): 95–111.

39. F. M. Dostoevsky, *Crime and Punishment*, trans. Constance Garnett (London: Heinemann, 1914), 377–78.

40. See Dostoevsky, *The Brothers Karamazov*, 297. Garnett has "responsible," which is a reasonable translation and captures one part of what is being said. "Guilt," however, highlights what Levinas would call the condition of being under accusation that I believe is also integral to what Dostoevsky is saying. On the role of this passage in Levinas, see A. Toumayan, "'I More Than the Others': Dostoevsky and Levinas," *Yale French Studies* 104 (2004): 55–66.

41. Dostoevsky, *The Brothers Karamazov*, 296.

2. Unknowing

The epigraph to this chapter is from Augustine, *Confessions*, trans. R. S. Pine-Coffin (Harmondsworth: Penguin, 1961), 21 (translation amended).

1. Augustine, *Confessions*, 211.

2. Whether Augustine was or was not a practitioner of apophatic theology in a radical sense is a moot point. Étienne Gilson emphasizes Augustine's insistence on God as being itself, an emphasis that, coupled with the theory of the human mind being directly illumined by the divine light, suggests that even though we may be dependent on divine initiative, knowledge, in a strong sense, is possible. See Étienne Gilson, *The Christian Philosophy of St. Augustine*, trans. L. E. M. Lynch (London: Gollancz, 1961), esp. intro. and part 1. In a more recent study, John Peter Kenney emphasizes why Augustine does not practice an apophatic theology of the kind found in Plotinus; despite occasional nods to divine unknowability, it seems that a direct relation to truth and to beauty (both of which served Augustine as divine names) allowed for a direct apprehension of God. John Peter Kenney, *Contemplation and Classical Christianity: A Study in Antiquity* (Oxford: Oxford University Press, 2013). While Georgiana Huian acknowledges a cataphatic element in Augustine, her study of *The Confessions* comes to an opposite conclusion, reading it as a study in apophatic anthropology and, therewith, also in apophatic theology. Georgiana Huian, *Augustin. Le coeur et la crise du sujet* (Paris: Cerf, 2020). John D. Caputo, commenting on Derrida's "Augustinian" *Circumfession*, suggests that the kind of longing exemplified in Augustine's text, as in Derrida's, is intrinsically oriented toward unknowing even when, like Augustine, it seems to be asking "what" it is that is to be known. Here, Augustine's tears are as important as his Platonic philosophizing. John D.

Caputo, "Shedding Tears beyond Being: Derrida's Confession of Prayer," in *Augustine and Postmodernism: Confession and Circumfession*, ed. John D. Caputo and Michael J. Scanlon (Bloomington: Indiana University Press, 2005), 95–114. Since my focus here is primarily on the post-Kantian tradition, I shall leave the historical and exegetical question to one side, commenting only that *read in a certain way* (Huian is exemplary here), Augustine's overall representation of the praying soul points to something very different from anything that could be recognized as "knowledge" in the modern research university.

3. Pseudo-Dionysius, "The Mystical Theology," in *The Complete Works*, trans. C. Luibhead (New York: Paulist, 1987), 141.

4. Anonymous, *The Cloud of Unknowing*, trans. C. Wolters (Harmondsworth: Penguin, 1961), 43.

5. Anonymous, *The Cloud of Unknowing*, 55.

6. Anonymous, *The Cloud of Unknowing*, 55.

7. Anonymous, *The Cloud of Unknowing*, 55.

8. Anonymous, *The Cloud of Unknowing*, 57–58.

9. Anonymous, *The Cloud of Unknowing*, 60.

10. Anonymous, *The Cloud of Unknowing*, 60.

11. Anonymous, *The Cloud of Unknowing*, 61.

12. Anonymous, *The Cloud of Unknowing*, 99.

13. Anonymous, *The Cloud of Unknowing*, 102.

14. Anonymous, *The Cloud of Unknowing*, 134.

15. The French School is a major focus of my study *The Phenomenology of the Devout Life* (Oxford: Oxford University Press, 2018).

16. See, e.g., George Pattison and Kate Kirkpatrick, *The Mystical Sources of Existentialist Thought: Being, Nothingness, Love* (London: Routledge, 2019), 9–13; see also W. Ezekiel Goggin and Sen Hannan, *Mysticism and Materialism in the Wake of German Idealism* (London: Routledge, 2022).

17. Søren Kierkegaard, *Eighteen Upbuilding Discourses*, trans. H. V. Hong and E. H. Hong (Princeton, NJ: Princeton University Press, 1990), 378; N. J. Cappelørn et al., eds., *Søren Kierkegaards Skrifter* (Copenhagen: Gad, 2006), 5:301. Further references to volumes in this edition will be given as SKS followed by volume and page number.

18. Kierkegaard, *Eighteen Upbuilding Discourses*, 309, translation adapted (SKS 5:302).

19. Kierkegaard, *Eighteen Upbuilding Discourses*, 322, translation adapted (SKS 5:313).

20. Kierkegaard, *Eighteen Upbuilding Discourses*, 399–400, translation adapted (SKS 5:380).

21. Søren Kierkegaard, *Upbuilding Discourses in Various Spirits*, trans. H. V. Hong and E. H. Hong (Princeton, NJ: Princeton University Press, 2009), 177 (SKS 8:312).

22. Kierkegaard, *Upbuilding Discourses in Various Spirits*, 193 (translation adapted) (SKS 8:222).

23. For more on Kierkegaard and the speculative philosophers' turn to mysticism, see Pattison and Kirkpatrick, *The Mystical Sources of Existentialist Thought*, 24–41.

24. Simone Weil, *Gravity and Grace*, trans. E. Craufurd (London: Ark, 1987), 23. Further references are given in the text. I am aware that this is a compilation that does not reflect the original structure of Weil's *Cahiers*. It does, however, reflect Weil as received in the Anglophone world in the postwar period.

25. The editor, Gustave Thibon, candidly admits that the order in which we find the aphorisms is not Weil's own but his.

26. Quoted from George Herbert, *The Works of George Herbert in Prose and Verse* (London: William Pickering, 1846), 217–18.

27. F. M. Dostoevsky, *The Idiot*, trans. Constance Garnett (London: Heinemann, 1951), 219. On the role of epilepsy in Dostoevsky's life and work, see Paul Fung, *Dostoevsky and the Epileptic Mode of Being* (London: Legenda, 2015).

28. Dostoevsky, *The Idiot*, 219.

29. The view that Dostoevsky's religion is ultimately more akin to speculative idealism than Christianity has been vigorously championed by Steven Cassedy in his study *Dostoevsky's Religion* (Stanford, CA: Stanford University Press, 2005).

30. Dostoevsky, *The Idiot*, 220.

3. Mystery

1. Nicholas V. Sakharov, *I Love Therefore I Am: The Theological Legacy of Archimandrite Sophrony* (Crestwood, NY: St. Vladimir's Seminary Press, 2002), 90–91. Another Orthodox thinker, André Scrima, has likewise spoken of apophatic anthropology. Both expressions point to the issue at the heart of this chapter.

2. Dom Cuthbert Butler, *Western Mysticism: The Teaching of SS Augustine, Gregory, and Bernard on Contemplation and the Contemplative Life* (London: Arrow, 1960), 66–67.

3. Butler, *Western Mysticism*, 87.

4. Butler, *Western Mysticism*, 89.

5. Augustine, *Confessions*, trans. R. S. Pine-Coffin (Harmondsworth: Penguin, 1961), 231. Further references will be given in the text by book (Roman numeral), chapter (Arabic numeral), and page number.

6. Butler, *Western Mysticism*, 91.

7. Butler, *Western Mysticism*, 129.

8. Butler, *Western Mysticism*, 195.

9. For a rich and insightful discussion of the apophatic dimension of the human search for self-understanding in Augustine's *Confessions*, see Georgiana Huian, *Augustin. Le coeur et la crise du sujet* (Paris: Cerf, 2020).

10. Cf. Emmanuel Mounier, who writes: "Le personnalisme est une philosophie, il n'est pas un système . . . son affirmation central étant l'existence de

personnes libres et créatrices, il introduit au cœur de ces structures un principe d'imprévisibilité qui disloque toute volonté de systematisation définitive."
E. Mounier, *Le personnalisme*, in *Œuvres* (Paris: Éditions de Seuil, 1962), 3:429.

11. N. A. Berdyaev, *The Beginning and the End*, trans. R. M. French (London: G. Bles, 1952), 104.

12. N. A. Berdyaev, *Spirit and Reality*, trans. George Reavey (London: Geoffrey Bles, 1939), 3.

13. Berdyaev, *The Beginning and the End*, 92–93.

14. Berdyaev, *The Beginning and the End*, 94.

15. Berdyaev, *Spirit and Reality*, 3–4.

16. Berdyaev, *The Beginning and the End*, 116.

17. Berdyaev, *Spirit and Reality*, 4.

18. Berdyaev, *The Beginning and the End*, 102.

19. Berdyaev, *The Beginning and the End*, 104.

20. N. A. Berdyaev, *Slavery and Freedom*, trans. R. M. French (London: Geoffrey Bles, 1943), 73.

21. N. A. Berdyaev, *Solitude and Society*, trans. George Reavey (London: Geoffrey Bles, 1938), 10.

22. Berdyaev, *The Beginning and the End*, 102. In this respect, it is plausible to see Berdyaev as anticipating some of the themes of postmodern philosophy. See Monika Wozniak, "Towards a New Understanding of Immanence and Transcendence in the Writings of Nikolai Berdyaev and Paul Tillich," in *Beyond Modernity: Russian Religious Philosophy and Post-Secularism*, ed. Artur Mrowczynski, Teresa Obolevich, and Pawel Rojek (Eugene, OR: Pickwick, 2016). Nevertheless, there are also passages in some later works, such as *Solitude and Society*, where he speaks of the human being's "original participation in the mystery of Being" that enables us "to apprehend being." Berdyaev, *Solitude and Society*, 7. This work reveals significant affinities with Gabriel Marcel, a personal friend, and it is possible that Marcel encouraged him to take a more positive view of being—as long as it is understood as essentially mysteriousness.

23. Berdyaev, *Spirit and Reality*, 4.

24. Berdyaev, *Spirit and Reality*, 31.

25. Berdyaev, *Spirit and Reality*, 31.

26. Berdyaev, *Spirit and Reality*, 33.

27. Berdyaev, *Slavery and Freedom*, 75–6.

28. Berdyaev, *Slavery and Freedom*, 76.

29. Berdyaev, *Slavery and Freedom*, 80. On the nonontological character of Berdyaev's concept of personality, see Romilo Aleksandr Knežević, *Homo Theurgos: Freedom according to John Zizioulas and Nikolai Berdyaev* (Paris: Cerf, 2020).

30. Berdyaev, *Slavery and Freedom*, 23; cf. *Solitude and Society*, 68.

31. Berdyaev, *The Beginning and the End*, 163.

32. Berdyaev, *The Beginning and the End*, 207.

33. Berdyaev, *Solitude and Society*, 67.

34. Berdyaev, *Solitude and Society*, 80.

35. This is a longstanding theme in Russian religious thought, going back to Peter Chaadaev and found in Dostoevsky, among others.

36. Berdyaev, *Spirit and Reality*, 21.

37. Berdyaev, *Spirit and Reality*, 33.

38. See, e.g., Berdyaev, *Solitude and Society*, 126, where Berdyaev refers to Max Picard—also a significant influence in Levinas's development of the idea of "the face."

39. G. Marcel, *The Mystery of Being*, vol. 1: *Reflection and Mystery*, trans. G. S. Fraser (London: Harvill, 1950), 155–56.

40. Marcel, *Mystery of Being*, 1:91.

41. Marcel, *Mystery of Being*, 1:90. Marcel opposes this to Sartre's account of the self's appearing in the world as a negation of givenness that is accompanied by anxiety and nausea.

42. G. Marcel, *The Mystery of Being*, vol. 2: *Faith and Reality* (London: Harvill, 1951), 2:62.

43. Marcel, *The Mystery of Being*, 2:17. Or, as Mounier puts it in his *Introduction aux Existentialismes*, "Le royaume de l'être est parmi nous." E. Mounier, *Introduction aux Existentialismes*, in *Œuvres*, 3:165ff.

44. Marcel, *The Mystery of Being*, 1:126.

45. Marcel, *The Mystery of Being*, 1:118.

46. Marcel, *The Mystery of Being*, 2:3.

47. Marcel, *The Mystery of Being*, 1:205.

48. Marcel, *The Mystery of Being*, 1:207–9.

49. Berdyaev, *Solitude and Society*, 7.

50. Berdyaev, *Solitude and Society*, 31.

51. Berdyaev, *Solitude and Society*, 43.

52. Marcel, *The Mystery of Being*, 2:162.

53. Marcel, *The Mystery of Being*, 2:162.

54. Gabriel Marcel, *Homo viator. Prolégomènes à une métaphysique de l'espérance* (Paris: Auber, 1945).

55. Marcel, *The Mystery of Being*, 2:158.

56. It is worth noting that Schelling played an important role in each of their intellectual trajectories. Tillich made a point of visiting Berdyaev in Paris shortly before the war and hailed *Slavery and Freedom* as "the expression of an unusual wisdom, profundity and universality." Paul Tillich, "Review of *Slavery and Freedom*," *Theology Today* 2, no. 1 (April 1945): 130–32; also, Paul Tillich, "Nicholas Berdyaev," *Religion in Life* 7, no. 3 (Summer 1938): 407–15. Berdyaev himself adopted Tillich's idea of the Kairos as the decisive moment of the divine-human encounter that cannot be identified on the basis of general historical laws but only through the fateful conjunction of freedom and destiny. On Schelling's relevance to the contemporary philosophical-theological situation, see John D. Caputo, *Specters of God: An Anatomy of the Apophatic Imagination* (Bloomington: Indiana University Press, 2022).

57. Paul Tillich, *Systematic Theology*, vol. 1 (Welwyn Garden City: James Nisbet, 1953), 83.
58. Tillich, *Systematic Theology*, 1:83.
59. Tillich, *Systematic Theology*, 1:86.
60. Paul Tillich, *My Search for Absolutes* (New York: Simon and Schuster, 1967), 68–70.
61. Tillich, *Systematic Theology*, 1:88.
62. Tillich, *Systematic Theology*, 1:88.
63. Tillich, *Systematic Theology*, 1:265.
64. Tillich, *Systematic Theology*, 1:265.
65. Tillich, *Systematic Theology*, 1:173.
66. Paul Tillich, *The Courage to Be* (London: Collins-Fontana, 1962), 156.
67. Paul Tillich, *The Shaking of the Foundations* (London: SCM, 1949), 56.
68. Tillich, *Shaking of the Foundations*, 56.
69. Tillich, *Shaking of the Foundations*, 57. Cf. Marcel: "The transhistoric depth of history . . . is, no doubt, the best short cut we can take towards the idea of Eternity." Marcel, *Mystery of Being*, 2:218.
70. Paul Tillich, *Systematic Theology*, vol. 2 (Welwyn Garden City: James Nisbet, 1957), 22.
71. Paul Tillich, *Systematic Theology*, vol. 3 (Welwyn Garden City: James Nisbet, 1964), 119.
72. For discussion, see Michael Theunissen, *Pindar. Menschenlos und Wende der Zeit* (Munich: C. H. Beck, 200), 958–70.
73. See, e.g., Tillich, *Systematic Theology*, 1:200.
74. Isa 43.19–19. Tillich, *Shaking of the Foundations*, 173.
75. In Wilhelm and Marion Pauck, *Paul Tillich: His Life and Thought*, vol. 1: *Life* (London: Collins, 1977), 51.
76. Tillich, *Systematic Theology*, 2:208.
77. On the interconnection between eschatology, apophaticism, and hope, see David Newheiser, *Hope in a Secular Age: Deconstruction, Negative Theology, and the Future of Faith* (Cambridge: Cambridge University Press, 2019).
78. Paul Tillich, *The Socialist Decision*, trans. Franklin Sherman (New York: Harper and Row, 1977), 111.
79. Tillich, *Systematic Theology*, 3:421.
80. For discussion of the relationship between Tillich's Marxism and mysticism, see George Pattison and Kate Kirkpatrick, *The Mystical Sources of Existentialist Thought: Being, Nothingness, Love* (London: Routledge, 2019), 192–212.
81. Tillich, *Shaking of the Foundations*, 181–82. Tillich's emphasis on the New bears comparison with the utopian philosophy of Ernst Bloch, whom Tillich referred to as a friend.
82. Tillich, *Shaking of the Foundations*, 184.
83. Tillich, *Shaking of the Foundations*, 185.
84. Paul Tillich, *The Boundaries of Our Being* (London: Fontana, 1973), 166.
85. Tillich, *The Boundaries of Our Being*, 170.

4. Words

1. William James, *The Varieties of Religious Experience* (London: Fontana, 1960), 367.

2. Dom Cuthbert Butler, *Western Mysticism: The Teaching of SS Augustine, Gregory, and Bernard on Contemplation and the Contemplative Life* (London: Arrow, 1960), 67.

3. Augustine, *Confessions*, trans. R. S. Pine-Coffin (Harmondsworth: Penguin, 1961), 197–98. Interestingly—but, in the light of Augustine's contribution to the philosophy of time, unsurprisingly—we note the particular emphasis on the limitations of speech being associated with its temporal character. Words are strung out in time, having a beginning and an end, whereas the intellectual "touch" of the eternal Wisdom is beyond and outside time.

4. See Martin Laird, *Into the Silent Land: The Practice of Contemplation* (London: Darton, Longman and Todd, 2006); Maggie Ross, *Silence: A User's Guide* (Eugene, OR: Cascade, 2014); Maggie Ross, *Silence: A User's Guide*, vol. 2: *Application* (Eugene, OR: Cascade, 2017).

5. Steven T. Katz, "Language, Epistemology, and Mysticism," in *Mysticism and Philosophical Analysis*, ed. Steven T. Katz (London: Sheldon, 1978), 26.

6. Katz, "Language," 29.

7. Katz, "Language," 63.

8. This kind of linguistic turn and an accompanying tendency to approach mysticism from a sociological and cultural rather than from an experiential perspective is reflected in a range of contemporary writers about mysticism in theology and religious studies. Don Cupitt and Denys Turner are two English theologians who divide on most major issues in philosophy but are united in not leaving mysticism to the proponents of wordless experience. See, e.g., Don Cupitt, *Mysticism after Modernity* (Oxford: Blackwell, 1998); Denys Turner, *The Darkness of God* (Cambridge: Cambridge University Press, 1995). Although less focused on "mysticism," the work of George Lindbeck popularized the view that religious language was to be approached as a "cultural-linguistic" phenomenon rather than as the expression of individual experiences. See George Lindbeck, *The Nature of Doctrine: Religion and Theology in a Post-Liberal Era* (London: SPCK, 1984).

9. Martin Heidegger, *Identity and Difference*, trans. Joan Stambaugh (New York: Harper and Row, 1969), 269. Further references are given in the text. For Parmenides, see G. S. Kirk and J. E. Raven, *The Presocratic Philosophers* (Cambridge: Cambridge University Press, 1963), fragment 344, 269.

10. The phrase "event of appropriation" is used here—unsatisfactorily—to translate Heidegger's term *Ereignis*. At one level, this is a very ordinary word translatable as "event" or "occurrence" and perfectly comprehensible to the person on the street. However, Heidegger also makes us attentive to the word *eigen*, buried, as it were, within *Er-eignis*. This is related to another famous Heideggerian term, *Eigentlichkeit*, conventionally translated as "authenticity." *Eigen* relates to what is one's own, thus "appropriation." *Ereignis* thus signals that

what happens when we understand something is both an event, something that happens to us, *and* an event in which we make what we understand our own. "Appropriation" is, however, an unfortunate term if it is allowed to have connotations of making one's own in the sense of ownership or even theft, since it is central to Heidegger's idea that the understanding that arises in the event of appropriation is not something we, as it were, "take" but something that is given to us.

11. These are from the final decade before the First World War, corresponding to the period of Heidegger's own student years, and cover a complex of issues that was widely debated at this time in the Germanophone world.

12. In *Daniel* Buber will consider the role of death in bestowing true existence on the individual, questioning whether "what we call death might be the way" and concluding: "The power of a life is the power of its unity. Whoso dies in the accomplished unity of his life gives utterance to an I that does not posit anything but is bare eternity." Martin Buber, *Daniel. Gespräche von der Verwirklichung* (Leipzig: Insel, 1922), 132, 151.

13. Martin Buber, *Die Rede, die Lehre und das Lied* (Leipzig: Insel, 1920), 23.

14. Buber, *Die Rede, die Lehre und das Lied*, 18.

15. A penchant for the prefix *Ur-* is also a feature of Heidegger's early writings, and there is also much here that calls Schleiermacher's second *Speech* to mind.

16. Buber, *Die Rede, die Lehre und das Lied*, 23.

17. Buber, *Die Rede, die Lehre und das Lied*, 25.

18. Buber, *Die Rede, die Lehre und das Lied*, 26.

19. Buber, *Die Rede, die Lehre und das Lied*, 30–32.

20. Buber, *Die Rede, die Lehre und das Lied*, 26.

21. Martin Buber, *Reden und Gleichnisse des Tschuang-Tse* (Leipzig: Insel, 1910), 40–41.

22. Buber, *Die Rede, die Lehre und das Lied*, 3–4.

23. Buber, *Daniel*, 29.

24. Martin Buber, *I and Thou*, trans. W. Kaufmann (Edinburgh: T. & T. Clark, 1970), 53.

25. Ludwig Wittgenstein, *Philosophical Investigations*, trans. G. E. M. Anscombe (Oxford: Blackwell, 1920), 2–3.

26. Anonymous, *The Cloud of Unknowing*, trans. Clifton Wolters (Harmondsworth: Penguin, 1961), 96.

27. Anonymous, *The Cloud of Unknowing*, 97.

28. Anonymous, *The Cloud of Unknowing*, 61.

29. A Monk of the Eastern Church, *On the Invocation of the Name of Jesus* (Oxford: Fairacres, 1970), 1.

30. However, to hear the name "Jesus" in the cry for "Help" is not to define "Help" by reference to a known name that is to be understood by reference to a determined historical identity. It is merely to indicate a possible horizon that might be opened from within "Help" (spoken, of course in the mode of

vocativity) and also to affirm that such a prayer is directed to someo*ne* and not simply to some*thing*.

31. The author of *The Cloud of Unknowing* himself comments that "in these matters height, depth, length, and breadth all mean the same" (97).

32. Anonymous, *The Cloud of Unknowing*, 61.

33. Søren Kierkegaard, *Without Authority*, trans. H. V. Hong and E. H. Hong (Princeton, NJ: Princeton University Press, 1997), 11–12; N. J. Cappelørn et al., eds., *Søren Kierkegaards Skrifter* (Copenhagen: Gad, 2006), 11:17–18. Further references to volumes in this edition will be given as SKS followed by volume and page number. Translation from Søren Kierkegaard, *Kierkegaard's Devotional Writings*, trans. and ed. George Pattison (New York: Harper and Row, 2010), 185.

34. Søren Kierkegaard, *Kierkegaard's Journals and Notebooks*, vol. 5, ed. and trans. N. J. Cappelørn et al. (Princeton, NJ: Princeton University Press, 2011), 379, journal entry NB5:22 (SKS 20:379).

35. See T. S. Eliot, "Little Gidding," in *Four Quartets* (London: Faber and Faber, 1959), 57 (ll. 198–99); for Kierkegaard, see Søren Kierkegaard, *Eighteen Upbuilding Discourses*, trans. H. V. Hong and E. H. Hong (Princeton, NJ: Princeton University Press, 1990), 399–400 (SKS 5:380).

36. Anonymous, *The Cloud of Unknowing*, 97.

37. Friedrich von Hügel (Baron), *Essays and Addresses in the Philosophy of Religion. Second Series* (London: Dent, 1933), 224.

38. According to a widely observed convention, the final verse, "Yea, Lord we greet thee, born this happy morning," is sung only on Christmas morning, emphasizing this response-character of the hymn (generally it has to be said, the connection between words and occasion is only loosely observed in the singing of Christmas carols). This is the logic unfolded by Heidegger in his commentary on the opening lines of Hölderlin's poem "The Ister." See Martin Heidegger, *Hölderlin's Hymn "The Ister,"* trans. William McNeill and Julia Davis (Bloomington: Indiana University Press, 1996), 6–11.

39. F. M. Dostoevsky, *The Brothers Karamazov*, trans. Constance Garnett (London: Heinemann, 1912), 682.

40. Dostoevsky, *The Brothers Karamazov*, 683.

41. Friedrich Hölderlin, *Poems and Fragments*, trans. Michael Hamburger (London: Anvil, 2004), 336 (German), 337 (English).

42. Zosima here echoes the teaching of Isaac the Syrian, an author whom Dostoevsky studied while writing *The Brothers Karamazov*. See Isaac the Syrian (Saint), "Homily 51," in *The Ascetical Homilies of Saint Isaac the Syrian* (Boston: Holy Transfiguration Monastery, 1984), 243–48.

5. Preaching

1. Paul Tillich, *Systematic Theology*, vol. 3 (Welwyn Garden City: James Nisbet, 1964), 128–30.

2. See, e.g., David Brown and Ann Loades, eds., *The Sense of the Sacramental Music, Place, and Time* (Oxford: Abingdon, 1995).

3. See David Brown's trilogy: David Brown, *God and Enchantment of Place: Reclaiming Human Experience* (Oxford: Oxford University Press, 2004); David Brown, *God and Grace of Body: Sacrament in Ordinary* (Oxford: Oxford University Press, 2007); and David Brown, *God and Mystery in Words: Experience through Metaphor and Drama* (Oxford: Oxford University Press, 2008).

4. John of Damascus, *On the Divine Images*, trans. David Anderson (New York: St. Vladimir's Seminary Press, 1980), 28–29.

5. Alexander Schmemann, *The World as Sacrament* (London: Darton, Longman, and Todd, 1966).

6. Edwin Muir, *Collected Poems* (London: Faber, 1960).

7. See George Lakoff and Mark Johnson, *Metaphors We Live By* (Chicago: Chicago University Press, 1980).

8. For a full discussion, see Helge Grell, *Skaberordet og billedordet. Studier over Grundtvigs teologi om ordet* (Copenhagen: Danske Boghandlers Kommissonsanstalt, 1980).

9. Martin Heidegger, *Being and Time*, trans. John Macquarrie and Edward Robinson (Oxford: Blackwell, 1960), 56/32. The translators give page numbers for the German first edition, and I shall give these following the English page number. Further references will be given in the text. Heidegger notes but does not dwell on other kinds of logos that do not have this apophantic function, e.g., "requesting." However, part of my argument here is that these too can also be "revealing," especially with regard to the word of preaching.

10. See Giorgio Agamben, *The Sacrament of Language: An Archaeology of the Oath* (Stanford, CA: Stanford University Press, 2010).

11. T. S. Eliot, "The Dry Salvages," *in Four Quartets* (London: Faber, 1959), ll. 6–7.

12. Martin Heidegger, *Unterwegs zur Sprache* (Stuttgart: Günther Neske, 1959), 30. Heidegger also speaks of the "Geheiß der Stille," which we could translate as "the call" of silence (33).

13. Jean-Louis Chrétien, *The Call and the Response*, trans. Anne A. Davenport (New York: Fordham University Press, 2004).

14. Jean-Louis Chrétien, *St Augustin et les actes de parole* (Paris: Presses universitaires de France, 2002), 96.

15. Chrétien, *St Augustin et les actes de parole*, 98.

16. Chrétien, *St Augustin et les actes de parole*, 86.

17. Chrétien, *St Augustin et les actes de parole*, 80.

18. Chrétien, *St Augustin et les actes de parole*, 31–32.

19. There might be much to comment on here about the challenge posed by the need for attention in an age in which electronic media are widely perceived as generating a sense of chronic distraction. See, e.g., Maggie Jackson, *Distracted: The Erosion of Attention and the Coming Dark Age* (Amherst NY: Prometheus, 2008).

20. See, for example, Bultmann's discussion of the futurity of the word, with particular reference to preaching, in his Gifford lectures: Rudolf Bultmann,

History and Eschatology (Edinburgh: Edinburgh University Press, 1975), 150–55.

21. Søren Kierkegaard, *Works of Love*, trans. H. V. Hong and E. H. Hong (Princeton, NJ: Princeton University Press, 1998), 253; N. J. Cappelørn et al., eds., *Søren Kierkegaards Skrifter* (Copenhagen: Gad, 2006), 9:252.

6. Promise

1. Mircea Eliade, *The Myth of the Eternal Return* (Princeton, NJ: Princeton University Press, 1974), 139–62.

2. Paul Tillich, *Theology of Culture* (Oxford: Oxford University Press, 1959), 31–39. Tillich also went on to see a duality within Judaism itself, distinguishing between what he saw as the authentically biblical prophetic call to historically enacted justice and the alien "pagan" emphasis on the promise of land. This, of course, raises difficult questions, and some may see it as revealing a certain antisemitism, though a similar argument was propounded in Franz Rosenzweig's *Star of Redemption*. These differences can be extended to a further distinction, namely, the distinction between religions that find expression in visual representation and those that believe the word to be the only adequate expression of divine will.

3. See, for example, Henri Lefebvre, *The Production of Space*, trans. N. Donaldson-Smith (1974; Oxford: Basil Blackwell, 1991); Edward S. Casey, *The Fate of Place: A Philosophical History* (Berkeley: University of California Press, 2013); Barney Werf and Arias Santa, eds., *The Spatial Turn: Interdisciplinary Perspectives* (London: Routledge, 2009). Like so much else in postmodern philosophy, the spatial turn often has a certain, often critical, relation back to the later Heidegger and the kinds of emphases that come to expression in his essay "Building, Dwelling, Thinking," in *Poetry, Language, Thought*, trans. Albert Hofstadter (New York: Harper and Row, 1971), 143–62. An excellent study of the theme of "place" in Heidegger is Jeff Malpas, *Heidegger's Topology: Being, Place, World* (Cambridge, MA: MIT Press, 2006).

4. On the futurity of the Christian Eucharist, see Geoffrey Wainwright, *Eucharist and Eschatology* (London: Epworth, 1971).

5. In terms of Agamben's analysis of sacramental oath swearing, a covenant both affirms what has been and is now the case in the relationship between the covenanting parties and commits them to future mutual obligations.

6. G. W. F. Hegel, *Elements of the Philosophy of Right*, trans. H. B. Nisbet (1821; Cambridge: Cambridge University Press, 1991), 23.

7. Vladimir Jankélévitch, *L'irréversible et la nostalgie* (Paris: Flammarion, 1974), 60.

8. See Søren Kierkegaard, *Concluding Unscientific Postscript*, trans. H. V. Hong and E. H. Hong (Princeton, NJ: Princeton University Press, 1991), 173–77; N. J. Cappelørn et al., eds., *Søren Kierkegaards Skrifter* (Copenhagen: Gad, 2006), 7:158–63. Further references to volumes in this edition will be given as SKS followed by volume and page number.

9. Martin Heidegger, *Being and Time*, trans. John Macquarrie and Edward Robinson (Oxford: Blackwell, 1963), 497 (note to 338 in the German edition).

10. See further discussion of this point in what follows.

11. Heidegger, *Being and Time*, 43–44 (German edition, 22).

12. See Aristotle, *Physics* IV.1–10. For Heidegger's discussion of Aristotle's idea of time and how time comes to be "covered up," see Martin Heidegger, *The Basic Problems of Phenomenology*, trans. Alfred Hofstadter (Bloomington: Indiana University Press, 1982), 227–74.

13. See Plotinus, *Ennead* III.7.11.

14. See my *Heidegger on Death. A Critical Theological Essay* (Farnham: Ashgate, 2013); also, see my "The Grace of Time: Towards a Kataphatic Theology of Time," in *Hermeneutics and Negativism: Existential Ambiguities of Self-Understanding*, ed. Claudia Welz and René Rosfort (Tübingen: Mohr-Siebeck, 2018), 145–60.

15. See Søren Kierkegaard, *The Concept of Anxiety*, trans. Reidar Thomte (Princeton, NJ: Princeton University Press, 1980), 88 (SKS4, 390–91).

16. I have considered this at greater length in my *A Metaphysics of Love* (Oxford: Oxford University Press, 2021), 194–201, with particular reference to the alternative views of Irene McMullin and Thomas Carlson.

17. Emmanuel Levinas, *Le temps et l'autre* (Paris: Presses universitaires de France, 1983), 19.

18. The same point is implied also in Kierkegaard. See my *Metaphysics of Love*, 91–96.

19. Levinas, *Le temps*, 20.

20. See the discussion in the preceding chapter.

21. The same logic also marks a difference between Levinas's and Sartre's accounts of why individual subjects cannot become the ground of their own existence, since, in Sartre's case, this is internal to the subject's way of being for-itself.

22. Franz Rosenzweig, "Zweistromland," in *Kleinere Schriften zu Glauben und Denken*, ed. Reinhold Mayer and Annemarie Mayer (Dordrecht: Martinus Nijhoff, 1984), 148–51.

23. Franz Rosenzweig, *Kleinere Schriften* (Berlin: Schocken/Jüdischer Buchverlag, 1937), 195.

24. See the essays in M. M. Bakhtin, *Art and Answerability*, trans. Vadim Liapunov (Austin: University of Texas Press, 1990); M. M. Bakhtin, *Toward a Philosophy of the Act*, trans. Vadim Liapunov (Austin: University of Texas Press, 1993).

25. See the discussion of Levinas and language in my *A Rhetorics of the Word* (Oxford: Oxford University Press, 2019), 203–11.

26. Clive Staples Lewis, *Till We Have Faces* (London: Geoffrey Bles, 1956).

27. See F. M. Dostoevsky, *The Brothers Karamazov*, trans. Constance Garnett (London: Heinemann, 1912), 253–54.

28. Dietrich Bonhoeffer, *Letters and Papers from Prison*, ed. Eberhard Bethge, trans. Reginald Fuller and others (London: SCM, 1971), 348–49.

29. Forty years ago, this last comment would have been uncontroversial. However, in the light of the growing popularity of transhumanism, I should note that I mean to emphasize "fully *human*" and am not intending to splice a transhumanist agenda onto a Christian theological argument. Transhuman beings may well come after us, but whether they will be beings capable of or interested in being bound by a covenant based on mutual love and promise is a whole other matter.

7. Height

1. Thomas Merton, *Confessions of a Guilty Bystander* (New York: Image, 1968).

2. Emmanuel Levinas, "Sur la mort dans la pensée de Ernst Bloch," in *Utopie—Marxisme selon Ernst Bloch: Un système de l'inconstructible: Hommages à Ernst Bloch pour son 90e anniversaire*, ed. Gérard Raulet (Paris: Payot, 1976), 76.

3. Levinas, "Sur la mort dans la pensée de Ernst Bloch," 76.

4. One thinks also of the debate surrounding the Anglican bishop John A. T. Robinson's 1962 book *Honest to God*, which called on religious believers to drop speaking of heaven as if it were literally or quasi-literally "up there"—or, as one British paper summarized Robinson's argument, "God is not a Daddy in the Sky."

5. It is striking that this goes against the grain of Tillich's view that "depth" was better suited to a modern religious consciousness than the "height" that traditional symbolism ascribed to God. The reasons for Tillich's preference are easy to see. Apart from the association of height with a pre-Copernican cosmology, it also reinforces monarchical images of God as ruling over and judging human beings, who are thereby reduced to the rank of humble servants without basic employment rights. Such images bespeak a God external to humanity, imposing an alien rule on human life, whereas, Tillich believed, depth redirected us to a dimension of existence that was immanent to our own humanity. Such a dimension of depth didn't lead to another world but, as Marcel put it, extended the mystery of being into the divine depth itself. However, we shall see that Levinas has his own ways of circumventing these objections.

6. Emmanuel Levinas, "Transcendence and Height," in *Emmanuel Levinas: Basic Philosophical Writings*, ed. A. T. Peperzak, S. Critchley, and R. Bernasconi (Bloomington: Indiana University Press, 1996), 11–31 (12–22 contain Levinas's own paper; the remaining pages are given to a transcript of the ensuing discussion. The original paper was published in French in 1962).

7. Emmanuel Levinas, *Totalité et Infini* (1961; Paris: Kluwer Academic, 2001). Further references will be given in the text.

8. Plato is by some distance the most frequently cited author in *Totality and Infinity*, although Descartes and Heidegger are also constant points of reference. Although quantitative data can be misleading (Levinas says at the outset that Rosenzweig is too omnipresent in the work to be cited), the connection is

important and not to be overlooked. If Levinas is often portrayed as breaking with the Greek tradition of philosophy, the evidence of *Totality and Infinity* suggests a reception in which there are positive as well as negative elements.

9. Against the now widespread misconception that any reference to the Genesis creation story by a Christian theologian implies acceptance of its literal truth, I emphasize that Levinas's (and my) references to the creation and, later, to the revelation on Sinai are absolutely without any implied claims as to the literal truth of these texts.

10. Levinas would have been familiar with the debate about the translation of the divine name brought to the fore in Rosenzweig and Buber's German translation of the Bible and therefore of Rosenzweig's use of "the Eternal" as a foil to the Christian "Lord." Yet the situation is complicated by the fact that, as Rosenzweig discussed, "the Eternal" itself could be used in such a way as to carry Aristotelian rather than biblical connotations. The key is to avoid what Rosenzweig saw as the (Christian) idea of lordship understood as domination and power over others rather than solidarity and power to assist them. Just how "seigneur" is to be interpreted is, of course, an open question, and I am not implying that Levinas intends a deliberate allusion to either Christian or Jewish liturgy. Nevertheless, his choice of words is striking.

11. It is possible that this distinction between "theology" and "ethics" is intended also to mark a distinction between a Christianity that is oriented toward and defined by theological statements regarding the nature of God and a Judaism based on the practice of obedience to Torah or divinely revealed Law. If so, it is questionable whether it stands up, since there are strong traditions within Christianity that likewise prioritize action over theory, viz. Luther's statement that "theology is a practical and not a theoretical science."

12. Michael Morgan speaks of his "affection for apparent paradox"—Michael L. Morgan, *The Cambridge Introduction to Emmanuel Levinas* (Cambridge: Cambridge University Press, 2011), 142.

13. On the distinction but also interinvolvement of the ethical demand and justice, see Michael L. Morgan, *Levinas's Ethical Politics* (Bloomington: Indiana University Press, 2016), 48–50.

14. Emmanuel Levinas, *Autrement que l'être ou au-delà de l'essence* (Paris: Kluwer Academic, 2001), 228. For discussion of Levinas's debt to Dostoevsky, see E. Toumayan, "'I More Than the Others': Dostoevsky and Levinas," *Yale French Studies* 104 (2004): 55–66.

15. F. M. Dostoevsky, *The Brothers Karamazov*, trans. Constance Garnett (London: Heinemann, 1912), 321.

16. As it relates to the widow and orphan, this injunction is repeated or alluded to at least twenty-eight times in the Hebrew Bible; references to the obligation to care for the alien or stranger are even more numerous.

17. For further discussion of such "height" imagery, see my paper "I Lift Up My Eyes to the Hills," in *Mountains, Mobilities, and Movement*, ed. Christos Kakalis and Emily Goetsch (New York: Springer, 2017), 237–54.

18. Morgan, *Cambridge Introduction to Emmanuel Levinas*, 142.

19. Hilary Putnam, "Levinas on Judaism," in *The Cambridge Companion to Levinas*, ed. Simon Critchley and Robert Bernasconi (Cambridge: Cambridge University Press, 2006), 45.

20. In the version of the teaching that Matthew's Gospel portrays as taking place on a mountain, Luke 6.12–49 suggests that Jesus and his disciples descended to the plain below the mountain to address the crowds.

21. In this connection, Dostoevsky's Zosima is often seen as epitomizing a distinctly kenotic model of Christian love.

22. This relates to an incident in the Exodus story when the Israelite camp is smitten by a plague of serpents. Moses is instructed by God to make a bronze serpent, which he was to place on a pole visible throughout the camp, so that anyone bitten by the serpents might look at it and be healed.

23. Levinas discusses this passage in interviews with Jill Robbins. Jill Robbins, ed., *Is It Righteous to Be? Interviews with Emmanuel Levinas* (Stanford, CA: Stanford University Press, 2001), 171–72.

8. Homecoming

1. Ernst Bloch, *Philosophy of Hope* (Oxford: Basil Blackwell, 1986), 3:1375–76.

2. This expression is from the title of a talk given by Levinas on November 28, 1975. The text is given in Emmanuel Levinas, *Dieu, la mort et le temps* (Paris: Grasset and Fasquelle, 1993), 31–36.

3. Simon Schama, *Landscape and Memory* (London: Fontana, 1995), 114.

4. The connection is made very explicit in an address Heidegger gave to university students in 1933, marking the anniversary of the execution for sabotage of a German student, Leo Schlageter, by French occupying forces. In this speech Heidegger especially emphasizes how "the young farmer's son" was shaped by the landscape of the Black Forest in which he grew up, inspiring him to die "for the German people and its Reich." Cited from William S. Lewis, "Martin Heidegger: Political Texts, 1933–1934," *New German Critique* 45 (1988): 96–114.

5. Martin Heidegger, *The Fundamental Concepts of Metaphysics: World, Finitude, Solitude*, trans. William McNeill and Nicholas Walker (Bloomington: Indiana University Press, 1995), 5.

6. Heidegger, *The Fundamental Concepts of Metaphysics*, 5.

7. Heidegger, *The Fundamental Concepts of Metaphysics*, 6.

8. Heidegger, *The Fundamental Concepts of Metaphysics*, 7.

9. Martin Heidegger, "Schöpferische Landschaft: Warum bleiben wir in der Provinz?," in *Denkerfahrungen. 1910–1976* (Frankfurt am Main: Vittorio Klostermann, 1983), 10.

10. Heidegger, "Schöpferische Landschaft," 12–13.

11. Martin Heidegger, *Erläuterungen zu Hölderlins Dichtung* (Frankfurt am Main: Vittorio Klostermann, 1996), 28.

12. Heidegger, *Erläuterungen zu Holderlins Dichtung*, 25.

13. This distinction could, of course, be used to exclude some inhabitants of a given location from full belonging, as when German Jews had their German identity revoked in the 1930s. However, it could equally be used to argue that neither ethnicity nor family roots are really relevant here: What matters is to be able to share in the visionary poetic word-event of "home."

14. Heidegger, *Erläuterungen zu Holderlins Dichtung*, 29–30.

15. Martin Heidegger, *Reden und andere Zeugnisse eines Lebensweges*, in *Gesamtausgabe* (Frankfurt am Main: Vittorio Klostermann, 2000), 16:574.

16. Heidegger, *Reden und andere Zeugnisse eines Lebensweges*, 575.

17. Heidegger, *Reden und andere Zeugnisse eines Lebensweges*, 575–76.

18. Heidegger, *Reden und andere Zeugnisse eines Lebensweges*, 576.

19. Heidegger, *Reden und andere Zeugnisse eines Lebensweges*, 578.

20. Heidegger, *Reden und andere Zeugnisse eines Lebensweges*, 578.

21. Heidegger, *Reden und andere Zeugnisse eines Lebensweges*, 579.

22. Heidegger, *Reden und andere Zeugnisse eines Lebensweges*, 580.

23. Heidegger, *Reden und andere Zeugnisse eines Lebensweges*, 581.

24. Heidegger, *Reden und andere Zeugnisse eines Lebensweges*, 603.

25. Heidegger, *Reden und andere Zeugnisse eines Lebensweges*, 607.

26. Heidegger, *Reden und andere Zeugnisse eines Lebensweges*, 607.

27. Edwin Muir, "One Foot in Eden," in *Collected Poems* (London: Faber, 1960).

28. Martin Heidegger, *Denkerfahrungen. 1910–1976* (Frankfurt am Main: Vittorio Klostermann, 1983), 89.

29. Heidegger, *Denkerfahrungen*, 88.

30. Heidegger, *Denkerfahrungen*, 108.

31. Heidegger, *Denkerfahrungen*, 112.

32. Seeing the issue in terms of language confirms the suggestion in note 13 that "belonging" is not a matter of ethnicity or localism but participation in poetic life. Although Heidegger does not explore this, it suggests that by reading the poet's words, a non-German can participate in the "homecoming" poetically enacted by Hölderlin, just as a German can participate in the poetic world of a Shakespeare or Dostoevsky. Literature in this way elevates and opens the local so as to make it potentially universal.

33. Anselm of Canterbury, *Volume One. Monologion, Proslogion, Debate with Gaunilo and a Meditation on Human Redemption*, trans. Jasper Hopkins and Herbert W. Richardson (London: SCM, 1974), 91–93.

34. Heinrich Ott, "Theologie als Gebet und als Wissenschaft," *Theologische Zeitschrift* 14 (1958): 120–32.

9. Humility

1. *Summa Theologiae*, Part II.2, Q.161, Article 5, reply to objection 2.

2. *Summa Theologiae*, II.2, Q.161, Article 1, reply to objection 5.

3. *Summa Theologiae*, II.2, Article 1, objection 5 and reply to objection 5.

4. Thomas à Kempis, *The Imitation of Christ*, trans. Leo Sherley-Price (Harmondsworth: Penguin, 1952), 29.

5. à Kempis, *The Imitation of Christ*, 28. Heidegger's farmer friends would doubtless agree.

6. à Kempis, *The Imitation of Christ*, 137.

7. Francis de Sales, Saint, *Introduction to the Devout Life*, trans. Michael Day (London: Burns and Oates, 1962), 97 (translation adapted).

8. De Sales, *Introduction to the Devout Life*, 98 (translation adapted).

9. De Sales, *Introduction to the Devout Life*, 100 (translation adapted).

10. De Sales, *Introduction to the Devout Life*, 101 (translation adapted).

11. De Sales, *Introduction to the Devout Life*, 104 (translation adapted).

12. In William. M. Thompson, ed., *Bérulle and the French School: Selected Writings* (New York: Paulist, 1989), 239.

13. Part 1, "The Art of Nature," offers a version of what Kant would later call the physico-theological proof and that would find its best-known exemplar in William Paley's *Natural Theology*.

14. Fénelon, François de S. de la M., "Démonstration de l'existence de Dieu," in *Œuvres*, ed. Jacques Le Brun (Paris: Gallimard, 1983), 2:596.

15. Fénelon, *Œuvres*, 2:602.

16. Fénelon, *Œuvres*, 2:605.

17. Fénelon, *Œuvres*, 2:617–18. With regard to the encounter with an inner infinity, comparisons have been drawn between Fénelon and Levinas, although Levinas would not describe the self as a "nothing." See Robert Spaemann, *Reflexion und Spontaneität: Studien über Fénelon* (1963; Stuttgart: Klett-Cotta, 1990).

18. Fénelon, *Œuvres*, 1:690.

19. In Thompson, *Bérulle and the French School*, 240.

20. Jean Baptiste Poquelin Molière, *Tartuffe, or The Hypocrite*, trans. Curtis Hidden Page (New York: G. P. Putnam's Sons, 1908), 25–26.

21. Molière, *Tartuffe, or The Hypocrite*, 98.

22. David Hume, *A Treatise of Human Nature* (London: J. M. Dent, 1949), 2:23.

23. Adam Smith, *The Theory of Moral Sentiments* (Oxford: Oxford University Press, 1979), 61.

24. Voltaire, Francois-Marie Arouet, *Philosophical Dictionary* (London: W. Dugdale, 1843), 2:568.

25. Immanuel Kant, "An Answer to the Question: What Is Enlightenment?," in *Practical Philosophy*, trans. Mary J. Gregor (Cambridge: Cambridge University Press, 1996), 17.

26. Ralph Waldo Emerson, *Works* (London: George Routledge, 1893), 579.

27. Emerson, *Works*, 11–12.

28. Carl Rogers, "'To Be That Self Which One Truly Is': A Therapist's View of Personal Goals," in *On Becoming a Person: A Therapist's View of Psychotherapy* (London: Constable, 1967), 163–82.

29. See, for example, Paul Tillich, *Systematic Theology*, vol. 1 (Welwyn Garden City: James Nisbet, 1953), 92–96.

30. Pindar, Isthmian Ode 5, l. 16; quoted in Michael Theunissen, *Pindar. Menschenlos und Wende der Zeit* (Munich: C. H. Beck, 2000), 225.

31. This is an etymology to which de Sales too refers.

32. See F. H. Heinemann, *Existentialism and the Human Predicament* (London: A. & C. Black, 1954).

33. F. Dostoevsky, *The Brothers Karamazov*, trans. Constance Garnett (London: Heinemann, 1912), 296–98, 335–36.

34. Dostoevsky, *The Brothers Karamazov*, 332–33.

35. Iris Murdoch, *The Sovereignty of Good* (London: Routledge & Kegan Paul, 1970), 71, 104. In line with Murdoch's logic, I am sympathetic to Michael W. Austin's attempt to rehabilitate humility in his *Humility and Human Flourishing: A Study in Analytic Moral Theology* (Oxford: Oxford University Press, 2018), but I'm not convinced that providing ethical reasons for being humble will produce the desired effect, not even when they're good reasons—unless they are grounded in a more fundamental conviction that humility best expresses who we really are.

Select Bibliography

Agamben, Giorgio. *The Sacrament of Language: An Archaeology of the Oath*. Stanford, CA: Stanford University Press, 2010.
Anonymous. *The Cloud of Unknowing*. Trans. C. Wolters. Harmondsworth: Penguin, 1961.
Anselm of Canterbury. *Volume One. Monologion, Proslogion, Debate with Gaunilo, and a Meditation on Human Redemption*. Trans. Jasper Hopkins and Herbert W. Richardson. London: SCM, 1974.
Aquinas, Thomas, Saint. *Summa Theologiae*. https://www.newadvent.org/summa/.
Augustine, Saint. *Confessions*. Trans. R. S. Pine-Coffin. Harmondsworth: Penguin, 1961.
Bakhtin, M. M. *Art and Answerability*. Trans. Vadim Liapunov. Austin: University of Texas Press, 1990.
———. *Toward a Philosophy of the Act*. Trans. Vadim Liapunov. Austin: University of Texas Press, 1993.
Berdyaev, N. A. *The Beginning and the End*. Trans. R. M. French. London: G. Bles, 1952.
———. *Slavery and Freedom*. Trans. R. M. French. London, Geoffrey Bles: 1943.
———. *Solitude and Society*. Trans. George Reavey. London: Geoffrey Bles, 1938.
———. *Spirit and Reality*. Trans. George Reavey. London: Geoffrey Bles, 1939.
Bloch, Ernst. *Philosophy of Hope*. Vol. 3. Oxford: Basil Blackwell, 1986.
Bonhoeffer, Dietrich. *Letters and Papers from Prison*. Ed. Eberhard Bethge. Trans. Reginald Fuller and others. London: SCM, 1971.
Brown, David. *God and Enchantment of Place: Reclaiming Human Experience*. Oxford: Oxford University Press, 2004.

———. *God and Grace of Body: Sacrament in Ordinary*. Oxford: Oxford University Press, 2007.

———. *God and Mystery in Words: Experience through Metaphor and Drama*. Oxford: Oxford University Press, 2008.

Brown, David, and Ann Loades, eds. *The Sense of the Sacramental: Music, Place, and Time*. Oxford: Abingdon, 1995.

Buber, Martin. *Daniel. Gespräche von der Verwirklichung*. Leipzig: Insel, 1922.

———. *I and Thou*. Trans. W. Kaufmann. Edinburgh: T. & T. Clark, 1970.

———. *Die Rede, die Lehre und das Lied*. Leipzig: Insel, 1920.

———. *Reden und Gleichnisse des Tschuang-Tse*. Leipzig: Insel, 1910.

Bultmann, Rudolf. *History and Eschatology*. Edinburgh: Edinburgh University Press, 1975.

Butler, Dom Cuthbert. *Western Mysticism: The Teaching of SS Augustine, Gregory, and Bernard on Contemplation and the Contemplative Life*. London: Arrow, 1960.

Caputo, John D. "Shedding Tears beyond Being: Derrida's Confession of Prayer." In *Augustine and Postmodernism: Confession and Circumfession*, ed. John D. Caputo and Michael J. Scanlon, 95–114. Bloomington: Indiana University Press, 2005.

———. *Specters of God. An Anatomy of the Apophatic Imagination*. Bloomington: Indiana University Press, 2022.

Chrétien, Jean-Louis. *The Ark of Speech*. Trans. Andrew Brown. London: Routledge, 2014.

———. *The Call and the Response*. Trans. Anne A. Davenport. New York: Fordham University Press, 2004.

———. *St Augustin et les actes de parole*. Paris: Presses universitaires de France, 2002.

Cupitt, Don. *Mysticism After Modernity*. Oxford: Blackwell, 1998.

Dalferth, Ingolf U. *Creatures of Possibility: The Theological Basis of Human Freedom*. Grand Rapid, MI: Baker Academic, 2016.

Dionysius, Pseudo-. *The Complete Works*. Trans. C. Luibhead. New York: Paulist, 1987.

Dostoevsky, F. M. *The Brothers Karamazov*. Trans. Constance Garnett. London: Heinemann, 1912.

———. *The Idiot*. Trans. Constance Garnett. London: Heinemann, 1951.

Eliade, Mircea. *The Myth of the Eternal Return*. Princeton, NJ: Princeton University Press, 1974.

Eliot, T. S. *Four Quartets*. London: Faber, 1959.

Emerson, Ralph Waldo. *Works*. London: George Routledge, 1893.

Fénelon, François de S. de la M. *Œuvres*. 2 vols. Ed. Jacques Le Brun. Paris: Gallimard, 1983.

Fichte, J. G. *Die Schriften zu J. G. Fichtes Atheismus-Streit*. Ed. H. R. D. Lindau. Munich: Georg Müller, 1912.

Gilson, Étienne. *The Christian Philosophy of St. Augustine*. Trans. L. E. M. Lynch. London: Gollancz, 1961.

Grell, Helge. *Skaberordet og billedordet. Studier over Grundtvigs teologi om ordet*. Copenhagen: Danske Boghandlers Kommissonsanstalt, 1980.

Hegel, G. W. F. *Elements of the Philosophy of Right* [1821]. Trans. H. B. Nisbet. Cambridge: Cambridge University Press, 1991.

Heidegger, Martin. *The Basic Problems of Phenomenology*. Trans. Alfred Hofstadter. Bloomington: Indiana University Press, 1982.

———. *Being and Time*. Trans. John Macquarrie and Edward Robinson. Oxford: Blackwell, 1960.

———. "Building, Dwelling, Thinking." In *Poetry, Language, Thought*, trans. Albert Hofstadter, 143–62. New York: Harper and Row, 1971.

———. *Erläuterungen zu Holderlins Dichtung*. Frankfurt a. Main: Vittorio Klostermann, 1996.

———. *The Fundamental Concepts of Metaphysics: World, Finitude, Solitude*. Trans. William McNeill and Nicholas Walker. Bloomington: Indiana University Press, 1995.

———. *Hölderlin's Hymn "The Ister."* Trans. William McNeill and Julia Davis. Bloomington: Indiana University Press, 1996.

———. *Identity and Difference*. Trans. Joan Stambaugh. New York: Harper and Row, 1969.

———. *Reden und andere Zeugnisse eines Lebensweges. Gesamtausgabe*, vol. 16. Frankfurt a. Main: Vittorio Klostermann, 2000.

———. "Schöpferische Landschaft: Warum bleiben wir in der Provinz?" In *Denkerfahrungen. 1910–1976*. Frankfurt am Main: Vittorio Klostermann, 1983.

———. *Unterwegs zur Sprache*. Stuttgart: Günther Neske, 1959.

Heinemann, F. H. *Existentialism and the Human Predicament*. London: A. & C. Black, 1954.

Hölderlin, Friedrich. *Poems and Fragments*. Trans. Michael Hamburger. London: Anvil, 2004.

Hügel, Friedrich von (Baron). *Essays and Addresses in the Philosophy of Religion. Second Series*. London: Dent, 1933.

Huian, Georgiana. *Augustin. Le coeur et la crise du sujet*. Paris: Cerf, 2020.

Hume, David. *A Treatise of Human Nature*. 2 vols. London: J. M. Dent, 1949.

Isaac the Syrian (Saint). *The Ascetical Homilies of Saint Isaac the Syrian*. Boston: Holy Transfiguration Monastery, 1984.

Jankélévitch, Vladimir. *L'irréversible et la nostalgie*. Paris: Flammarion, 1974.

John of Damascus. *On the Divine Images*. Trans. David Anderson. New York: St. Vladimir's Seminary Press, 1980.

Kant, Immanuel. "An Answer to the Question: What Is Enlightenment?" In *Practical Philosophy*, trans. Mary J. Gregor. Cambridge: Cambridge University Press, 1996.

———. "Religion within the Boundaries of Mere Reason" [1793]. In *Religion and Rational Theology*, ed. and trans. Allen Wood and George di Giovanni. Cambridge: Cambridge University Press, 1996.

Kempis, Thomas à. *The Imitation of Christ*. Trans. Leo Sherley-Price. Harmondsworth: Penguin, 1952.

Kenney, John Peter. *Contemplation and Classical Christianity: A Study in Antiquity*. Oxford: Oxford University Press, 2013.

Kierkegaard, Søren A. *The Concept of Anxiety*. Trans. Reidar Thomte. Princeton, NJ: Princeton University Press, 1980.

———. *Concluding Unscientific Postscript*. Trans. H. V. Hong and E. H. Hong. Princeton, NJ: Princeton University Press, 1991.

———. *Eighteen Upbuilding Discourses*. Trans. H. V. and E. H. Hong. Princeton, NJ: Princeton University Press, 1990.

———. *Kierkegaard's Devotional Writings*. Trans. and ed. George Pattison. New York: Harper and Row, 2010.

———. *Purity of Heart Is to Will One Thing*. Trans. Douglas Steere. London: Fontana, 1961.

———. *The Sickness unto Death*. Trans. E. H. Hong and H. V. Hong. Princeton, NJ: Princeton University Press, 1980.

———. *Søren Kierkegaards Skrifter*. Ed. N. J. Cappelørn et al. Copenhagen: Gad, 2006–2013.

———. *Upbuilding Discourses in Various Spirits*. Trans. H. V. Hong and E. H. Hong. Princeton, NJ: Princeton University Press, 2009.

———. *Without Authority*. Trans. H. V. Hong and E. H. Hong. Princeton, NJ: Princeton University Press, 1997.

———. *Works of Love*. Trans. H. V. Hong and E. H. Hong. Princeton, NJ: Princeton University Press, 1998.

Katz, Steven T. "Language, Epistemology, and Mysticism." In *Mysticism and Philosophical Analysis*, ed. Steven T. Katz. London: Sheldon, 1978.

Kneževic, Romilo Aleksandr. *Homo Theurgos: Freedom according to John Zizioulas and Nikolai Berdyaev*. Paris: Cerf, 2020.

Lakoff, George, and Mark Johnson. *Metaphors We Live By*. Chicago: University of Chicago Press, 1980.

Levinas, Emmanuel. *Autrement que l'être ou au-delà de l'essence*. Paris: Kluwer Academic, 2001.

———. *Dieu, la mort et le temps*. Paris: Grasset and Fasquelle, 1993.

———. "Sur la mort dans la pensée de Ernst Bloch." In *Utopie—Marxisme selon Ernst Bloch: Un système de l'inconstructible: Hommages à Ernst Bloch pour son 90e anniversaire*, ed. Gérard Raulet. Paris: Payot, 1976.

———. *Le temps et l'autre*. Paris: Presses universitaires de France, 1983.

———. *Totalité et infini* [1961]. Paris: Kluwer Academic, 2001.

———. "Transcendence and Height." In *Emmanuel Levinas: Basic Philosophical Writings*, ed. A. T. Peperzak, S. Critchley, and R. Bernasconi, 11–31. Bloomington: Indiana University Press, 1996.

Lewis, William S. "Martin Heidegger: Political Texts, 1933–1934." *New German Critique* 45 (1988): 96–114.

Malpas, Jeff. *Heidegger's Topology: Being, Place, World.* Cambridge, MA: MIT Press, 2006.

Marcel, Gabriel. *The Mystery of Being I: Reflection and Mystery.* Trans. G. S. Fraser. London, Harvill, 1950.

———. *The Mystery of Being II: Faith and Reality.* Trans. R. Hague. London, Harvill, 1951.

Merton, Thomas. *Confessions of a Guilty Bystander.* New York: Image, 1968.

Molière, Jean Baptiste Poquelin. *Tartuffe, or The Hypocrite.* Trans. Curtis Hidden Page. New York: G. P. Putnam's Sons, 1908.

A Monk of the Eastern Church. *On the Invocation of the Name of Jesus.* Oxford: Fairacres, 1970.

Morgan, Michael L. *The Cambridge Introduction to Levinas.* Cambridge: Cambridge University Press, 2011.

———. *Levinas's Ethical Politics.* Bloomington: Indiana University Press, 2016.

Mounier, Emmanuel. *Le personnalisme.* In *Œuvres*, tome III. Paris: Éditions de Seuil, 1962.

Muir, Edwin. *Collected Poems.* London: Faber, 1960.

Newheiser, David. *Hope in a Secular Age: Deconstruction, Negative Theology, and the Future of Faith.* Cambridge: Cambridge University Press, 2019.

Ott, Heinrich. "Theologie als Gebet und als Wissenschaft." *Theologische Zeitschrift* 14 (1958): 120–32.

Pattison, George. "The Grace of Time: Towards a Kataphatic Theology of Time." In *Hermeneutics and Negativism: Existential Ambiguities of Self-Understanding*, ed. Claudia Welz and René Rosfort, 145–60. Tübingen: Mohr-Siebeck, 2018.

———. *Heidegger on Death: A Critical Theological Essay.* Farnham: Ashgate, 2013.

———. "I Lift Up My Eyes to the Hills." In *Mountains, Mobilities, and Movement*, ed. Christos Kakalis and Emily Goetsch, 237–54. New York: Springer, 2017.

———. *A Metaphysics of Love.* Oxford: Oxford University Press, 2021.

———. *A Phenomenology of the Devout Life.* Oxford: Oxford University Press, 2018.

———. *A Rhetorics of the Word.* Oxford: Oxford University Press, 2019.

———. "'Water the Earth': Dostoevsky on Tears." In *Litteraria Pragensia: Studies in Literature and Culture* 22, no. 43 (July 2012): 95–111.

Pattison, George, and Kate Kirkpatrick. *The Mystical Sources of Existentialist Thought: Being, Nothingness, Love.* London: Routledge, 2019.

Pauck, Wilhelm, and Marion Pauck. *Paul Tillich: His Life and Thought.* Vol. 1: *Life.* London: Collins, 1977.

Putnam, Hilary. "Levinas on Judaism." In *The Cambridge Companion to Levinas*, ed. Simon Critchley and Robert Bernasconi, 33–62. Cambridge: Cambridge University Press, 2006.

Robbins, Jill, ed. *Is It Righteous to Be? Interviews with Emmanuel Levinas*. Stanford, CA: Stanford University Press, 2001.

Rogers, Carl. "'To Be That Self Which One Truly Is': A Therapist's View of Personal Goals." In *On Becoming a Person: A Therapist's View of Psychotherapy*. London: Constable, 1967.

Rosenzweig, Franz. *Kleinere Schriften zu Glauben und Denken*. Ed. Reinhold Mayer and Annemarie Mayer, 148–51. Dordrecht: Martinus Nijhoff, 1984.

Sales, Francis de (Saint). *Introduction to the Devout Life*. Trans. Michael Day. London: Burns and Oates, 1962.

Schleiermacher, F. D. E. *The Christian Faith*. Trans. and ed. H. R. Mackintosh and J. S. Stewart. Edinburgh: T. & T. Clark, 1989.

———. *Speeches on Religion to Its Cultured Despisers*. Trans. R. Crouter. Cambridge: Cambridge University Press, 1988.

Sakharov, Nicholas V. *I Love Therefore I Am: The Theological Legacy of Archimandrite Sophrony*. Crestwood, NY: St. Vladimir's Seminary Press, 2002.

Schama, Simon. *Landscape and Memory*. London: Fontana, 1995.

Schmemann, Alexander. *The World as Sacrament*. London: Darton, Longman, and Todd, 1966.

Smith, Adam. *The Theory of Moral Sentiments*. Oxford: Oxford University Press, 1979.

Spaemann, Robert. *Reflexion und Spontaneität: Studien über Fénelon* [1963]. Stuttgart: Klett-Cotta, 1990.

Theunissen, Michael. *Pindar. Menschenlos und Wende der Zeit*. Munich: C. H. Beck, 2000.

Thompson, William M., ed. *Bérulle and the French School: Selected Writings*. New York: Paulist, 1989.

Tillich, Paul. *The Boundaries of Our Being*. London: Fontana, 1973.

———. *The Courage to Be*. London: Collins-Fontana, 1962.

———. *My Search for Absolutes*. New York: Simon and Schuster, 1967.

———. "Nicholas Berdyaev." *Religion in Life* 7, no. 3 (Summer 1938): 407–15.

———. "Review of *Slavery and Freedom*." *Theology Today* 2, no. 1 (April 1945): 130–32.

———. *The Shaking of the Foundations*. London: SCM, 1949.

———. *The Socialist Decision*. Trans. Franklin Sherman. New York: Harper and Row, 1977.

———. *Systematic Theology*. Vol. 1. Welwyn Garden City: James Nisbet, 1953.

———. *Systematic Theology*. Vol. 2. Welwyn Garden City: James Nisbet, 1957.

———. *Systematic Theology*. Vol. 3. Welwyn Garden City: James Nisbet, 1964.

———. *Theology of Culture*. Oxford: Oxford University Press, 1959.

Toumayan, A. "'I More Than the Others': Dostoevsky and Levinas." *Yale French Studies* 104 (2004): 55–66.

Turner, Denys. *The Darkness of God*. Cambridge: Cambridge University Press, 1995.
Voltaire, Francois-Marie Arouet. *Philosophical Dictionary*. Vol. 2. London: W. Dugdale, 1843.
Wainwright, Geoffrey. *Eucharist and Eschatology*. London: Epworth, 1971.
Weil, Simone. *Gravity and Grace*. Trans. E. Craufurd. London: Ark, 1987.
Wittgenstein, Ludwig. *Philosophical Investigations*. Trans. G. E. M. Anscombe. Oxford: Blackwell, 1920.
Wozniak, Monika. "Towards a New Understanding of Immanence and Transcendence in the Writings of Nikolai Berdyaev and Paul Tillich." In *Beyond Modernity: Russian Religious Philosophy and Post-Secularism*, ed. Artur Mrowczynski, Teresa Obolevich, and Pawel Rojek. Eugene, OR: Pickwick, 2016.

Index

Abraham à Sancta Clara, 118–19
Agamben, G., 74–75, 79, 93
Anselm of Canterbury, 121
apophaticism, 14, 19, 34, 36, 38, 43, 44, 52; of the self 43, 88, 145n2, 147n1, 147n9
Aristotle, 89–90, 136
attention, xii, 26–32, 57, 77–79, 108, 111, 135, 154n19
Augustine of Hippo, 17–18, 30, 35–36, 59, 64, 76, 77–78, 90, 99, 145n2
Austin, M. W., 162n35
autonomy, 2, 22, 33, 105, 122, 123, 131–37. *See also* freedom; the self

Bakhtin, M. M., 15
Barth, K., 74
being, 5–12, 16, 23–25, 28, 31, 34–50, 54–59, 72–73, 76–78, 87–94 passim, 97–100 passim, 102, 104, 113, 118, 121,127–29, 135. *See also* ontology
Berdyaev, N. A., 37–40, 42–43, 46, 47, 48, 85, 108, 110, 111, 149n56
Bernanos, G., 100
Bloch, E., 97, 99, 110–11
Brown, D., 70–71
Buber, M., 57–59, 152n12
Butler, Dom Cuthbert, 34–37, 51, 52

Caputo, J. D., 145–46n2, 149n56
Chrétien, J.-L., 6–7, 77–78, 144n19
Christ, Jesus, 12, 19, 30, 49, 61, 69, 70, 71–72, 94, 106–8, 124–25, 137

Cloud of Unknowing, The, xii, 17–22, 25, 26, 29, 30, 52, 59–61, 62, 64
covenant, 83–86, 93, 95, 155n5, 157n29
Cupitt, D., 151n8

Dalferth, I., 143n8
Descartes, R., 39, 98, 128, 137, 157n8
Dionysius the Areopagite, 18–19, 30
Dostoevsky, F. M., 12–16, 32–33, 59, 86, 94–95, 103, 134, 137–39

Eliade, M., 84–85, 95
Eliot, T. S., 64, 76
Emerson, R. W., 132–33
eschatology, 44, 47–49, 86–87, 111
ethics, 4, 101–2, 108, 132, 158n11
experience, religious experience, 3–6, 12, 13–16, 17–18, 20, 21, 23–25, 32–33, 34–35, 37, 39, 40–44, 49, 51–54, 55, 57, 58–59, 61, 65, 66, 79, 92, 110, 113–15, 119, 121, 133, 135, 141, 143n7

faith, 3–4, 5, 34, 69, 74, 80, 95–96, 119, 121, 124
Fenélon, F., 125, 127–29, 138
Fichte, I. H., 37
Fichte, J. G., 2, 3–5, 6, 11, 37, 39
freedom, 3–6, 11–12, 15–16, 28, 37–40, 43, 46–47, 86–87, 94, 131–32, 134. *See also* autonomy

Gilson, É., 145n2
God. *See* being; Christ, Jesus; grace; love

171

grace, 1, 2–3, 20, 21, 22, 28–30, 64, 70, 81, 126
Grundtvig, N. F. S., 71–72
Guyer, P., 143n7

heart, the, 11, 18, 25, 42, 62, 64–65, 67, 78, 126
Hegel, G. W. F., 37, 38, 72
Heidegger, M., 6, 35, 38, 54–57, 58, 67, 72–74, 76–77, 79, 80, 88, 89–92, 96, 110–22, 133, 135–36, 151–52n10, 152n15
Heinemann, F., 136
history, 3, 39–40, 47, 49, 50, 84–87, 94, 109, 112, 133
Hölderlin, F., 47, 67, 117, 119
home, homecoming, 110–22, 160n13
Hügel, F. von, 64
Huian, G., 145n2
Hume, D., 131
humility, 100, 123–39

Isaac, of Syria, 153n42

Jankélévitch, V., 87
Jesus. *See* Christ, Jesus
John of Damascus, 71
Johnson, M., 71
justice, 87, 98, 102–3, 105–6, 108–9, 155n2

Kant, I., Kantianism, 1–2, 4, 6, 11–12, 15, 16, 22, 35, 37, 130, 131–32, 134, 135
Katz, S., 52–53
Kempis, Thomas à, 124
Kenney, J. P., 145n2
Kierkegaard S., 6–12, 16, 22–26, 29, 31–32, 62–63, 64–65, 72, 79, 81, 87–90, 93, 125, 134, 139
knowledge, 4, 5, 11, 14, 17–19, 20, 21, 22–26, 29, 31, 34–36, 38, 43, 44–46, 50, 51, 87–90, 98, 100–5, 110, 116, 124, 127, 145n2

Laird, M., 52
Lakoff, G., 71
language, 51–82, 92–95, 108–9, 119–20, 122, 136
Levinas, E., 91–94, 96–109, 110, 136–17, 156n21, 156–57n8, 157n9, 157n10, 158n14, 161n17
Lewis, C. S., 94
Lindbeck, G., 151n8
listening, 57, 59, 62, 74, 76–79, 81, 112
love, 13, 30, 99, 124; God's love, 9, 28, 29, 31, 45, 61, 95, 106, 125; of God, 11, 18, 19–22, 23, 25, 26, 28, 31, 60, 129, 132, 138–39; of others 3, 26, 41, 87, 92, 108, 122, 137, 138–39, 142

Marcel, G., 40–43, 46, 82, 108, 111, 148n22, 150n69, 157n5
Molière, J. B. P., 130

Morgan, M. 158n12, 158n13
Muir, Edwin 71, 119
Murdoch, I., 139
mystery, 12, 14, 16, 33, 34–50, 51, 54, 61, 91, 94, 115, 117, 122, 138, 148n22
mysticism, 22, 25, 34, 46, 49, 52–53, 55, 151n8

Nancy, J.-L., 143n7
Newheiser, D., 150n77
Novalis, 112–13
new, the, 23, 27, 39, 47–50, 68, 83, 85, 109, 111, 112, 116, 117, 121, 127, 141
Nietzsche, F., 132–33, 137
non-being 46, 47–48, 90
nothingness, 10, 17–18, 22–24, 27, 29, 33, 51, 82, 90, 98, 118–19, 121, 127–29, 138, 139, 141
novelty. *See* the new

Olier, J.-J., 125, 127–28
ontology, 11, 37–40, 44, 52, 91, 93, 97, 121
Ott, H., 121

Paul, St. 81, 88, 102
Pindar, 135
Plato ,98–99, 113, 157n8
Plotinus, 88, 89, 90, 145n2
preaching, 68–82
promise 75, 79, 81, 83–95, 96, 142

Rogers, C., 133
Rosenzweig, F., 8, 59, 92–93, 157n8, 158n10
Ross, M., 52

sacrament, sacramentality, 68–72, 74–75, 83
Sakharov, V. N., 34
Sales, F. de, 125–27, 130, 139
Sartre, J.-P., 41, 98, 134
Schama, S., 112
Schelling, F. W. J., 37, 149n56
Schleiermacher, F. D. E., 4–6, 63
Scrima, A., 147n1
self, the, 1–16, 17, 21–22, 23–26, 27, 28, 31, 33, 34–37, 40–41, 43, 44, 53, 58–59, 60, 61–66, 89, 91, 92, 93, 98–100, 105, 108–9, 123, 124, 131–39; annihilation of, 12, 17, 23, 26, 30, 33, 90, 91, 123. *See also* autonomy
Shpet, G., 68
silence, 12, 13, 50, 51–54, 57, 59, 62, 70, 77, 81, 82
Smith, A., 131
solidarity, 16, 109, 112, 138, 158n10
space, spatiality, spatial turn, 28, 46–47, 60, 68, 83–86, 90, 111–12, 120, 137, 138
subject, subjectivity, 22, 23, 30, 33, 35, 38, 42, 43, 44, 87, 91
Suzuki, D. T., 141

tears, 13–15, 138, 145n2
Thomas Aquinas, 124
Tillich, P., 39, 43–50, 70, 84, 85, 108, 110, 111, 135, 148n22
time, 9, 18, 25–26, 33, 39–40, 47–49, 58, 79–81, 83–95, 110–11, 120, 121
Toumayan, E., 145n40

Voltaire, F. M.-A., 131

Weil, S., 26–32, 79, 108, 139
will, 1–2, 4–5, 10, 11, 20, 23, 25, 29–30, 31, 64, 67, 132–33
Williams, B., 136
Wittgenstein, L., 52, 59

George Pattison is a retired Anglican priest and scholar. He has held posts in Cambridge, Aarhus, Oxford, and Glasgow universities and has published extensively on existential philosophy, especially Kierkegaard, Heidegger, Tillich, and Russian religious philosophy. His previous books include *A Metaphysics of Love: A Philosophy of Christian Life, Part III*; *A Rhetorics of the Word: A Philosophy of Christian Life, Part II*; and *A Phenomenology of the Devout Life: A Philosophy of Christian Life, Part I*.

Perspectives in Continental Philosophy
John D. Caputo, series editor

Recent titles:

Irving Goh, ed., *Jean-Luc Nancy among the Philosophers.*
Neal DeRoo, *The Political Logic of Experience: Expression in Phenomenology.*
John D. Caputo, *Radical Theology: Expositions, Explorations, Exhortations.*
Michael Naas, *Class Acts: Derrida on the Public Stage.*
Adam Kotsko, *What is Theology? Christian Thought and Contemporary Life.*
Galen A. Johnson, Mauro Carbone, and Emmanuel de Saint Aubert, *Merleau-Ponty's Poetics: Figurations of Literature and Philosophy*
Ole Jakob Løland, *Pauline Ugliness: Jacob Taubes and the Turn to Paul.*
Marc Crépon, *Murderous Consent: On the Accommodation of Violent Death.* Translated by Michael Loriaux and Jacob Levi, Foreword by James Martel
Emmanuel Falque, *The Guide to Gethsemane: Anxiety, Suffering, and Death.* Translated by George Hughes.
Emmanuel Alloa, *Resistance of the Sensible World: An Introduction to Merleau-Ponty.* Translated by Jane Marie Todd. Foreword by Renaud Barbaras.
Françoise Dastur, *Questions of Phenomenology: Language, Alterity, Temporality, Finitude.* Translated by Robert Vallier.
Jean-Luc Marion, *Believing in Order to See: On the Rationality of Revelation and the Irrationality of Some Believers.* Translated by Christina M. Gschwandtner.
Adam Y. Wells, ed., *Phenomenologies of Scripture.*
An Yountae, *The Decolonial Abyss: Mysticism and Cosmopolitics from the Ruins.*
Jean Wahl, *Transcendence and the Concrete: Selected Writings.* Edited and with an Introduction by Alan D. Schrift and Ian Alexander Moore.

Colby Dickinson, *Words Fail: Theology, Poetry, and the Challenge of Representation.*

Emmanuel Falque, *The Wedding Feast of the Lamb: Eros, the Body, and the Eucharist.* Translated by George Hughes.

Emmanuel Falque, *Crossing the Rubicon: The Borderlands of Philosophy and Theology.* Translated by Reuben Shank. Introduction by Matthew Farley.

Colby Dickinson and Stéphane Symons (eds.), *Walter Benjamin and Theology.*

Don Ihde, *Husserl's Missing Technologies.*

William S. Allen, *Aesthetics of Negativity: Blanchot, Adorno, and Autonomy.*

Jeremy Biles and Kent L. Brintnall, eds., *Georges Bataille and the Study of Religion.*

Tarek R. Dika and W. Chris Hackett, *Quiet Powers of the Possible: Interviews in Contemporary French Phenomenology.* Foreword by Richard Kearney.

Richard Kearney and Brian Treanor, eds., *Carnal Hermeneutics.*

A complete list of titles is available at http://fordhampress.com.

www.ingramcontent.com/pod-product-compliance
Lightning Source LLC
Chambersburg PA
CBHW020412080526
44584CB00014B/1291